ROUTLEDGE LIBRARY EDITIONS: HUMAN RESOURCE MANAGEMENT

Volume 40

T0362348

GRADUATES IN INDUSTRY

GRADUATES IN INDUSTRY

Routledge
Taylor & Francis Group

LONDON AND NEW YORK

First published in 1957 by George Allen & Unwin Ltd

This edition first published in 2017
by Routledge
2 Park Square, Milton Park, Abingdon, Oxon OX14 4RN

and by Routledge
711 Third Avenue, New York, NY 10017

Routledge is an imprint of the Taylor & Francis Group, an informa business

British Library Cataloguing in Publication Data
A catalogue record for this book is available from the British Library

ISBN: 978-1-138-80870-6 (Set)
ISBN: 978-1-315-18006-9 (Set) (ebk)
ISBN: 978-0-415-78853-3 (Volume 40) (hbk)
ISBN: 978-0-415-78856-4 (Volume 40) (pbk)
ISBN: 978-1-315-22325-4 (Volume 40) (ebk)

Publisher's Note
The publisher has gone to great lengths to ensure the quality of this reprint but
points out that some imperfections in the original copies may be apparent.

Disclaimer
The publisher has made every effort to trace copyright holders and would welcome
correspondence from those they have been unable to trace.

GRADUATES

IN INDUSTRY

1957

LONDON
POLITICAL AND ECONOMIC PLANNING
16 QUEEN ANNE'S GATE

GEORGE ALLEN & UNWIN LTD
40 MUSEUM STREET

Made and printed in England by
STAPLES PRINTERS LIMITED
at their Rochester, Kent, establishment

CONTENTS

CHAPTER V

TRAINING

CHAPTER VI

IN THE FIRST JOB

ACKNOWLEDGEMENTS

THIS report, like its forerunner, *Graduate Employment*, has been carried out under the guidance of an Advisory Group, which met at P E P; and has been sponsored by the Human Relations Joint Committee of the Department of Scientific and Industrial Research and the Medical Research Council and has been made possible by a grant under the Conditional Aid Scheme for the Use of Counterpart Funds derived from the United States Economic Aid.

P E P wishes once more to record its thanks for this grant and for the kindness of the Vice-Chancellors and heads of colleges of the universities and Principals of the university colleges in Great Britain, in making available the addresses of graduates. It is grateful also to the Federation of British Industries, secretaries of university appointments boards and other bodies and individuals for much valuable help and advice; and to the Social Survey for carrying out one of the two series of interviews on which this report is based.

The Group wishes to thank the members of the P E P Research Staff whose diligence and good work made this report and its predecessor possible. In particular, it wishes to record its high appreciation of the work of its Senior Research Officer, Miss J. H. Lidderdale, O.B.E., whose ability and experience were invaluable in carrying through a complicated and difficult project.

INTRODUCTION

Two major, and in some respects distinct and unconnected, developments in the life of this country converge in the recruitment of university graduates by industry. There is, on the one hand, the extension of public education in successive stages to the present provision of free secondary education for all children and of substantial financial help for the increasing numbers going on to a university. On the other, there have been immense advances in scientific and technological knowledge and its application to industry. These could not have been achieved without an army of administrators and managers, of scientists and technologists with their supporting technicians, many of whom have, and must have, graduate or roughly equivalent professional qualifications.

These two developments, academic and industrial, have proceeded side by side: they have accelerated at much the same time, they have converged and are now inextricably intertwined. But industry has had relatively little time in which to get to understand the objectives and methods of its new partner. It is faced with major questions of educational policy and of the right use of qualified manpower. What kind of graduates does it need? And in what numbers?

Although it is essential, if this country's standard of living and position in world affairs is to be maintained, that industry should get the kinds of men it needs in the right numbers, it is equally essential that it should recruit no more graduates, or any other qualified men, than it needs. In other words, it should use graduates only for work that calls for the qualifications they have acquired and should employ them fully and effectively in this work, if only because other employers, as vital as industry to the well-being of the country, must also be able to get the graduates they need.

This new relationship between universities and industry calls for close and continuous study: the speed and direction of its development is of outstanding importance, not only to the universities and to industry, but to the country as a whole.

It was with these thoughts in mind that P E P decided to undertake a survey of the partnership between the universities and industry, as it had developed after the years of reconstruction immediately following World War II. Three separate enquiries seemed to be called for: one into the employment entered by university graduates; one into the views of the universities on the whole question of education for industry; and a third into industry's views on this question and into the developments that were taking place in industry in the recruitment and employment of university men.

The investigation into the employment entered by graduates has already been carried out and a report on it was published in October 1956.* The ascertaining of the views of the universities on education for industry has been postponed, with great reluctance, because of shortage of time and of staff. It is, however, P E P's intention to return to this. The third enquiry is the subject of the present report.

A fairly considerable mass of material had already appeared on the subject of the graduate in industry. This consisted to a large extent of the expression of views and opinions or of exhortations or of surveys devoted to particular problems or aspects of industry. What seemed to be needed was an attempt to get at the facts of the situation as a whole, as it existed at some given juncture—how many graduates, and what sort of graduates, were going into industry; why it was that industry recruited graduates at all; how far those it recruited were what it wanted; what steps were taken by employers to equip their graduate recruits for work in industry by training and so on, and to use them effectively and intelligently.

The terms of reference

The terms of reference governing the present enquiry, as approved by the Department of Scientific and Industrial Research, for whom it was carried out, were:

> To investigate the policy and practice of British industrial undertakings in respect of the recruitment, training and employment of university graduates.

It seemed important to seek information not only from those who formed and those who carried out graduate employment policy but also from graduates who experienced the policies in practice. By this means it was hoped it would be possible to see in the round the way in which the policies were working out in fact, their impact on graduates, and the impact of management

---

* *Graduate Employment: A Sample Survey* (P E P), 1956. 30s.

and graduates on one another. Procedure by way of random samples seemed best; by this means it would be possible to achieve a picture, or at least a sketch, showing how the recruitment and employment by industry of university graduates had developed in the country as a whole.

Scope of the enquiry

In the terms of reference, "British" was taken to mean an undertaking operating solely or mainly in the United Kingdom. Industry was defined (as for the preceding survey on graduate employment) as comprising mining and quarrying; oil extracting, refining, distribution, etc.; manufacturing; building and contracting and civil engineering; public utilities—gas, electricity, water, and transport by rail, road and air.

"University" was taken to mean the universities in Great Britain. For reasons that seemed decisive, the enquiry as a whole, including the surveys that are the subject of the present report, was limited to men graduates. The reason most relevant to the present report was that the attitude of many employers to the employment of women graduates is very different from their attitude towards the employment of men. This is particularly marked in industry. Broadly speaking, it is true to say that industrial firms do not regard women graduates as possible recruits for management and, as yet, are prepared to employ them only, if at all, in specialist posts without promotion prospects comparable to those offered to men.

"Recruitment" and "training" are reasonably precise terms; they presented little or no difficulty. "Employment", on the other hand, lent itself to various interpretations, the most ambitious of which would have meant investigating how university graduates were employed in industry from their first day at work to their retirement. This was clearly out of the question within the scope of a single enquiry. But in any case, fairly rigid limits to the interpretation of employment were necessarily imposed by the procedure adopted, as explained below. None of the men who would be interviewed would have worked in industry for much more than four years since graduating; some would have worked for an even shorter period, if after graduating they had done other work or had completed their national service before going into industry.

It was thought desirable, as far as possible, to raise with members of management only those subjects which would be within the experience of their graduate recruits. In investigating employment, it was therefore decided to take things no farther than the stage of the work first undertaken, either on entry to the firm or after training, as the case might be. This meant that, among other things, policy and practice regarding "executive development"— that is, the deliberate and sustained coaching of members of management for senior positions—which has rightly been receiving increased attention in recent years, fell outside the scope of the enquiry. Even so, a considerable range of subjects remained to be examined within the bounds of a questionnaire that should not be made intolerably long.

In considering recruitment, a fundamental question of policy came first: why employ graduates? Some investigation of managements' views on this prior question was clearly needed. Their attitudes to it and the policy they adopted would vary; and might be expected to colour much else in their practice in employing graduates. After strategy come tactics: having decided to employ graduates, what steps were taken to recruit them— advertising, for example, application to university appointments boards, or some other method or methods? Finally, what methods of selection were adopted in choosing the candidates that presented themselves?

Training, again, had three aspects, or phases. In theory, at any rate, training on entry into a firm could not be undertaken without reference to the education that had preceded it. How far was the graduate recruit already equipped to play his part? Some questions were clearly needed on the relationship between university education and training in industry. Training itself seemed to have two sides: the introduction (sometimes mysteriously dubbed "induction") of a graduate to the firm as a whole, to enable him to grasp the structure and organisation of the firm and its place in the industry of which it was a part and his own place in the firm; and his training, in the strict sense, for the work upon which he was to be set.

With an assessment of the situation at the stage when the graduate was settled in his first job (whether or not after introduction and training) the other end of the span of this research is reached. But in order to have some means of assessing the value placed on graduates at this stage in their career, as compared with other recruits, and of the graduate's views on his employment and prospects, some information was also sought on the question of salaries.*

The methods employed

Both the decision to proceed by way of random samples and the nature and scope of the samples taken were determined by an earlier decision to investigate the employment entered by graduates, the subject of the preceding enquiry already mentioned, by means of a random sample. This is the "main" sample. The two samples taken for the present enquiry are sub-samples of this main sample. There was, indeed, no other means of obtaining representative samples relating to the employment of graduates in industry. There was no reliable and comprehensive information about what firms employed graduates, nor about the employment, whether in industry or elsewhere, entered by graduates. A considerable amount of information was in the hands of university appointments boards, of course, but it would have yielded a biased sample, since graduates also can, and do, obtain employment in industry through channels other than their appointments board.

The main sample

In the investigation of the employment entered by graduates, questionnaires were sent to one in two of the 13,500 men who graduated in an arts subject or in science or technology in the academic year 1949-50. Six thousand eight hundred and forty-one questionnaires were issued. About 1,500 probably failed to reach their destination and 4,535 completed forms were returned, though some came in too late to be used. This was a response of 66 per cent. The final sample consisted of 3,961 men, that is, some 30 per cent of all the men graduating in the three faculties already mentioned.

As background to the present report, the figures of employment entered, set out in *Graduate Employment* (Table 23), are reproduced here in full.

---

* A P E P broadsheet devoted to the salaries received has already been published: *Salaries of Graduates in Industry*, PLANNING No. 408, March 1957. 2s. 6d.

TABLE I

FIRST PAID EMPLOYMENT AFTER GRADUATING IN 1950

First career employment	Graduates entering	
	No.	%
Civil Service	124	3·1
Civil Service/scientific	218	5·5
Local government service	141	3·6
Teaching (maths. and science)	265	6·7
Teaching (other)	660	16·7
Universities	166	4·2
Commerce	296	7·5
Industry, as defined for the purpose of the enquiry:		
Mining and quarrying	44	1·1
Oil	49	1·2
Manufacturing industry	929	23·4
Building and contracting	78	2·0
Public utilities	68	1·7
Consultant engineers	50	1·3
Research associations, etc.	53	1·3
Armed Services	62	1·6
The Churches	172	4·3
Law	164	4·1
Cultural occupations	61	1·5
Others	128	3·3
All career employments	3,728	94·1
No career employment*	233	5·9
TOTAL	3,961	100

* These men had spent the period between graduating and the time of the survey in a number of ways, including studying for a higher degree and in national service. The number unemployed for any period was extremely small.

It will be seen that 1,168 of the 3,961 men went into industry, as defined for the purpose of the enquiry. As these 3,961 represent some 30 per cent of the actual numbers graduating in the three faculties in 1950, the actual numbers of men who went into industry after graduating must have been some 4,000.

From this main sample, which was representative in the statistical sense, it was possible to draw the two sub-samples decided upon for the present enquiry.

The sample of industrial undertakings (the case studies)

There were some 700 industrial firms,* other than nationalised industries, to which the graduates in the main survey went. A sample of one in nine was drawn, making a total of seventy-seven, and out of these it was possible, in the time set aside for this purpose in the winter of 1954-55, to study forty-seven out of the fifty-seven which were good enough to agree to being interviewed. This is, of course, a small sample, being only some 7 per cent of the total number of firms, as defined, to which graduates in the main sample had gone. Metal and metal goods manufacturing, electrical engineering, motor vehicles, food, and building and contracting are over-represented as compared with the seventy-seven firms drawn; non-electrical engineering and textiles somewhat under-represented. There was also no opportunity of ascertaining how far, if at all, the firms interviewed varied in their policy and practice from the sample from which they were drawn. It is, however, at least a random sample, in that no element of choice entered into its selection.

Of the forty-seven firms studied, which were in all parts of the country, 9 were electrical engineers; 9 produced consumer goods of various sorts (4 of these were in the food industry); 7 were metal manufacturers or made metal goods; 6 were in the building, contracting and civil engineering industry; 4 produced vehicles or aircraft; 4 were in the chemical and allied trades and the remaining eight were in five other categories. These firms ranged in size from three with less than a hundred employees to two with more than 30,000.

In addition to these forty-seven firms, all of which were in the private sector of industry, it was decided to study one of the nationalised industries. The gas industry was chosen for this purpose. The twelve area gas boards into which it is divided are to a large degree autonomous in regard to staffing policy, and the four selected for study, after consultation with the Ministry of Fuel and Power, as it then was, all agreed to co-operate.

A total of fifty-one undertakings, therefore, forty-seven firms and four area gas boards, were studied. For convenience, they are called collectively "the case studies" although, as will be seen, it

---

* As defined in Appendix B.

B

was not possible, within the time available, to go into anything like the detail normally involved in the conduct of case studies.

One hundred and thirty-four people were interviewed at the management level, of whom 54 were directors of a firm or members of an area gas board, and 206 graduates, all of whom had been to a university since World War II.

The graduate interview sample

The second of the two surveys is of a random sample of graduates who had worked in industry after graduating, though not necessarily immediately after graduating, in 1950, and who were still in the country. This sample will be referred to as "the graduate interviews". Seven hundred and fifty were selected at random for interview and 594 were successfully contacted in the winter of 1954-55. This is 80 per cent of the sample. Five hundred and seventeen of these graduates, 87 per cent, were still in industry when they were interviewed. They were all questioned about the first industrial undertaking in which they had worked, whether or not they were still in it.

About a fifth of these men went into the chemical and allied trades, and nearly a quarter into electrical engineering. Nine per cent went into firms manufacturing metal or metal goods; and another 9 per cent went into firms producing consumer goods in the widest sense—textiles, clothing, food, for example. Some 60 per cent of the men were still with the firm about which they were interviewed.*

Their distribution among the branches of industry faithfully reflects that in the main sample, as shown in the industrial sections of Table 1, except that mining (other than the National Coal Board) and electricity supply are a little under-represented. Both are such small categories that a deviation of this order could have arisen by chance, though the low figures for mining might be accounted for by the fact that a large proportion of graduates going into mining were abroad at the time of the interviewing.

The graduate interview sample also faithfully reflects with very minor variations the other characteristics in schooling, university record and so on, of the graduates in the main sample. It is, in short, a representative sub-sample.

* Further details of this sample are given in Appendix A and of the branches of industry entered in Appendix F.

Relationship of the two samples

Although the two sub-samples are not strictly comparable, the replies from the 594 graduates in the larger, graduate interview, sample serve as a check on those from the graduates in the case studies. The results suggest that the firms studied constitute a reasonably representative cross-section of those recruiting graduates in the period 1950-55 and can be used to fill out and to illustrate the more impersonal information derived from the graduate interview sample.

Interviewing procedure

Two rather different methods were adopted in collecting the information needed. The 594 men in the larger sample were all interviewed at home by the Social Survey, acting on behalf of P E P, in accordance with the Social Survey's normal procedure. In effect, this meant that these graduates were required to answer questions (which they had not previously had an opportunity of considering) put to them verbally by an interviewer; and they were given an opportunity to expand what they had said, or to make any comments on the questions put or on any subjects raised in their minds by them, only at the end of the interview. As none took advantage of this opportunity, these interviews were, in the event, limited to answers to the questions put and were straightforward "set" interviews.

A somewhat looser method was adopted in the studies of industrial undertakings. Each interview, whether of a member of management or of a graduate, was a compromise between a "free" interview, in which the ground to be covered is in the control of the person being interviewed, and a "set" interview, in which the ground to be covered is to a very large extent determined beforehand by the questions to be put and answered. It was thought that this procedure would be more likely than the set interview to establish the actual policy and practice of each firm in employing graduates and would also lend itself more readily to the seeking of opinions relevant to the subject. It also had advantages over the free interview in providing a certain minimum of information on each firm from which to draw comparisons.

A number of questions was therefore asked, but a break was made at eight points, that is, at the end of each group of questions, to allow the person being interviewed to make any comments he chose. Members of management and, although to a much smaller extent, their graduate recruits took advantage of these breaks and their remarks were taken into account in analysing replies to the set questions. The conduct of these interviews and their analysis called for considerable experience. They were carried out by three members of the P E P research team and were recruited for the purpose.

The questionnaires

The 594 graduates who were interviewed by the Social Survey were asked the questions set out in the questionnaire reproduced in Appendix C. The 206 graduates who were interviewed in the firms and gas boards that were the subject of case studies were asked questions closely similar to these, but because of the freer method of interviewing adopted no provision was made for the pre-coding of answers, and the two series are not absolutely identical. They are, nevertheless, so very similar that replies to them can be considered together. These questions fall under one or other of the heads of the enquiry, such as selection methods, or training.

Members of management in the fifty-one case studies were asked a series of questions which also fall under these heads. These are set out in Appendix D. It was not necessary to put all these questions to every member of management in any one firm. Once the questions seeking information on purely factual matters had been answered, only those questions seeking opinions were put to the remaining members of management. The interviews with managements preceded those with their graduate recruits.

The graduates themselves

As a result of the way in which the sub-samples were necessarily taken and of the scale upon which it was decided that each should be conducted, the emphasis of the present enquiry is on graduates. Before going on to consider the results of these interviews, some notes on the background of the eight hundred graduates in the two sub-samples might be useful.

They all filled in the questionnaire about their schooling, university record and post-graduate career which was the basis of the material reported on in *Graduate Employment*.* The 594 graduate interview men were rather older than the others. Twenty-one per cent of them were twenty-six years old or more on graduating in 1950; 49 per cent were twenty-three to twenty-six years old. The graduates interviewed in the case studies were not confined to the year 1950 for graduation. (Had this been done, there would in many cases have been too few or no graduates to interview.) They had, however, all graduated since the war. Only 17 per cent were twenty-six years old or more in 1950 and 38 per cent were twenty-three to twenty-six years old. The number of men who were rather older than the normal run reflects the interruption of the war.

Of the graduate interview men, 27 per cent, and of the case study men, 19 per cent, had been educated in an independent or public school included in the Headmasters' Conference, and 61 per cent of the graduate interview men and 68 per cent of the case study men had been educated at a grammar school not a member of the Conference or at its Scottish equivalent, a Scottish senior secondary school.

In both groups there were about two science graduates and two technology graduates for each arts graduate. They came from a representative cross-section of universities in Great Britain. About a fifth came from Oxford or Cambridge; 10 to 17 per cent were London Internal graduates and about a third were at other English universities or university colleges; 14 to 16 per cent had obtained a London External degree through a technical college or by other means. About one in ten had obtained a First and four in ten a Second Class Honours degree. The remainder got a Third or Fourth Class degree or a Pass or Ordinary degree. Almost all had studied full-time. All the 594 men in the graduate interview sample had graduated in 1950. Fifty-seven of the 206 men in the case studies had done so. Of the remainder, 28 had graduated between 1947 and 1949 and 112 between 1951 and 1954. Nine did not answer. Some 6 per cent of them all had gone on to take a higher degree.

---

* The 594 in the graduate interviews had of course already filled in this questionnaire, as they were part of the main sample. The 206 graduates in the case studies did so at the time the survey was made in the winter of 1954-55. The questionnaire is set out in Appendix A of *Graduate Employment* and is therefore not reproduced here.

Presentation of the evidence

The evidence falls under six broad heads: the major policy decision to recruit or not to recruit graduates; education for industry; the selection of graduates; their introduction; their training; and an assessment of the situation as seen by members of management and of graduates three or four years after the graduates' entry to the firm. Each chapter is devoted to one of these. Each starts with an introduction to the subject treated, goes on to a detailed review of the answers to the questions put and ends with a summing up of their outcome.

The emphasis of the enquiry as a whole was on graduates, and, as is usually the case in interviewing, the more critical, though as objective in their judgments, often replied to questions more freely than the others. This gave rise to some difficulty in maintaining a balanced presentation of the evidence. If some loss of perspective has been incurred at times in quoting criticisms and suggestions, it is compensated for in the summaries of the outcome of the answers given.

CHAPTER I

WHY EMPLOY GRADUATES?

THE question whether to employ university graduates is part of the wider question what amount and sort of labour is needed to carry out the work to be done and what amount and sort of labour is available. In industry an increasingly larger proportion of jobs needs to be filled by men with academic achievements beyond those of the secondary school and Higher National Certificate, or with above-average capacity for administration and leadership, or both.

Side by side with this higher standard has gone the increasing proportion of school children reaching a university. Before the war there were some 50,000 full-time students; now there are some 88,000. It would not be true to say that every young man with the makings of a good manager or a good scientist gets swept into the stream. For a variety of reasons, this does not happen. Some are too eager to start earning in their teens, or their parents want them to do so. Some public school boys of good calibre give up the idea of going to a university if they fail to get into Oxford or Cambridge. Some children, mainly of professional people, though well able to profit by going to a university, cannot get to one because their parents' income is above the modest upper limit within which grants may be made. Again, a long period of professional training, for example to be an accountant or solicitor, may make it difficult for parents to provide for a university education as well. It is true, nevertheless, that a larger proportion than ever before of the more intelligent children of university age in fact go to a university and this proportion is still increasing.

There is, however, no exact correspondence between the proportion of the population going to a university and the proportion of work that needs to be done by university people either in industry or elsewhere, nor between the qualifications acquired at a university and the qualifications sought by employers. The present shortage of scientists and technologists, for example, is too well known to need stressing, and it is complicated by shortages at lower levels—of technicians and laboratory assistants.

Reactions to this situation are likely to vary widely between different industries and different firms: the outlook of each will be governed by different considerations. There is, first, the nature of the work to be done. It may be highly complicated, as much of the work in electrical engineering or in the manufacture of aircraft, or it may be comparatively simple. Secondly, the nature of the work may be fairly stable, or it may be undergoing, or about to undergo, fundamental changes either in the end-product or in the process of production.

The size of the undertaking is another matter of considerable importance. Size will be governed to some extent by the nature of the product and by the effect and assessment of competition both at home and abroad. With increases in size may come increases in the responsibilities and problems of management.

Moreover, the nature and the amount of work to be done may not be adequately sized up. The firm may underestimate the effort it must make to maintain or to improve its relative position, and, as a consequence, it may underestimate the quality of the men it should recruit and also, therefore, its dependence, in the present situation, on the universities as a source of recruitment. That this may be true of some sections of industry at any rate was suggested in a White Paper on the recruitment of scientists and engineers by the engineering industry.* Shortage of labour at all levels may inhibit a firm from setting itself a standard higher than that determined by market conditions.

Even if the facts of the present and future situation are correctly assessed, the subsequent reactions to them may not be entirely uniform. A firm may realise that management succession will not be secured unless a certain proportion of recruits is capable of being promoted to higher posts. In spite of this, it may resist recruiting from the universities because it feels that the graduate is not as well fitted for its purpose as the young man who joins as a schoolboy and acquires his academic or professional qualifica-

* Advisory Council on Scientific Policy. Committee on Scientific Manpower. *Report on the Recruitment of Scientists and Engineers by the Engineering Industry* (H.M.S.O.), 1955. 1s. 6d. The committee suggested that the figure of 25 per cent shortage of university graduates estimated by the firms examined (mostly in the aircraft industry) "may well be an underestimate. The demand for such men is rising all the time with the increase in the general level of industrial activity, and the increased awareness of firms of their need for trained technologists". Paragraph 9.

tions by studying part time. On the other hand, a firm which may not have grasped the implications for its management succession of the universities' near-monopoly of intelligent young people may nevertheless recruit graduates for the sake of "being in the swim"—it may recruit in the right market but for wrong reasons.

The answers of the fifty-one undertakings studied to the question why they employed graduates, with which the present chapter opens, are, indeed, as diverse as might be expected from this brief review of the sort of reactions that could be made to it.

Old and new employers of graduates

Perhaps the first thing to note is how many graduates these undertakings had on their books at the time of the survey and how long they had been recruiting from the universities as a matter of deliberate policy.* The number of graduates in any undertaking naturally influences outlook on such things as further recruitment, on the measures to be taken to attract graduates, and on the need for the introduction of formal training schemes. Eighteen "old" employers had been employing graduates since before 1945—one had done so for forty years. Twenty-five "new" employers had recruited graduates only since the end of the war. These firms, at the time of the survey, could not have had more than nine years' experience of employing graduates as a deliberate policy: one had had only a few months'. The four gas boards have been included among the new employers as a more positive policy towards the recruitment of graduates was introduced after nationalisation in 1949, though graduates, most of them with degrees acquired after part-time study, had in fact been employed before then.

Eight firms, a sixth of all the private enterprise undertakings studied, had decided, either as a deliberate policy or because of the special circumstances in which they were placed, to recruit no graduates. But it happens that they had all, incidentally or unwittingly, taken on a man who had graduated in 1950. A return will be made later in this chapter to these eight firms: their attitude is of particular interest.

This distribution of old and new employers is itself worth some consideration, though the number of firms is small. Among the eighteen old employers none had fewer then 500 employees; ten

* See also Appendix F, Table F3.

employed at least 5,000 people. Two had under ten graduates and ten had a hundred graduates or more. (One, which did not or could not say how many graduates it had, was in fact a heavy recruiter. It certainly had many more than a hundred graduates and is therefore grouped among those with a hundred graduates or more.) Among the twenty-five new employers, six had less than 500 employees, and another eleven employed under 5,000 people. Ten had less than ten graduates altogether, and only four had a hundred or more.

Seventeen firms, a third of all these forty-three undertakings, had less than twenty-five graduates each, twelve had less than ten. There were nearly twice as many new firms as old ones among employers of less than twenty-five graduates. No firm with less than 2,000 employees had as many as twenty-five graduates. Only two out of the thirteen graduate-employing firms with between 2,000-4,999 employees had a hundred graduates but four out of six with 5,000-9,999 employees had a hundred graduates or more; and (excluding the area gas boards, which had well below this number) all those with 10,000 or more employees had at least a hundred graduates. Six firms, all with several hundred graduates, have been classed as giant employers of them.

Generally speaking, therefore, the larger the firm the larger the number of graduates employed. Equally, the heavier concentrations of graduates were also to be found in those industries with relatively complicated products or processes. Two out of three of the chemical firms had a hundred graduates or more, and six out of the eight electrical engineering firms. On the other hand three out of five of the firms in the metal manufacture and metal goods category had less than fifty graduates. Six of the nine consumer-goods firms had under twenty-five graduates.

Reasons for employing graduate scientists and technologists

In examining the replies to the question why graduates were taken on, no clear-cut divisions emerge. Many firms qualified their remarks in one way or another and in some firms the members of management interviewed were divided in their views. Opinions on the need for or the desirability of employing graduates shade off from positive to negative and are complicated and influenced by such things as geographical situation, the relative newness of the recruitment policy and the experience of members of management interviewed when they themselves first went into industry. In some instances it was found that a director or personnel officer had himself started out during the depression of the 1930s and felt some resentment towards a generation of young men who had been enabled to go to a university at the public expense, and to whom fears of unemployment were unknown. The material, in short, does not lend itself to exact analysis.

All but one of the forty-three firms who reported that they had a policy to employ graduates (though, possibly, on a very small scale) had some graduate scientists or technologists or both, but three were mainly concerned with arts graduates and with the problem of management succession. Of the remaining thirty-nine, all but three said that they employed scientists and technologists because some of their work had to be carried out by people who had achieved a certain standard of knowledge, though a degree was not necessarily the minimum standard required and might, indeed, be more than was required. For most firms, in fact, a degree was not essential, or was essential only for a proportion of the work for which they recruited graduates. Typical replies were:

We are in need of their trained knowledge.

They are essential for various of our development and design tasks.

The reason for taking on graduates given next in order of frequency was that they were needed as potential managers. But this reason was given only once for every twice that the graduates' knowledge was mentioned and was never given as the sole reason for taking on a scientist or technologist. Among the ten firms employing under 2,000 people that are here relevant, only four, in various industries, gave "management" as a reason; among the eighteen medium-sized firms, nine gave this as a reason; and among the seven large firms and four gas boards, all with 10,000 or more employees, three firms (a metal manufacturer, a vehicles manufacturer and a food concern) and two gas boards gave this as a reason. None of the four large electrical engineers gave management as a reason. Of the sixteen firms giving management as a reason for taking on graduates, nine had under fifty graduates, and six of the nine were new employers; of the remaining seven, five had more than a hundred graduates, and only one was a new employer. Typical replies here were:

We want the best men available for higher executive posts and look to graduates to form the nucleus for these posts.

The trained mind learns the business more quickly and is therefore more suitable for management later.

The remaining reason given may be broadly described as the general educational value of a graduate. It was mentioned, however, by only eleven of the thirty-nine undertakings concerned with the recruitment of scientists and technologists. Seven of them were medium sized, two small and two large. Most were old employers. It is exemplified by:

We need a class of brain found in graduates.

Modern industry needs the outlook of the educated man.

As might be expected, for work at an advanced level on development or reasearch, graduates were recruited because only they were considered capable of carrying it out. This work was naturally concentrated to a large extent in those industries with complex products or processes: the chemical manufacturers, the electrical engineers and one of the vehicle firms are the main examples. For work below this level there was some evidence that graduates were sometimes employed because there was no one else to be had: laboratory assistants and others were in even shorter supply. A member of management in one firm said: "It is the semi-qualified staff who are really short", and scientists in this firm complained of being employed in too junior work. A member of management in another firm said: "It is now difficult to get lab. boys. We don't want to give menial tasks to [graduate] chemists but we may have to". For other work, only five firms insisted that graduates were recruited because they were essential.*

Examination of these replies goes to show that recruitment was undertaken with varying degrees of enthusiasm. One of the chemical manufacturers, all the electrical engineering firms except one large one, two of the vehicle and aircraft manufacturers, the textile firm, two in building and one gas board could be said, on the whole, to have recruited graduates as graduates, that is, not just because they were "bright", or as second best. These fourteen undertakings, not quite a third of all the sample, could be said to have had a relatively positive attitude to the employment of

* See page 18.

science and technology graduates, though many had reservations to make of one kind or another. All but the three smallest electrical engineers and the gas boards were old employers. Typical replies from these firms were:

> Only science graduates could do the work.
>
> This is a class of work which only graduates can do.

Next comes a category of ten firms which recruited from the universities because, in effect, they wanted what they described as "good brains", and looked for them where they were likely to be found. The one old employer among them, a large food concern, had always recruited good brains, whether from the universities or from schools, and now that a much larger proportion of them was going to a university, the company had realised that it would have to depend more heavily on the universities and less heavily on the schools. In general the new employers in this group could be said to be out to get good brains rather than graduates as such. These firms were of various sizes and in various product categories. Two had a somewhat divided attitude. Members of management at the headquarters of one were much more enthusiastic than those at the unit visited, which was not well placed geographically to attract recruits.* In the other there was also a marked difference in enthusiasm; those at the board level were much more sanguine of finding good brains at universities. At a lower level a member of management thought that "the case for the employment of graduates had been over-sold". Typical replies from other firms in this group were:

> Most of the good brains are going to universities now and we recruit from universities chiefly because we want trained engineers.
>
> The educational system has changed. If we want to get a proper share of brains we must go to universities.

Outside this group, six other firms also said they were keen to get good brains, but they offered the graduates which they recruited work on testing, for example, with little or no prospects of advancement to top-level posts. All had under twenty-five graduates; three were in the consumer-goods industries.

The attitude of these recruiters of good brains recalls observations made by Lord Eustace Percy (as he then was) in an address

---

* The term "unit" is used to denote the section of the firm in which graduates (as well as management) were interviewed. See Appendix B.

at the conference organised by the Federation of British Industries in 1949 on "Industry and the Universities". He made the point that industry, ever since the Education Act of 1902, had been chasing "the new secondary scholar through his school, trying to catch up with him", and now has to chase him through the university. It is perhaps not surprising that firms took part in this chase with varying degrees of eagerness and that many of them could be said to look upon a university less as a seat of learning than as a labour market.

A more negative attitude was taken by four firms and two gas boards which were, or had become, reluctant to go to the universities because of continual difficulties in getting enough graduates or because the graduates they had succeeded in getting had proved disappointing in one way or another. One gas board was, however, divided in its views, a senior member being more enthusiastic than his colleagues.

Finally, there were two firms—one metal manufacturer with under fifty graduates, one non-electrical engineer with less than ten—which were outspoken in their dislike of having to go to universities. The first said:

> It is not our policy to recruit from the universities, but we have had to recognise that it is increasingly difficult to recruit at the school age. Those of school age we have seen have become duller in the last twenty years and we have had to widen our net, and bring in a few graduates. . . . But it is not a policy we like.

The second said that jobs formerly being done by craftsmen were now being done by graduates, and it much regretted the disappearance of the craftsman, or rather of his skill.

In short, half the old employers of graduates, four out of the six giant employers, and all but one of the electrical engineers were among the fourteen firms with a relatively positive attitude towards the recruitment of graduates. Rather more, sixteen, were primarily concerned to recruit good brains and went to the universities as likely places in which to find them. At the other end of the scale came all but one (the largest) of the metal and metal goods manufacturers, the non-electrical engineers and two of the gas boards with a somewhat reluctant approach.*

* One gas board, which was prevented by redundancy of staff from developing a graduate recruitment policy, has been omitted from this analysis of attitude to recruitment.

Reasons for employing arts graduates

The employment of arts graduates was on a much smaller scale. For four firms, however, all of them very large employers of graduate scientists and technologists, information is lacking. One was certainly, and the other three were probably, fairly heavy recruiters of arts graduates. Apart from these four, the arts graduates amounted to a ninth of the total number of graduates.*

Of the thirty-two undertakings with some arts graduates for which figures were obtained, half had less than nine—ten had fewer than four—twelve had ten or more. Of these twelve, all but one of the firms and one out of the two gas boards had more than fifty graduates altogether. They were divided equally between new and old employers of graduates. Five of the twelve had more than twenty-five arts men. With one exception, they were large firms. All were in different industries. Their arts-graduate strength ranged from thirty-one to eighty-four.

Reasons for recruiting and attitude towards recruiting arts men varied considerably. Ten firms, including five large ones, were decidedly favourable to the employment of arts graduates and had the possibility of eventual promotion to management in mind for them. Only one, however, appeared to be really enthusiastic. It had started "without much conviction", but its scheme for arts men had been "a terrific success" and was to be expanded. Here again, firms recruited graduates not as such but as likely to have personality or a good background—either social or educational—as well as brains. All these firms mentioned these personal, rather than academic, qualities as those they sought. Typical of the replies given was the statement that:

> Arts graduates are taken on to ensure the flow of intellect and quality into the organisation.

This attitude to the recruitment of arts graduates has, indeed, become familiar. The University of Oxford Appointments Committee, for example, has more than once drawn attention to this tendency. In its report for 1954 it pointed out that:

---

* In *Graduate Employment* it was shown that industry recruited from men graduating in 1950 in the proportion of four scientists or technologists to one arts graduate: the latter formed a fifth of the total. The proportion among these firms, though not an exact figure, indicates an advance in the recruitment of arts graduates by industry.

Eighty-five per cent of notifications [for arts men for industry and commerce] revealed interest in how the candidate worked and what part he played in college and university life, rather than in the subject he read.

Next comes a group of eight firms and a gas board which recruited graduates for somewhat limited purposes, at least in the first instance. Recruitment was confined to personnel work, accountancy or economic research, for example. They are followed by a group of four firms which recruited arts graduates with some reluctance or because there seemed no alternative:

They are the hardest to fit in and find jobs for.

Finally, three firms and one gas board had experimented with the employment of arts graduates, but had decided against any further recruitment. Two of these found that an arts degree did not provide a sufficient grounding in science; one did not feel that they "mucked in" well enough and had in fact taken them on only in "the chaos of the post-war years where many gaps had to be filled"; and the gas board had set its face against any further recruitment from universities.*

When these four that had decided against recruiting any more arts men are added to the eleven firms that had never done so (though they employed science and technology graduates), a more balanced view of the attitude of firms to this question is reached. At one end of the scale, there were ten firms which were relatively favourable to recruiting arts men, followed by nine which recruited them for limited purposes, and, at the other end of the scale, fifteen which had never recruited them or had ceased to do so. The sort of reasons given by the last were that the arts graduate could not talk to a craftsman (in a vehicles firm) in his own terms; or that technical knowledge was required for administration and the preparation of contracts (in a reinforced concrete firm).

On the whole, it is clear that the employment of arts graduates was by no means widespread, but that of the twelve undertakings known to have ten or more arts men, eight were still recruiting them, and with some success, not primarily as graduates, but as young men with good brains and some personality, and three for their specialist knowledge—mostly a degree in commerce or

---

* The remaining five either had no views or were divided in their views.

economics. The gas board had decided against recruiting any more if it could help doing so.

Firms employing no graduates

As has been seen, in the sample of fifty-one firms studied, eight turned out not to have employed graduates except incidentally or unwittingly, and in ones or twos. Yet each, in fact, took on one man who graduated in 1950, and thus appeared in the sample.

The line dividing them from some of the firms just reviewed, and classed as having some sort of graduate employment policy, is a fine one, but of all the eight now to be considered it can be said that none had intended, nor intended for the future, deliberately to seek a graduate of any sort, as such.*

At the time of the survey, three—a quarrying firm, a firm in the chemical and allied trades and a firm making metal goods— had no graduates; four—another manufacturer of metal goods, a firm of electrical and a firm of non-electrical engineers, and a firm of builders and contractors—had one graduate each, and the remaining one, which manufactured vehicles, had two.

These graduates were employed either incidentally or accidentally. For example, the only graduate in one of the metal-manufacturing firms, a small family firm, was the son of the director. He had been taken into the firm to succeed his father, to whom the fact that his son had been to a university was entirely irrelevant. The vehicle manufacturers had taken the two graduates on their books apparently without knowing that they were graduates.

Three of these firms had under a hundred employees; two had under five hundred; one (the firm in the building and contracting trade) had between 1,000 and 2,000 employees; the electrical engineers had between 3,000 and 4,000 employees, and the vehicle manufacturer had considerably over 10,000 employees. Five out of the eight, therefore, were small firms.

The reasons given by these firms for not employing any graduates as such fall, broadly, under two heads: that graduates

* These firms are shown in Table F3 in Appendix F. They were asked questions only on why they did not employ any graduates or any graduates as such, and whether they had any views on the value to them of university men. These questions fall within the ambit of heads I and VIII of the questions to management set out in Appendix D. Questions under other heads, Recruitment, for example, were irrelevant.

were unsuited to or not needed in the firm; or that the firm could not offer suitable conditions and prospects to graduates.

In the first category comes the vehicle manufacturer, perhaps the most interesting of all these eight, because it is so much the largest. It firmly believed that other kinds of recruits were best suited to it. It wanted people to grow up with the firm and to have "a background of the industry from the start". It had various apprentice schemes for the training of youths for production and development work and took in grammar school boys to train for administrative work. The top management regarded this policy as satisfactory and did not propose to recruit any graduates as such from universities. Each year, however, it was offering two of its apprentices the possibility of taking a degree at the local university after three years with the firm. (It is interesting to note that there were no arts graduates either in this or in the other two vehicle manufacturing firms included among the forty-three with a deliberate graduate recruitment policy).

The electrical engineers, who made electrical accessories, and one of the metal manufacturers, regarded the nature of their product as not requiring graduate labour and took in boys from school. The electrical engineers, for example, considered that the pace of technical advance could be satisfactorily set by the firm from which they obtained their machines and that the ingenuity called for in obtaining the best use of these machines could be and was provided by non-graduate technicians. They were, in fact, prospering.

The civil engineering contractors considered that there were no degrees immediately relevant to its needs. This firm, however, had a decidedly critical attitude towards graduates, and this was perhaps the real reason for its decision against employing them. The managing director of the firm said that they had "no faith in degrees only, which are usually obtained to compensate for some personal deficiency". The small firm of non-electrical engineers had rather the same point of view, reinforced by its feeling that the works operatives would be prejudiced in favour of technical-college-trained and works-trained men:

This may be an old-fashioned Yorkshire prejudice, but it will take a lot of breaking down.

The men who come up the hard way are hard to beat. . . . Still, nowadays, when university education is free, it is a great temptation to parents. There are going to be far too many graduates. What's to be done with them all? They want money and who is to give it them when they know nowt? (A director in the same firm.)

The metal manufacturer whose son had, incidentally, gone to a university said that in his view the firm was too small to entertain the idea of employing any graduates. But, apart from this, he was not convinced of the advantages of employing graduates:

One can always tell a public school man, but the same cannot be said of graduates.

The other metal manufacturer was more outspoken. It was their deliberate policy "not to take any notice of degrees". They were interested only in whether candidates "can do the job". Their processes of manufacture were, however, in their view, simple and "did not need specialised technical skills".

This, and the other four small firms in this group, in effect, said that it would not be proper for them to employ graduates because they were not in a position to do so. All five said that the size of the firm (none had more than 500 employees) did not allow them to entertain the idea of employing graduates. Three said that they could not afford graduates' salaries; two that they could not train them, and two that they could not offer them enough scope in their work or prospects of advancement. Three were family firms.

With the exception of the second metal manufacturer, however, these five small firms appeared to be conscious of the handicap imposed by their size and recognised in some degree the risks they were running in having to confine their recruitment to non-graduates. These risks, however, were not all of the same order. For the quarrying firm, for instance, they could not be regarded as anything but marginal.

THE QUALIFICATIONS SOUGHT

IN this review of the reactions to the question why graduates were employed or were not employed, some indication has been given of the graduate strength of each firm, the sort of work for which graduates were recruited and what impelled the firm to seek them. Broadly, as was expected, the scale and range of recruitment was closely related to the size of the firm and the nature of its product. Not much has been said, however, about the academic qualifications and personal qualities sought.

Academic qualifications

In recruiting science and technology graduates, fifteen undertakings preferred, if they could, to obtain science and technology graduates, or only science or only technology graduates, with a First or a Second Class Honours degree, both for research and for production. Seven of these, including a gas board, were large; eight had more than a hundred graduates; four were electrical engineers. But three, including two large electrical engineers, were prepared to accept a lower class Honours or a Pass or Ordinary degree for production work. Seven firms wanted a First or a Second only for research. Four of these were large firms; five had more than a hundred graduates. Twelve firms were content with Pass degrees or thought that class of degree was immaterial. Of these none were large firms and only one had more than a hundred graduates. Seven had under twenty-five. Four were in the consumer goods industries and three were builders and contractors. Another four firms, all with four graduates, and three gas boards had no views on qualifications: they were interested, rather, in the subject in which the degree was taken. Only one had more than fifty graduates.

As might be expected, it was in the chemical and allied trades, in electrical engineering and in vehicle and aircraft construction that higher academic achievements were most frequently sought, and least frequently in building and contracting and the gas boards. Again all the eight large firms (those with at least 10,000 employees) aimed at a First or a Second for research or for research and production: and five of these were giant employers of graduates.

In sum, therefore, although only a minority of firms and only one out of the three gas boards set their sights high, this minority includes all the major claimants on scientists and technologists: broadly speaking, the larger the firm and the larger the graduate strength, the higher the academic standard sought in these faculties.

Turning to the qualifications expected of arts graduates, it has already been seen that many of the thirty-two firms employing arts graduates were more interested in personality than in academic achievements. Only nine firms and a gas board, in fact, sought arts graduates with a First or a Second. Four and a gas board were large; four were among the small band of five with more than twenty-five arts graduates; and one had decided against recruiting any more, after taking on two arts graduates.

Eight firms and three gas boards had no views on the academic qualifications that their arts graduates should possess. Only three of them had more than ten arts graduates. Three, including one of these, had decided not to have any more. The remaining firms made no stipulation about class of degree. Here again the larger the graduate strength, the higher the academic standard sought.

Generally, it may be said that, except for a very important minority of firms interested mainly in scientists and technologists, the academic calibre sought was not exacting. There appear to be two reasons for this. The first, and more important, is a distinct anti-academic bias. This was displayed by a number of firms mainly in an aversion to "brilliance" or to First Class Honours degrees, whether held by a scientist, technologist or arts man. Examples of this point of view were:

> We are not shown Firsts by appointments boards—we don't think they would fit in, anyway.
>
> In the main, we don't think a First man is as a rule the man we want.
>
> Brilliant academic distinction doesn't mean a thing as far as personality is concerned.
>
> We don't seek people with Firsts as they often tend to have no sense of humour.

This point of view is reinforced by the very limited value set on higher degrees by many firms—to which a return will be made in the next chapter.

Secondly, the standard of some employers must have been affected to some extent by the difficulty of getting men with relatively good degrees. Only twelve firms said they were getting as many graduates of the kinds they wanted and, of these, seven were small, and none had more than eleven graduates altogether; four were medium-sized and one a giant employer of graduates with a large measure of "glamour".

Personal qualities

The impression gained, however, is that shortage of supply was not the main influence in determining the attitude of firms to the qualifications sought. Again and again throughout the interviews it was personal qualities rather than paper qualifications that seemed to engage the attention of directors and others concerned with graduate recruitment. This concern with questions of adaptability, responsiveness, ability to get on with, and eventually to lead, others is readily seen as the obverse of the tendency, already noted, to discount the purely academic. In speaking of these qualities, a few members of management gave the impression that they expected the graduate recruit to be already relatively mature. Most, however, implied that they hoped only that the recruit would give promise of developing these qualities as he gained experience in the firm.

It would be wrong to suppose that this preoccupation with personal qualities was largely confined to arts graduates. This was not so. It was most often in discussing science or technology graduates (with which, of course, most were concerned) that this preoccupation was displayed. The qualities sought first and foremost were what might be called social: that is, such things as humour, ability to mix well, wide interests, tact, poise, being a man of the world. Only a little different from these, but mentioned rather less frequently, came qualities of character: leadership, responsibility, independence, honesty, ambition, drive. Typical replies were:

> We must have the right personal qualities even in people going into research.

> They must have personality, have their feet on the ground and be good mixers. No back-room boys!

> We want graduates who will do the work without fuss and fit into the organisation.

A long way behind came mental (as distinct from academic) abilities: common sense, logical thought, powers of expression.

These personal qualities were sought in both scientists and technologists, though with more emphasis on the latter. There was little evidence of the old conception of an engineer as someone concerned first and last with machines. For arts graduates there appeared to be less insistence on social qualities and more on mental qualities—on powers of expression and so on. This may have been due to the fact that many firms were at a rather early stage in their employment of arts graduates and were not yet sure what qualities to seek in them. Others were too preoccupied with scientist and techologists to give their views on the personal qualities they should look for in arts graduates.

Be this as it may, the paramount desire was to find recruits who would "fit in", get along with the shop floor and be generally tactful; in short, good mixers. For every three mentions of social qualities there were two of qualities of leadership and drive, of qualities of character, and one of mental capacities, of the capacity for "elegant thought" as one man put it! All but two of the twenty larger employers of graduates looked for social qualities of one kind or another and all the giant employers did so.

Preoccupation with social and allied qualities was, indeed, so striking that it is worth asking whether it was not, perhaps, rather more than the obverse of the anti-academic bias found in so many of the employers—a bias against mere bookishness more common in England, in which most of the firms were to be found, than in Scotland or Wales. May they not also be connected with recent new thinking on personnel relations, and the functions of management and, more widely, the structure and health of industrial society? These undertakings were, perhaps, consciously or unconsciously, attempting to redress earlier conceptions of labour as a commodity to be bought and sold and, generally, to counteract the tendency to think of production as having none but an economic purpose. The difficulties into which industry has been led by an inadequate grasp of its purpose and functions and, therefore, of the qualities to be looked for in better educated recruits, were recognised earlier in the United States than in this country: but here, too, much headway had already been made by the time of this survey, and the objectives in recruitment just considered are some evidence of it.* The relevance that the stress laid by employers on social qualities has to university education is considered in the next chapter.

This analysis of the qualifications and qualities sought has been in very general terms. At this point, therefore, in order to give

* It is twenty years since Professor T. N. Whitehead analysed so brilliantly the causes of the weakness of industrial concerns. "How does it happen that a poverty of social activity is found particularly within the walls of industry itself? . . . The ulterior purpose of business activity has been erroneously supposed to be the accumulation of wealth for its own sake, as distinct from its social function." *Leadership in a Free Society* (Harvard University Press), Fifth printing, 1950. $3.50. Page 31.

greater definition to the practices of these undertakings, consideration is given to the measures taken to recruit graduates: the assessment of need, the means taken to attract graduates to the firm, and the results achieved.

IDEALLY, the aim of any undertaking should be to assess, as a continuous process, and as precisely as possible, the number and kinds of recruits it needs. There are many things to be taken into account: the standard of product to be achieved and the scale on which it is to be produced, the assessment of competition, both at home and abroad, the likelihood of changes in the process of production, following on research or development work conducted by firms or by others, for example. Such an assessment implies an analysis of the work to be done and the qualifications needed to carry it out. Assessment of the jobs for which graduates are or will be needed is part of the wider assessment. This is by no means a simple process. Industry as a whole has a far more complicated task in this respect than, for instance, the civil service or the teaching profession.

The assessment of need

In considering the replies to the questions on how it was decided how many graduates to take on, it should be borne in mind that it was only in a minority of firms that graduates were considered essential for all or for some of the work for which they were recruited. Replies to the question: *Are these jobs confined to graduates?* showed that only five firms, four with under thirty graduates and one with over a hundred, would not consider other candidates for the work for which they recruited graduates.

Six firms, of which four had more than a hundred graduates, had an intermediate type of recruitment. They recruited non-graduates or men promoted from existing staff for all work other than research or development, for which graduates were needed. (These terms were not defined and may not have been used in the same sense by all those using them.) One with over a hundred graduates, interested almost entirely in arts graduates, had a small range of vacancies for which graduates only were accepted; another, with over fifty graduates, had a small range reserved for graduate scientists and engineers for production and research work.

A typical reply from a firm with this type of recruitment, in which only a proportion of the work was reserved for graduates, was:

> We have some very able men with no university qualification: lab. technicians or foremen with, for instance, Higher National Certificate. We think it important that we should provide careers for those men and second them into the graduate staff area and we are slowly arranging that. In future there will be an area of overlap, particularly in the production departments. Some jobs may be staffed by either graduates with limited experience or experienced non-graduates. It is very much what happens in the army—you often meet a ranker captain or major but rarely a ranker staff officer.

For all the work for which they also recruited graduates, all the other undertakings were prepared to accept non-graduates—men with professional qualifications or with a Higher National Certificate, for example—or, less specifically, and more frequently mentioned, "company-trained men" or "any suitably qualified applicants", this last most frequently in reference to work on sales:

> Vacancies are open to anyone. There is a promotion and education scheme for everyone in the firm. This removes a frequent cause of hostility to graduates.

> Others are eligible if they make the grade, but we have proved it's the graduate who gets to the top.

Large firms

The five giant employers of graduates and the other three manufacturing firms in the private sector of industry employing at least 10,000 people appeared, with one exception, to review their needs in a systematic and sustained manner, in that they said they made annual or more frequent surveys in which they made allowance for probable wastage in staff, and for trends or expansion in output. Their replies, however, in most cases, were not very full. The reply of one of the electrical engineering firms, a giant employer of graduates, though fuller than the others, reflects their general tenor:

> We must crystal gaze to 1984! We as a company must go up with industry and we must increase our output 6 per cent per annum.

To achieve this, we need a staff increase of 4 per cent per annum. Our normal wastage due to turnover is 3 per cent. At an intelligent guess we need 120 this year, plus this figure for the next five years.

The exception, an electrical engineering firm, replied to the questions on how it decided how many graduates to take on by saying that it got hold of as many suitable candidates as it could. This was not in fact an answer to the question and, in view of the size of the undertaking, probably did less than justice to the firm's actual practice in assessing need. In the circumstances of shortage, the answer given is understandable.

These large undertakings were also asked: *Are the qualifications required for specific jobs defined in advance?* For undertakings of this size, this was perhaps a tall order. But it was the purpose of the question to discover how far each job was graded in terms of the demands it would make on the academic qualifications and personal qualities of the recruit that filled it. One, an electrical firm, said "No", six gave qualified replies, and one, a giant employer of graduates said "Yes" without developing this in any way. Of the six which qualified their replies, four said they decided what man might fill what job, one at the stage of selecting candidates, three at the training stage. In another firm, metal manufacturers, the qualifications needed for each particular job were defined in some departments and not in others. The last of the six had, in effect, a two-tier system of recruitment. At headquarters, which acted on behalf of a very wide range of factories, the specification of qualifications for all individual vacancies was not attempted. But at the unit visited, which recruited in part through headquarters, the qualifications needed for each vacancy were said to be defined in advance of taking steps to recruit.

In effect, therefore, except in one firm, it seems that the vacancies that might be filled by graduates were assessed in a generalised way, as though they were interchangeable within wide categories such as production or research. In fact, in half these large firms all candidates were said to be recruited with a range of possible jobs in mind for them, and in the others some at any rate were recruited in this way. In the company which was the exception, a giant employer of graduates, the qualifications required for each vacancy were said to be defined in advance and each man was recruited with a specific vacancy in mind for him. But at that time the company was giving a training course only to those graduates destined for the sales department and was better placed than the others to foresee individual vacancies at the stage of assessing need. Most of these concerns, therefore, appear to have laid down the qualifications sought only in general terms. A specification might have taken the form, for example, of "Someone with a degree or a professional qualification in mechanical engineering; a good mixer", or x men with these qualifications, and the successful candidates would be allocated, either immediately or after training, to the vacancy that seemed most appropriate.

The four gas boards also fall into this group of large concerns employing more than 10,000 people. The smallest of them was not in a position to recruit because of redundancy precipitated by nationalisation, and one was giving up the recruitment of graduates and did not feel it need explain the steps it took to assess needs. Of the other two, one said it reviewed its needs in the light of wastage and of any new developments in the board; but it did not specify qualifications except in broad terms. The remaining board took on some eight a year. This was about as many as they found that they could attract to them. They would have liked more but recognised that limitation to eight had its advantages, since this was the maximum number that could be trained at its larger plants, where facilities existed for this purpose.

Medium-sized firms

Recruitment in the medium-sized firms was naturally not on the scale of the large organisations. Of the nineteen firms in this group, only six had between a hundred and two hundred graduates and nine had less than fifty. Half these firms appear to have assessed regularly what their requirements would be, though, again, some were more forthcoming than others in describing the considerations taken into account in building up an estimate. Some confined their replies to the administrative arrangements for making an assessment:

> We work out what the turnover is likely to be. We also have a number of contracts and get an idea how many we will want.

> The staffing committee . . . meets four or five times a year, when future requirements are assessed.

> We get an estimate each year and with our knowledge of the sort of

losses we have and how much departments will expand we calculate accordingly.

We ask the departments for their estimates of their needs for a year.

We allow for wastage and use the departments' estimates as a guide, because there is some inter-departmental transfer.

Four, of which only one had more than fifty graduates, regarded their intake as static, or limited for the time being, or rapidly tailing off within the following four years; two appeared to feel their way as vacancies arose. Two—one with more than fifty, the other with more than a hundred graduates—said they were in the hands of the market, though their replies imply that they had a fairly clear notion of requirements:

It is impossible to get anywhere near the figure the Board want. So it is no good assessing a figure. At the moment we are about thirty-two short and we are frantic.

All I can get. We are chronically short.

Eight of these nineteen firms, including three with more than a hundred graduates, said that they defined the qualifications needed for each vacancy but said no more than that. Six, including three with more than a hundred graduates, said "Yes" when asked if qualifications were defined in advance, but qualified this in some way or another:

Yes, in so far as we seek a degree.

Yes, but some are taken on blind, not knowing where expansion is going to be.

Yes and no: we try to get a specification.

For scientists, yes, for arts, no.

A firm of civil engineers said they specified in the sense that they wanted civil engineers only. Another firm, in the consumer-goods industry, with over a hundred graduates, said "Yes, but not very clearly".

Two gave a qualified "No":

No: but leadership is essential. (A firm mainly interested in arts graduates.)

No, except that a man must have a degree or its equivalent.

In effect, therefore, this amounted to the same reply as that just quoted: that nothing more was aimed at than a specification of the common denominators for all relevant vacancies. Two said "No" more decisively:

No, they are difficult to define.

No. Nine out of ten are taken on without any particular job in view.

Small firms

Of the twelve small firms, only two had more than ten graduates. The recruitment of graduates was on a scale commensurate with the existing graduate strength. Three said, in effect, that they looked ahead and, for example:

... recruited from the point of view of the long-term future—five years is short.

The others filled vacancies as they arose, in the light of the "flow of work and projects" or "the specific jobs available". One said:

One graduate is all that is needed.

Five said, without further comment, that they defined the qualifications needed for each vacancy and four of them recruited with a specific vacancy in mind for each candidate. Seven gave qualified answers such as:

It is a flexible specification. If we are looking for someone on the production side we would specify science.

Character first, qualification second, every time.

If they have a university degree, that is all that is needed.

Four out of these seven nevertheless recruited graduates with a specific vacancy in mind for each man sought.

In summing up, it should first be emphasised that, within the compass of a relatively short interview, questions relating to the assessment of graduate intake could not be many or detailed. The answers just considered, however, convey the impression that all the large firms and half the medium-sized firms made periodic assessments of their need for graduates in a regular manner and based them on estimates of future production and of wastage. In most of the other firms, with demands shading off from some thirty graduates to a single one, no reference was made to any regular periodic review. Replies were, however, in many cases scanty, and in three cases took the form of a reference to the shortage of the graduates sought. What is clear is that in most firms the assessment of need would have to have been made in the light of the fact that non-graduates were eligible for the work for which graduates were sought. The general practice, though less common in smaller firms, was also not to differentiate the qualifications needed for each individual vacancy, but to express them, as it were, in terms of the factors common to each range of possible vacancies. The specification in broad terms of the qualifications needed was due no doubt in part to the eligibility of non-graduates over a wide field, but also perhaps to the importance attached to personal qualities, which do not lend themselves readily to precise definition in terms of vacancies to be filled, and lastly also to the fact that, in cases in which training was to follow recruitment, the actual vacancies to be filled could not always be known at the stage of assessing needs.

ATTRACTING GRADUATES TO THE FIRM

HOWEVER its needs were assessed, every firm had, by some means or another, to persuade graduates to apply for work with it. The steps taken to attract graduates are now reviewed.

TABLE 2

METHODS OF RECRUITMENT

(Used in five or more undertakings)

	Firm size					
Method	1-499	500-1,999	2,000-4,999	5,000-9,999	10,000 and over	Total
	Number of firms					
Advertising	4	3	11	2	8	28
Technical and Scientific Register	—	—	1	2	2	5
University appointments boards given vacancies . . .	1	4	7	3	4	19
Contacting of graduates through university appointments boards	—	—	6	4	6	16
Ties with university departments	1	6	6	4	7	24
Contacting of graduates through university departments .	—	—	3	2	3	8
Vacation work . . .	—	—	1	3	2	6
Professional contacts . .	—	1	3	—	1	5
Number of firms in size group .	6	6	13	6	12	43

All the undertakings were asked what methods they had adopted of attracting graduate recruits and, in particular, whether they had any direct contact with universities.

For the sake of brevity, Table 2 sets out in summary form the methods said to be adopted; methods used by less than five firms are excluded. Advertising was the method most frequently mentioned, but close behind came the making of contacts with heads of university departments and other senior members of universities and the notification of vacancies to university appointments boards.

This relates, however, to all the undertakings, and includes, therefore, those with only a very small or intermittent demand for graduates. Of the eighteen firms and two gas boards with fifty or more graduates on their books all but one, a gas board, had a sustained demand, and six have been classified as giant employers of graduates. They are more pertinent since it is into the employment of the (comparatively small number of) larger firms that most men go and it is their recruiting campaigns that are likely to make the biggest impact. Advertising was mentioned by fourteen firms, of whom three mentioned "prestige" advertising; and all except one notified university appointments boards of their vacancies* and eleven went further. For instance, they went to see the secretaries of the boards and arranged talks to undergraduates through them. Moreover, a similar number, including five out of the six giant employers of graduates, had a second line of communication with universities in the form of personal contacts with heads of departments and other senior members. A typical reply to the question on methods adopted was:

A team of experts go to universities and interviews anyone interested. Professors and appointments boards submit suitable men to us.

Others took more elaborate steps:

We run vacation courses, and invite students to spend some days in our factories, we organise recruiting visits to universities, and have contacts, both official and personal, with various departments in universities. We also give some universities untied grants.

* The exception, a large firm with over a hundred graduates, said, "Appointments boards are useless. Too many firms are wooing graduates. . . . But advertisements won't woo them. We rely on hard cash." But the firm had contacts with senior members of universities and paid visits to universities and thought them useful.

A pamphlet, which describes the activities of the firm, gets around. This gives the conditions of work, which includes the provision of excellent accommodation in a country setting, which appeals to a number of students. We take over the local hotel and entertain about thirty professors yearly. Our policy is to make them our friends. We also present equipment to colleges from time to time and see that our nameplate is on it.

We go round to universities, keep in close touch with appointments boards and arrange conferences with appointment board officers. University staffs are invited to the works and are kept in touch with what we do. Visits are also arranged for first-year students and this year we are starting a big two-day visit for third-year students to include a tour of establishments.

The reply of the only large employer of graduates which succeeded in getting all the graduates it required was:

By making friends with universities and heads of departments; by ensuring that university appointments boards really know the quality and conditions of work in the company; by visits to and from universities and direct contact with them all; by press publicity, prestige advertising and the distribution of literature about the firm; and by paying the expenses of applicants to enable them to look at the work. They are met by car, and shown round. Offers from various departments are made to them.

Some firms mentioned still further tactics. Good or high salaries were mentioned by two, one a giant employer; and an electrical firm, particularly badly off for graduates, had started a summer school as a means of attracting more. The reputation of the firm was spoken of by three, one a giant employer, as a magnet for graduates. A metal manufacturer summed up their methods as "everything except bribery and corruption".

The way graduates heard of openings

The figures in Table 2 do not give the whole picture. Further light is shed on the methods adopted by turning to the answers given by graduates to the question how they heard about the opening in the firm about which they were interviewed. These figures are indicative of the results achieved by the various methods adopted. A firm would not be slow to note the results of its various campaigns, and within the resources at its disposal would adjust its tactics accordingly.

The replies of the graduate interview sample of 594 men* show that 35 per cent heard of their opening through a university appointments board, a visit from a representative of a firm or through an introduction from a professor or tutor. This means that, broadly speaking, about a third of the graduates heard of their opening through some initiative of the firm taken at universities (though not all the jobs found through university appointments boards would have been notified to them by the firms concerned: some boards inform graduates of vacancies advertised in the Press). Another 18 per cent heard of the opening through some other type of initiative taken by the firm: advertising vacancies or notifying the Technical and Scientific Register or a labour exchange.

Almost a quarter said that they heard of the opening through having made a personal application to the firm. This is not necessarily an answer to the question; but a general enquiry to a firm whether a vacancy is available is by no means an unknown method of seeking work. (It was in fact mentioned by some of the firms studied and the graduates in them. The answers of the latter to another question, on their reason for applying for the job, show that it was the type of work offered, the reputation of the firm or, rather less frequently, its location, or sometimes two of these combined, that moved them to make a personal application.) How these graduates came to hear of the firm to which they applied is not known. Of the remaining quarter the largest category was the 12 per cent who heard of the opening through knowing someone in the firm. Here the initiative could have been taken either by the student or by the person in the firm.

As is shown in Tables 3, 4 and 5, these figures varied with the graduate's university, faculty and the size of the firm. The numbers are small, but they suggest that there were marked differences in tactics at different universities. Table 3 shows that almost 40 per cent of the graduates from Oxford and Cambridge heard of the opening through their committee or board, but for

* This sample is described in Appendix A. It is concerned with the first job in industry of 594 men who graduated in 1950. The channels through which the graduates in the firms studied heard of the opening were much the same, though rather more mentioned their university appointments board or an advertisement and rather fewer having made a personal application. The graduate interview sample of 594 men is, however, representative in the statistical sense and is therefore used here.

D

TABLE 3

HOW DID YOU HEAR OF THE OPENING?

Graduate's university

Method	London: Int.	London: Ext.	Oxford and Cam.	English univs.	English univ. colls.	Welsh univ. colls.	Scottish univs.	Total
			Percentage of graduates mentioning a given method					
Advertising . . .	16	18	6	11	25	4	2	11
Ministry of Labour .	2	2	4	4	—	4	4	3
Technical and Scientific Register . . .	5	4	1	4	—	4	9	4
University appointments board . . .	10	4	39	29	8	20	11	21
Visit from representative of firm . . .	16	6	2	11	8	8	20	10
Personal introduction .	6	5	8	5	17	12	5	6*
Personal application .	26	25	14	22	25	32	29	23
Knowing someone in firm . . .	6	8	20	13	17	12	16	12
Other channels . .	25	6	6	2	—	4	2	4
No answer . . .	10	20	1	1	—	—	2	6
Number of graduates at university .	103	93	107	199	12	25	55	594

* Some three-fifths of these introductions were from the graduate's professor or tutor.

those who took an external degree of London University, either from a university college or otherwise, less than 10 per cent heard of the opening by this means. A visit from a representative of the firm or "talent scout" was mentioned most frequently by

TABLE 4

HOW DID YOU HEAR OF THE OPENING?

Faculty

Method	Arts	Science	Technology	Total
	Percentage of graduates mentioning a given method			
Advertising	8	14	10	11
Ministry of Labour . . .	8	3	1	3
Technical and Scientific Register .	—	8	2	4
University appointments board .	24	26	15	21
Visit from representative of firm .	—	9	16	10
Personal introduction . . .	6	6	7	6
Personal application . . .	21	20	26	23
Knowing someone in firm . .	23	8	11	12
Other channels	5	1	6	4
No answer	5	6	6	6
Number of graduates in faculty .	132	218	244	594

men who obtained an internal degree at London University and by those who graduated in Scotland. As might be expected, an advertisement was more frequently mentioned by men with an external London degree than by others. "Other channels" bulked large only for London internal people. This was composed of a large number of different organisations, the professional engineers' institutes, the Institute of Personnel Management and so on. London students are, of course, exceptionally well placed to use other agencies such as these.

There are also marked differences when the graduates are considered as scientists, technologists or men with an arts degree. About a quarter of the men with an arts degree mentioned their university appointments board, and another quarter knew someone in the firm to which they went. No man with an arts degree mentioned hearing of his opening from a representative of the firm. The scientists used their university appointments board a little more than the arts men, and advertisement a good deal more—14 per cent of them, as against 8 per cent of the arts men. The scientists were the only ones who mentioned the Technical and Scientific Register to any extent: eight per cent heard of their

TABLE 5

HOW DID YOU HEAR OF THE OPENING?

Size of firm entered

Method	1-499	500-1,999	2,000-4,999	5,000-9,999	10,000 and over	Not known	Total
	Percentage of graduates mentioning a given method						
Advertising . .	16	10	18	8	8	21	11
Ministry of Labour .	4	4	4	—	3	3	3
Technical and Scientific Register . .	2	4	4	5	4	6	4
University appointments board . .	14	19	22	29	21	9	21
Visit from representative of firm . .	—	—	5	8	17	3	10
Personal introduction.	12	13	4	3	6	—	6
Personal application .	11	15	30	24	25	18	23
Knowing someone in firm . . .	33	18	8	13	6	27	12
Other channels . .	4	7	5	1	3	9	4
No answer . .	5	7	1	8	6	3	6
Number of graduates in firm size .	57	67	80	86	271	33	594

opening through it. The technologists mentioned their university appointments board a good deal less frequently than the others—15 per cent, against 24 to 26 per cent; and a visit from a representative of the firm much more frequently than the scientists—16 per cent, as against 9 per cent.

Table 5, which gives this information in relation to the size of the firm to which the graduate went, shows, broadly speaking, that the number of graduates who mentioned appointments boards and a visit from representatives of the firm, goes up with the size of the firm; as the size of the firm increases, it goes down for advertising and knowing someone in the firm. What stands out is the very steep rise, as the size of the firm increases, in the proportion mentioning a visit from a representative of a firm. Not one graduate who went into a firm with under 2,000 employees mentioned this. Of those who went into firms with between 2,000 and 10,000 employees, 5 to 8 per cent mentioned such a visit; but 17 per cent of those who went into a firm larger than this said that they had heard of the opening through such a visit, and it is into large firms such as these, with 10,000 or more employees, that nearly half the graduates went.

In sum, attracting graduates to the firm was achieved both by indirect and by direct means. Four out of ten of the graduates heard of the opening either through their own initiative, in writing to enquire, or through personal contacts made either by knowing someone in the firm or through an introduction, given in a number of cases by a professor or tutor. Five out of ten heard of the opening through some initiative taken by the firm and the greater part of this initiative was directed towards the universities.

Graduates' impressions of information provided

It is worth noting that, in spite of some evidence among firms of a sense of pressure in trying to secure graduates, very few of their graduates interviewed made any complaint that the information given them was inadequate or misleading.

The 183 graduates interviewed in the case studies, of whom fifty-eight had had some intervening career employment before joining their firm, were asked whether, in applying for the job about which they were interviewed, they felt they had been given all the information they needed, and whether this information had turned out to be realistic. (Those who had joined their firm before graduating were not asked this question.)

Three-quarters of this number made no kind of critical comment; less than a fifth made very mild adverse comments on the paucity of information they had been given, and some of them pointed to the difficulty that firms would have in giving a realistic picture to persons unfamiliar with industry. Only sixteen graduates in twelve firms and one in a gas board (less than a tenth of the whole number) said that the information they had been given had proved misleading. Of these, only two were arts graduates.

Only one critical comment was made among the graduates in the smaller firms; more were made by those in the larger medium-sized and large firms.

The "fading of the rosy picture" of which some of the graduates complained was made more explicit by others. Promises which failed to materialise were made with regard to the degree of responsibility given, the conditions of work, the research facilities available, training and a promise of work abroad. Three examples, shown in relation to the graduate's reason for applying for the job, are given:

A technology graduate with previous industrial experience had seen an advertisement in one of the national daily papers, wanted to improve his situation and joined the firm about which the question was put. "The products are well known and it's an important firm." He felt that the information given at the interview was not realistic: "I was shown well-equipped laboratories, to the point of luxury, costly. But I wasn't told that these were used only by one small section of the development departments. Not only were they not available for research generally, but attempts to use the apparatus are jealously opposed by those in the departments".

An arts graduate had applied to a firm because he understood that it offered good training and good pay. His interviewer "mentioned features which would have ready appeal and left out the less appealing ones". A technology graduate in the same firm said, "The company appeared to offer a course on production engineering and paid well while doing it", but "seventy-five per cent" of the information "painted rather too glowing a picture".

A science graduate said that he got an impression that he would be a member of a fairly large, efficient section with superiors of wide experience and so on—"People I could learn from. I didn't find the standards I expected or hoped for."

As has been said, however, the great majority of the graduates had nothing critical to say about the information provided by the firm they entered. Whatever other effects recruitment drives may have had, such evidence as the case studies provides goes to show that firms rarely yielded to the temptation to overpaint the picture.

THE RESULTS

How far were these endeavours rewarded? Members of managements were asked: *Are enough graduates of the right kind being attracted to the firm?* The question was addressed both to the qualitative as well as the quantitative aspects of the results of recruitment campaigns: it did not ask merely whether enough graduates were being attracted. Of the 126 members of management interviewed at various levels, twenty-one felt that they had not the experience to answer or did not do so; the remainder replied.

Many elements must enter into the forming of an opinion on this question: the relative importance of graduates to the firm and to particular departments in it, the academic and other standards aimed at, the attitude to graduates of the person being questioned, for example. With the exception of six firms, members of management were in broad agreement with one another. In three of the exceptions, a less senior member of management concerned with a particular department complained of shortages of graduates in his department, although a senior man thought requirements were being met. In the remaining three, a senior man was not satisfied and a less senior man took another view. One less senior man thought in effect that, in recruitment for research, the sights were being set too high—that graduates were being put on to too junior work. In another, a less senior man thought that the situation had improved and enough good engineers were then being attracted to the firm; in the third, one man thought that insufficient engineers of any quality were being attracted; another member of the firm thought enough graduates were being brought in though "the quality was not always what we want".

Secondly, though the question was concerned with the number and quality of recruits, it was clear from their answers that members of management did not always address themselves to both aspects. Some answers convey the impression that it was difficulties in finding recruits for a particular section of the work, perhaps production or sales, or in attracting certain types of graduates, a man with an Honours degree, for example, that precipitated an answer "No". This would not necessarily mean that recruitment for other work or of other types of graduates might not have been meeting with reasonable success. Similarly, an answer "Yes" might equally ignore or discount shortfalls or disappointments at various points that were not at that juncture of particular concern. The answers must therefore be considered with these reservations in mind. They convey, at any rate, the emphasis—whether on shortages or otherwise—which those questioned elected to adopt.

Firms attracting enough graduates of the right kind

Senior members of management in nine firms held they were recruiting successfully as regards both the quantity and quality of the graduates being attracted, and in three others, all small firms with two graduates each, they protested that they had no experience which would enable them to answer, or did not answer. At another stage in the study of these three small firms, however, the member of management interviewed made it plain that his very limited requirements were in fact being met. These firms, therefore, are grouped under this category.

These twelve firms, in which satisfaction was expressed both with the number and with the kinds of graduates available, may be regarded as special cases. They include seven of the twelve small firms, in which, as several members of management pointed out, the number needed was small, three firms which were recruiting mainly arts graduates and two which were seeking graduates to fill management positions at a later stage and which were in a position to recruit the small numbers they needed over a period long enough to enable them to bide their time. The two firms with the largest number of graduates (both had well over a hundred), the chemical manufacturer and a vehicles firm, were each, in the view of members of management interviewed, particularly well placed to attract graduates. The chemical manufacturers had exceptionally close contacts with universities, and its products and research were recognised to be attractive to graduates. The senior member of management in the vehicles firm considered that "all its requirements had always been met" and that this was on account of the firm's "glamour". (A colleague, however, considered that there was a serious shortfall in the engineering department.)

The remaining firms

Senior members of management in twenty-seven firms and the two gas boards that are here relevant (those with active graduate recruitment policies), when asked if they could get enough graduates of the right kind, answered "No", with varying degrees of emphasis and elaboration. They constitute 67 per cent of the total number of members of management replying.

As has been seen, the answers do not lend themselves to any rigid classification, and an understanding of their nature can best be got from quoting some of them. (Where answers from other members of management fill out the replies of the senior man, they are included also):

> Definitely no . . . we have been trying for many years to get about fifteen [electrical engineers] from universities each year. The results have been rather poor. Last year I visited eleven and contacted eight more universities and technical colleges and interviewed fifty-six students . . . of whom nineteen were offered training in the firm, but only four accepted. Three others indicated that they would come after National Service. Another member of management said: We are particularly short in the upper strata, first-class brains. We only require a small number, for example, six, but we cannot get them.

> Not enough engineers; not enough mechanical engineers especially.

> No, the production side of the house doesn't attract graduates. I feel this is the fault of the universities, who have been very slow in this direction. The cry from most graduates is for research and development. There has been a big demand [for our product] so sales attracts them also. But here in this production department the bias of our need is in the direction of electrical engineers, demand for whom exceeds the supply.

> No, neither in quality nor quantity. Another member of management said: There is a deficiency in the number of men of satisfactory calibre. . . . But we won't lower our sights, and we know that taking on a few good men is better than diluting.

> No. We have an unsatisfied demand. There is an absolute shortage of chemical engineers. There are not enough to fill [our vacancies] of any quality and there is a shortage of good chemists. Mechanical engineers are now drying up.

From our point of view we get all we require, although the quality is not always what we want.

No, especially scientists. The textile trade has not the appeal of some others. It may be a question of security, the memory of unemployment in the Thirties. (A textile firm.)

The official answer is "No". We tend to be short of chemists. But I think it depends on what sort of job you can offer a chemist. There's something about saying "And all my foremen are university chemists". But, does one really need a university chemist for all jobs? (Another member of the same textile firm, not so senior.)

We are not getting enough of the right kind [of arts men]. We prefer to come away with nobody rather than be satisfied with what we can get.

No. We are often having to put up with the second best. We are short of mechanical engineers. (A large electrical engineering firm.)

No, too many people are wanting the top 15 per cent of university people. (Another member of management in the same large electrical engineering firm.)

An isolated or unattractive location was a severe handicap in recruitment, especially to smaller firms. Night shift work in metal manufacturing was a standing difficulty for the firms in this trade. One firm which suffered also from being in an isolated place, had painfully built up a graduate strength of six, but had failed to get any more and replied to the question with some bitterness:

No graduates of either the wrong or right kind are being attracted.

Again, a branch of an industry that had become outclassed by another and newer branch in the attractiveness of the work it had to offer, also felt the pinch: vehicles were outclassed by aircraft, heavy electrical engineering by electronics. Textiles were considered to be labouring under the double disadvantage of memories of the effects on the trade of pre-war depression and of the relatively greater attraction of other industries. The gas industry, with "its smell and its dirt", was outclassed, so it seemed to the boards, by almost every other.

No doubt because of the heavy representation of electrical engineering and building and contracting firms in the sample, emphasis was laid on the shortage of graduates in engineering, mainly mechanical engineering, but also on chemical engineering. Eight firms and two gas boards spoke of their failure to get enough engineers; three of their failure to get scientists. The type of shortage was, however, generally implied, not stated, and was left to be inferred from the context of the firm or the department of it under discussion. As might be expected, no reference was made to any shortage in numbers of arts graduates. In fact, only six firms mentioned them at all.

Certain overtones could also be detected in the course of the interviews. Disappointment in recruiting engineers or scientists seemed often to have engendered a feeling that it was always the other fellow who had landed the biggest fish. This feeling is exemplified in the remark already quoted, made in one of the giant electrical engineering firms, that too many people were "wanting the top 15 per cent of university people"; or that "the best were creamed off for research". It may have entered into and complicated the assessment of the results of recruitment efforts. This feeling was also reinforced for a number of firms by the behaviour of scientists and technologists at interviews. Stories were told of graduates appearing with notebooks to take down details of the employment offered, in order to measure up the advantages or disadvantages of work offered at their leisure. To a natural sense of disappointment in the results of recruitment or some aspect of it, therefore, there was sometimes added irritation at the way graduates had been taking advantage of their scarcity value.

As has been seen, except for more advanced research, the general practice was to take on non-graduates for work for which graduates were also recruited. In many instances the graduates' academic qualifications were preferred to those of the non-graduates also recruited, and thirty firms gave the knowledge gained by scientists and technologists at the university as their sole reason for employing them. But other evidence goes to show that it was the ability to get on with others, to mix well, to show qualities of leadership and power of thought and analysis, which employers hoped also to find in recruiting from the universities. It was qualities such as these which it was hoped would sooner or later differentiate the graduate recruit from his fellows, and justify his promotion to positions of increasing responsibility. Indeed, the mere fact that their recruit had been to a university seems to have led some firms to have assumed that these qualities would have been fostered and developed in him during his undergraduate years almost automatically. But comment on the quality of graduates often reflected disappointment in the qualities of those recruited. Some further examination of the views of management on the question of university education is therefore indicated. This is the subject of the next chapter.

SUMMING UP

THIS chapter has attempted a brief review of the attitude of forty-seven firms in the private sector of industry and of four gas boards towards the question whether to employ graduates; and of the practice of those with a positive policy to recruit graduates, first in assessing the number and kinds of graduates they wanted and then in recruiting them. It has also indicated their views about the results of their efforts to attract graduates to them.

It follows from the nature of the sample of firms* that there was a very wide variation, both in size and in product. At one end of the scale there were three with less than a hundred employees and at the other, nine with more than 10,000. The ten main heads under which their products have been grouped are a further indication of their diversity. Products ranged from quarrying to electrical engineering, from smelting metal to baking bread. At the time the survey was made, three had no graduates at all, fourteen had a hundred or more. Again, the proportions in which arts graduates, scientists or technologists were employed, if they were employed at all, varied from firm to firm.

The policy of these undertakings also varied. One of the four gas boards was hoping to dispense with the recruitment of graduates, and another had not been in a position to take on more than one since nationalisation in 1949. Eight firms, six of them small, had apparently never recruited, nor intended ever to recruit, a graduate, except quite incidentally; twenty-one out of the remaining thirty-nine firms had started to recruit only since the end of the war, that is, since the Education Acts of 1944 and 1946 radically altered the conditions under which recruitment had to operate. Most of the firms which had been recruiting since before the Acts came in were large, had relatively complex products and were heavy employers of graduates. Most of the firms which had started since then were smaller and their graduate strength was much less substantial. In short, a sixth of the undertakings had not

* Explained in Appendix B.

yet accepted the need to employ graduates or felt that they were not in a position to do so, and half had started to employ graduates only since the end of the war.

Did these newcomers recruit graduates because they had come to the conclusion that it was men with a university education that they needed? Or did they do so because they wanted to bring in young men of promise and recognised that the universities were the most likely place in which to find them? All firms, and especially the newcomers, were faced with a situation so novel and, because of shortage of supply of scientists and technologists and of technical staff at other levels, with a situation so difficult, that any attempt to assess their policy and practice or to generalise about them is fraught with difficulty. Nevertheless, there are three points which emerge from their replies deserving of consideration.

First, whether it recognised it or not, each of these undertakings was faced with the problem of securing enough recruits of the right calibre to enable it at least to survive. The prevailing conditions of increasing international competition and of fundamental new developments in materials and industrial processes would affect some more directly than others; but all had to meet their challenge in some degree. Secondly, whether or not it had had any experience of recruiting graduates before the Education Acts ensured that a much larger proportion of able school-leavers went on to a university, each had to think out what would be the implications of these changes for its own future.

How far had these undertakings gone in this process? The impression received is that most of the larger firms, mainly those in the newer and more complex industries included in the studies, which had been recruiting graduates before the introduction of the present educational system, and which already had substantial numbers of them, were reasonably well attuned to these changes. They recognised the need to secure men of good intellectual calibre and were happy to go to the universities for them. Outside this group there was a fairly rapid falling off in adjustment to these changes. An intermediate group of firms recognised the need to bring in good brains, but regarded the necessity to recruit them from universities with varying degrees of warmth. Lastly, there were firms which were reluctant to go to the universities, or which did so but were prepared to employ graduates only in work of a somewhat routine nature, or which were not proposing to recruit a single graduate except quite incidentally. This last group, though composed for the most part of small firms, amounted to some third of all the undertakings. It included five out of the seven metal or metal-goods manufacturers, and two out of the four gas boards. In the event, and contrary to what might have been expected, there was almost no evidence of any firm recruiting merely to be "in the swim".

As might be expected, attitude to the recruitment of graduate scientists was the least inhibited. Towards the recruitment of graduate engineers, attitudes ranged from conviction that they were essential to the concern, to a determination to recruit none, on the ground that they were ill-suited to the needs of the undertaking. Towards arts graduates there was an even wider range of attitude; the number of undertakings which had never recruited any (eleven) or had decided to stop doing so (four) was high, but this must be considered in the light of the relative newness of the recruitment of arts graduates by many branches of industry.

Altogether, the studies make clear how much the period through which these undertakings were passing was one of transition. All the undertakings seemed to be aware in some degree of the new relationship of industry to the universities, but they varied considerably in the extent to which they had accepted its implications for themselves.

The second point that must be made in considering the findings of this chapter is that university men, particularly scientists and technologists, constitute one of the most valuable of the nation's assets. The greater the competition for them, the greater becomes the responsibility of any employer, whether he be in industry, in the civil service or in any other walk of life, not to recruit more than he needs, and to use any he has secured as effectively as possible. For example, at the time of the survey, manufacturing industry was probably recruiting about one-third of the scientists coming out of the universities of Great Britain.* To take a hypothetical case, if, as a result of a careful survey of its needs, industry had reduced a year's recruitment of scientists by 10 per cent, it would have made available for other employment some 150 scientists, every one of whom would have been eagerly sought by other employers, in particular for the teaching of mathematics and science in schools.

* *Graduate Employment.* Table 28, page 71.

The first step towards the avoidance of any wasteful use of graduates must be the assessment of the work to be done in terms of the qualifications and qualities used to carry it out. The work to be done will vary in kind, in complexity and in volume. Graduate recruits will have different paper qualifications, and will vary widely in general ability and personality. How many graduates of any particular kind and quality are really essential to the carrying out of any particular job?

The point that stands out in examining the practice of firms in assessing their need for graduates is that for much of their production and administrative or non-technical work and for some of their research work recruitment of graduates was not regarded as essential. For this work the qualifications required could be stated in terms wider than those that would be called for if university men alone were to be considered. Steps may be taken at a later stage to distinguish among the graduates and others recruited, those of good, indifferent or poor quality. But it cannot be denied that the more broadly requirements are stated, the greater the danger becomes of failing to grade work according to the demands it will make on the academic and other qualities of the man who is to carry it out, or of losing sight of any grading that has been done, and therefore, of failing, at any rate in the initial stages of employment, to get the maximum benefit from the human resources secured.*

The third point that calls for comment is the energy that seems to have been put into the hunt for graduates by firms needing more than an occasional one or two. For every graduate in the survey secured for any particular firm, how many, whether they were eventually secured for industry or for other employment, were wooed by one or other of the talent scouts who went from one university to the next in attempts to secure the graduates they needed? And how many thousands of pounds a year were being poured out in these campaigns? Moreover the pace has certainly quickened since the survey was made. In a debate in the House of Lords on engineering and scientific education, one "moderate-sized engineering company" was said to have been spending at the rate of £20,000 a year on advertising for staff.† But the

---

* Some evidence on the extent to which the graduates interviewed were being employed in suitable work is examined in Chapter VI.

† *Hansard.* House of Lords, 21 November 1956. Col. 426.

financing of these campaigns is not as germane to this present enquiry as their effects on those feeling their impact. The Secretary of the Cambridge Appointments Board, describing the "annual scramble for scientists and engineers and for the more capable and 'leaderly' arts graduates", has said:

> Each year the courtship grows a little more feverish, every device being exploited to acquire prestige in the university and to excite the interest of the promising undergraduate and his mentors.*

Though little evidence on this point has emerged from these surveys—no question was directed to it—and though no evidence has been taken from the universities themselves, it may well be asked what the effect of these campaigns must be on both senior and, particularly, on junior members. It may be argued that, in existing conditions, and in the conditions then prevailing, there is no short-term alternative to these campaigns, and, indeed, that other competitors for graduates outside industry may well have to intensify their efforts also. The Civil Service Commission has, in fact, recently taken some steps in this direction. It is, nevertheless, fair to ask whether the larger firms which are setting the pace in conducting these recruiting campaigns have considered carefully enough what their effects are likely to be and whether there is anything they could do to mitigate them. The intrusion into university life, with its unhurried tread and with its bias towards learning and research for their own sake, of an almost endless stream of propaganda designed to advertise the spoils awaiting the newly-fledged scientist or technologist must be, to say the least, disturbing.

The only solution, and it is a long-term one, is an increase in the number of scientists and technologists leaving the universities every year. The current plans for increasing the numbers of university students, together with those for colleges of higher technology, promise well to go some way at any rate towards this solution, if staffing and other problems are successfully solved. But in any case these plans will not yield results for some years.

---

* J. G. W. Davies, "The Appointments Boards", *Financial Times: Careers Supplement*, 12 November 1956. Page 8.

CHAPTER II

INDUSTRY AND UNIVERSITY EDUCATION

THE last chapter considered policy and practice in recruiting university graduates. It revealed, among the fifty-one undertakings studied, wide differences in outlook on the suitability of graduates for their purposes. Before going on to examine the next step in the recruitment of graduates—the methods of selection adopted—it seems desirable to examine the views of the members of management interviewed on university education and to set beside them the graduates' replies to allied questions.

The six questions put under this head were designed to discover managements' views on the general question of the advantage to industry of university education; on the requirements of their own firms, both as regards first degree courses and higher degrees; and whether they had taken any steps to get put into practice any ideas on courses they may have had. The aim, in short, was to draw them out on the whole problem of the relationship of industry to the universities, a subject of the first importance both for industry and for the future prosperity of the country. Parallel questions were put to the graduates on the value they set on their time at a university and on their first degree course and any higher degree.

The subject, however, as has been suggested already, is complicated in more ways than one. Industry, which draws recruits not only from universities but also from schools and technical colleges, is primarily concerned with education as equipment for work, rather than for life, and with the harnessing of knowledge to industrial processes. On the other hand, though some of the alumni of a university may eventually become industrialists, others may also go on to become parsons or ambassadors, professors or town clerks, in fact almost anything under the sun. A university is not primarily interested in what its undergraduates are going to do: its first interest is in teaching and research for their own sake—and in subjects it considers worthy of study. Problems which may appear to industry to be of the first importance and to call for study at the university level may not necessarily be acceptable from the academic point of view. By their very nature, industry and the universities start with fundamental differences in outlook on the scope and purpose of education. Yet they are both confronted with the fact that industry has become, and that only recently, the largest single user of university men.

At the time of the survey, the views of industry on the vocational aspects of university education had been undergoing some modification. They had been tending towards a fuller appreciation of the non-vocational aspects of most university education and away from earlier emphasis on the vocational aspects and on specialisation. It was an object of the first four questions put to members of management to discover how far this trend would be reflected in their replies.

THE ADVANTAGES OF UNIVERSITY EDUCATION

THE first question put to members of management was a very general one: *Do you consider a university education, as compared, for example, with a technical college education, an advantage to industry?* The question was put not only to the thirty-nine firms with a deliberate graduate recruitment policy and to the gas boards, but also to the eight firms then recruiting a graduate only incidentally, if at all, which had nevertheless appeared in the sample because each had taken on one of the men who graduated in . 1950.* It was answered by all but four of the 126 members of management in the first group and all but one of the eight in the second group.

Seventy of these 134 members of management said "Yes" (but three, all in one firm, answered the question in relation only to their firm) and in the course of their replies many made reservations of one kind or another. Eight said "No": of this eight, four were in firms classed as old employers of graduates; one had only his firm in mind. Another six said that it was not possible to give an exact reply, though most went on to elaborate. The remainder, forty-five, a third of them all, said neither "Yes" nor "No", but proceeded to make some reservation or to point out one or more ways in which a university education, as compared with other kinds, was in their view an advantage to industry, without committing themselves to a positive "Yes". Though members of management were asked to give their views separately in relation to scientists, to technologists and to arts men, very few

* Chapter I, page 11.

E

made any explicit distinction. Twenty-three, in the event, made specific references to arts men and, of these, twenty answered "Yes", two "No", and one was unable to give a firm answer.

Advantages of various kinds were put forward and various reservations made in answering the question. (There were seventy-one references to some advantage and sixty-four reservations of one kind or another.) The replies are most conveniently considered in relation to each of the subjects raised under one or other head—advantages and reservations.

The advantages seen in a university education fall into four broad groups. They are given in ascending order of frequency.

i. The graduate wins in the end (three replies). For example:

> The technical school man wins in the first year or so, but the graduate ultimately has the advantage.

ii. The more advanced or specialised work done at a university (five replies). For example:

> The degree man goes that amount further in his knowledge.

iii. Development of personality and the power of leadership, ability to get on with others (twenty-three replies, of which two related only to arts graduates). For example:

> A university education gives self-confidence; a university man ... can, generally speaking, take responsibility earlier.

> We want both university and technical college men but we look to the university for leaders.

> A university education gives more, a residential university especially.

> There a young man can develop personality and strength of character. This is more important than academic qualities.

iv. Training of the mind, development of the power of thought, education in the widest sense (forty replies, including seven relating only to arts graduates). For example:

> Life at a university is fuller. The student meets more people and learns to think and later when he is in a job, he is more able to cope.

> They are spoon fed at technical colleges, whereas at universities they are trained to think.

> A university education provides balance and broadmindedness. A harder education cramps a man's mind. A university education doesn't do as much harm as other sorts.

The first two categories are heavily outweighed by the last two. In short, the advantages of a university education, as compared, for example, with a technical college education, were thought to lie hardly at all in any purely academic superiority, but in the development of the powers of leadership and of thought.

The obverse of this lack of emphasis on the relative academic advantages of university education is to be seen in the replies of those few—eight—members of management who saw no advantage at all in a university education. Most based their argument on the ground that the training provided elsewhere was better than that provided at a university:

> There is no advantage. The [local technical college] is best.

> It's still best on the shop floor. University textbook knowledge is not applied.

Managements' reservations

The reservations made in answering "Yes" or in making a non-committal reply fall into five broad groups. They are also given in ascending order of frequency.

i. Family or school background is also important (seven replies). For example:

> School and home background are of fundamental importance in people.

> Technical college men don't do so well later and haven't such a good school background.

ii. The older universities are better (eight replies). For example:

> Broadly, a university education is better, but there are many exceptions. Oxford and Cambridge provide the cultural opportunities needed.

> It depends on the colleges. You are more likely to get managerial qualities in a man from a residential university such as Oxford or Cambridge.

> If a man comes from Cambridge, we'll take him even if he's failed.

> We would rather take a Cambridge arts man and spend two years training him to be an engineer than a technology graduate from somewhere else.

iii. Closely allied to these, but more broadly stated, were thirteen

replies to the effect that it all depended on the university, or on
the conditions in which a man had spent his undergraduate years.
For example:

> I'm all out for the university graduate but preferably one who has
> been in residence full time.
>
> Provincial universities with a tradition of digs or living at home are
> hopeless.
>
> It all depends on the university and the technical college. Our local
> technical college is better than our local university.
>
> It all depends on which university—some have no university life and
> produce a man as from a technical college.

iv. Reservations were also made by thirteen members of management on a different count—that it all depended on the individual.
For example:

> A university education is an advantage provided the man is adaptable.
>
> A university won't change a man's drive and a non-graduate with
> push and drive may get better results.

v. The reservation most frequently made, however, took a different form. Twenty-three members of management qualified
their assent to the idea that a university education had advantages
for industry or amplified a non-committal reply by pointing out
that industry needed non-graduates as well as university men or
that there was little to choose between them. For example:

> There is something to be said for each. The graduate has wider
> knowledge but academically there is not much to choose.
>
> Both are good in their own way and cannot be compared.
>
> For research, yes, for general engineering, fifty-fifty.

Broadly, the upshot of these replies amounts to this: that, on
balance, there were advantages for industry in university education, compared with other kinds, but that these advantages were
of a social or broadly educational, as opposed to an academic,
order, and that certain universities, those with a collegiate system
or providing halls of residence, were more likely than others to
provide these advantages.

These replies have been considered so far purely in terms of the
individuals making them. The question was not concerned with

the relevant advantages of a university education to any particular firm. The size, product and graduate-recruitment policy of each firm might, nevertheless, colour these replies—and, indeed, as has been seen, one or two members considered the question only in relation to their firm. A brief review may therefore be useful.

The metal manufacturers, the metal-goods manufacturers and, but to a lesser extent, the builders and civil engineers were slightly more inclined to non-committal or negative replies than the others. Among the forty-nine members of management in the eighteen firms and two gas boards with more than fifty graduates, only two considered a university education to have no advantages over other kinds; and only two gave a non-committal answer. Among the fifty members of management in the fourteen firms which have been classified as having a positive attitude to the employment of graduates,* and which largely overlap with those with fifty graduates or more, no one considered a university to have no advantage for industry and only seven (in three firms) gave a non-committal answer.

At the other end of the scale, only one out of the eight members of management, a metal-goods manufacturer,† in the firms classified as employing a graduate only incidentally, if at all, would agree that a university education had advantages for industry over others. His reply, however, was: "In general terms, yes. Here, no". Of the others, three would not commit themselves and made reservations of one kind or another; and another three said "No". (One did not answer.)

Graduates' views

The general trend of the replies from managements is reflected in the replies from graduates to a question on the value of going to a university. Those with a first degree obtained after full-time study were asked: *If you could start all over again would you still choose to go to a university: if so, why; if not, why not?*

Ninety-eight per cent of the 552 men in the graduate interviews and 95 per cent of those in the case studies said they would. This result is perhaps not surprising since the question was entirely personal to the graduates themselves, who had all taken the opportunity offered them of going to a university.

* Chapter I, page 6.
† Chapter I, page 13.

The reason most frequently given for being prepared to go to a university again was, in effect, that a university broadens the outlook:

It's not just what you learn but whom you meet and what you do in your spare time.

I learnt to mix with people of every opinion and race.

Two out of every three men in the graduate interviews mentioned this. But less than half said that they would return for purely academic reasons.

Half also mentioned better employment prospects. These proportions were broadly reflected in the case-study graduates. Typical replies were:

It's an easy way of getting more money and a more interesting job.

Education is recognised these days as a means of making more money.

A degree is a mode of entrée second to none.

The most common reason given by the 2 to 5 per cent of the graduates who would not go to a university again was simply that they saw no advantage in it. Other replies, some from only one graduate, were that a job not requiring a degree would now be preferred, that practical experience was more useful or that a technical college training was better for industry.

In general, graduates, as might be expected, were a little more solidly in favour of a university education than the members of management interviewed and laid rather more stress on its academic advantages. But they were at one with their seniors in mentioning more frequently than any other the social or broadly educational advantages of a university education.

SHOULD THE UNIVERSITIES DO MORE?

The next question put to members of management followed logically from the first. It, again, was a general one: *Do you consider that universities should do more to meet the needs of industry? If so, what?* This again was put to the 134 members of management in the thirty-nine firms with a deliberate graduate recruitment policy, to the gas boards and to the eight firms then recruiting a graduate only incidentally, if at all.*

* The subsequent four questions on education were not put to these eight firms as they were considered inappropriate to them.

This question was followed by another, related this time to the undertaking to which the member of management belonged: *What, from your experience, would be the ideal university first degree course for your purposes? What would be its content and its length?* This was put to the 126 members of management in the thirty-nine firms with a deliberate graduate recruitment policy and to the gas boards. It was felt not to be appropriate to the other eight firms and was not put to them. Because of the outcome of the replies to this second question, as indicated below, it is convenient to consider the two together.

Three members of management said they did not know what answer to give to the first question, whether the universities should do more to meet the needs of industry, and eleven had no views. In saying that they had no views, most were entirely detached in their attitude, but one, a director of one of the eight firms mentioned above, said, "I have no views and no time to theorise". A negative answer was given by forty-three, of whom half were from firms classed as old and half from new employers of graduates. The remainder, seventy-seven, over half the members of management, thought that universities should do more to meet the needs of industry and proceeded to make suggestions of one kind or another. There was a slight tendency for a larger proportion of those in the gas boards and in the consumer goods industry to say "No", but there was very little in this. Twelve of those who answered "No" (of whom three were referring to arts graduates) did not elaborate their answer.

Eight had no views on what would be the ideal university first degree course for their purposes; eighteen did not answer. Of the remaining hundred, the majority mentioned an existing course or courses, or more often a subject of study.*

---

* References to existing courses or subjects of study were: "Any technological subject" (3); engineering (7); civil engineering (3); mechanical engineering (10), of which three were to the course at Cambridge and one to "any provincial university"; electrical engineering (9); gas engineering at Leeds (1); production engineering (2); chemical engineering (11), of which one reference was to the course at Cambridge; "general engineering design" (6) (Total 52). To scientific subjects the references were: Mathematics (7); chemistry (9); physics (8); metallurgy (3); "any" or "general" science (2); biology (1) and zoology (1) (Total 31). References to non-technical subjects were: Philosophy, Politics and Economics ("Modern Greats"), Oxford (2); "an arts course at Cambridge" (1); "a general arts course" (1); commerce (1); accountancy (1); "no preference for any arts course" (3) (Total 9). Grand total: 92.

Twenty-five replies included suggestions regarding the content or objectives of courses, twelve regarding the length of courses.* There were thirteen replies which included statements such as "We must have a sound standard" or "Men rather than intellects". In these circumstances it is more convenient to take the twenty-five replies regarding the content of courses with replies on the same subject in answer to the earlier question, though this related to industry as a whole and not to the needs of a particular firm.

Over a third of the ninety-two references to existing subjects of study or courses, as constituting an ideal first degree course, came from those forty-three members of management who, on one ground or another, had said that universities should not or could not do more to meet the needs of industry. The remainder came from those who had had suggestions to make on this count.

Negative answers

Of the forty-three people who gave a negative answer to the question whether the universities should do more to meet the needs of industry, a small number, five, did so on grounds of principle: that the universities would be wrong to have any regard for the needs of industry. A typical answer was:

> The last thing a university should do is to take any notice of industry ... and industry should be wise enough not to influence the universities.

The replies given by another ten came very near to this but they were based on the argument that the universities could not do more for industry because it was the universities' job to educate, industry's to train. For example:

> The universities are doing all they possibly can. They provide the fundamental knowledge that is essential. After that, industry must provide the training.

Six, of whom one was referring only to arts graduates, thought that universities could not do more because the needs of industry were so varied. Eleven had no suggestions to make as they thought

---

* Seven of the twelve replies on the length of courses were: "Three years"—apparently the existing length of the course to which reference was being made. The others were miscellaneous, for example: "Four years" (for scientists); or "Length all right"; or "No longer than at present: the sooner we get our hands on him the better" (for engineers).

the universities were doing well enough already. For example, from a firm interested only in graduate scientists and technologists:

> No. They are doing very well on the technical side—they couldn't do better.

Less complimentary, but to substantially the same intent, were:

> No, now they have stopped looking down their noses at us—especially Oxford and Cambridge.

> No. Most professors are only too aware of the needs of industry.

One man wondered whether the universities were not

> ... trying to do too much for industry. ... The standards of entry are lower now. The pre-war graduate was a better article on average.*

WHAT THE UNIVERSITIES COULD DO

MORE than a hundred suggestions were put forward by the members of management who considered that the universities could do more to meet the needs of industry. Only a minority of the suggestions had to do with social or manpower questions—the question, for example, of producing more engineers. The majority had to do with problems connected with various types of courses or with steps that should be taken by senior members of universities to improve their knowledge of industry and to ensure that students heading for industry acquired some practical experience or an understanding of its history, structure and organisation before starting work.

Three of the nine suggestions on social questions were pleas for the provision of more halls of residence; the remainder had to do with the development of personality. As has been seen, these subjects were closely allied in the minds of many members of of management:

> They must be persuaded to increase facilities for residence. Their role is not exclusively turning out scientists. More attention should be given to turning out the complete man.

Seventeen suggestions were to the effect that universities should produce more men for industry. Two of these had to do with the

* The remaining ten replies (to make the total of forty-three) were simply "No".

more leaderly type of arts men, the remainder with scientists and technologists. Replies typical of the latter were:

> They should specialise in chemistry, physics, mechanical engineering and mathematics.
>
> Turn out more scientists!
>
> The engineering side should be increased.

One suggestion (from a member of management in a large electrical-engineering firm) was more thoroughgoing and also more realistic, since it implied some appreciation of the fact that the provision of more men for industry might entail substantial adjustments in university policy:

> Change their policy! They should regard the teaching of engineering and science as fundamental. First they should make it possible for a large proportion of their students to be scientists and engineers. Then they should encourage arts people to have some appreciation of science.

This suggestion applied to all universities without distinction. Another suggestion, also concerned with increasing the output of scientists and technologists, discriminated between the older and the newer universities:

> The older universities, no, the modern, yes. They should be more closely tied up with technical colleges. The technical colleges should provide the engineers and technicians and the universities the scientists.

On the other hand, two men expressed some anxiety lest the policy to increase the size of the university population be at the expense of the most gifted students:

> I feel that the potential genius gets bogged down: with so many going through, the brighter men are being held back.
>
> My view is that the universities are so busy educating the masses that they lose the top men in the wash.

Analysis of general replies on contents of courses

Ten members of management made some suggestions on the objectives of university teaching in relation to the wider question what universities could do for industry and seven others in relation to the narrower question on an ideal first degree course for their firm.

In effect, four members of management (all in firms with some fifty or more graduates) thought that the overriding objective of university teaching should be the education of the mind:

> What the universities can produce is a first-class mind and I think we must leave the universities to determine the best way to produce it.

> We are not fussy provided the graduates are taught how to think.

> The universities should cultivate practical sense and an enquiring mind. No discoveries can be made without these.

Secondly, four members of management touched on the question of specialisation in a general way. (A few others made suggestions for widening specific courses, which are considered later in this section.) Two were in favour of specialisation, two against:

> Don't broaden university courses. Specialists are essential. Broaden before and after the university. A jack-of-all-trades will be useless to the industry of the future.

> The tendency of the universities is to be too narrow. They should broaden education and not cram knowledge before the humanities.

Two referred in a general way to the need to develop a command of language. A few others did so also when discussing specific subjects:

> The universities should foster the ability to explain and expound, especially to juniors.

> Every course should include ... reading and writing essays.

Lastly, one member of management, in a firm with more than fifty graduates, in reply to the wider question what the universities could do for industry, suggested that the quality of university teachers should be improved:

> People with good minds are bitterly disappointed in their teachers.

The teaching of science

Members of management in six firms had something to say about the teaching of science in general for industry as a whole.

Three of them thought that the universities should aim at providing "fundamental" science, leaving "the rest" to industry:

> The universities should provide fundamental training in mathematics, physics and chemistry, with plenty of English. The latter is the real trouble.

Another also made a plea for the broadening of science teaching, but added that he thought the universities were tending already to broaden syllabuses. One thought the best scientists came from Cambridge; another that more emphasis should be given to "applied science", though he "recognised the value of an academic degree and theory"; another that there was a

> language weakness in the teaching of science. Graduates often have no German or French, which is essential.

On the teaching of chemistry, two members of management in four firms (of which two were chemical manufacturers) had something to say:

> All chemistry should include some chemical engineering, however elementary.

> The universities should provide an extra year for the solving of problems and testing whether a chap can think at all.

The other two were concerned with the needs of their own industry. A food manufacturer put in a plea for the teaching of the chemistry of foodstuffs. He recognised that this was too specialised to rank as a course on its own and was grateful for its inclusion in a wider course on industrial fomentation at Manchester. The other, interested in research on leather, thought that his firm's needs could best be met by a "basic" degree in science followed by another in the chemistry of leather.

Physics came in for very little attention as such, but it was mentioned at certain points in relation to other subjects. One member of management thought it "more useful" than chemistry; another in an electrical-engineering firm would prefer to recruit physicists to engineers:

> It is easier to make an engineer out of a physicist than a physicist out of an engineer.

The teaching of technology

Rather more suggestions were put forward on the teaching of the various branches of engineering than on science. One member of management held that engineers should have a "scientific grounding" so that they could understand "not only what happens but why" and that the best way of achieving this might be for engineers to take a first degree in science and to follow this with one in technology. In another case the normal first degree was thought to be "not sufficient" and "wider knowledge of physics" was needed, with the result that "the only practical course" was a post-graduate year in which some specialisation could follow a broad first degree that included physics. The "increasing complexity of life" called for more "specialised training", according to another member of management, but if specialised first degree courses were rejected, the solution might be a "more general" course followed by "specialist" courses later. Finally it was suggested that courses for undergraduate engineers should include something on the "humanities" (suggested twice) and "English".

Cambridge was said to offer the best engineering courses. Other comments were made on courses in the various branches of engineering. To meet its needs a firm interested in vibration control wanted a greater emphasis on mathematics and thermodynamics and workshop experience in mechanical engineering courses. For an electrical engineering firm a greater knowledge of electricity was required than was found in the "pure mechanical man". Some of the civil engineering firms would have liked a greater knowledge of the industries which would be encountered —for example, timber. A civil engineering firm employing a graduate only incidentally suggested that universities should have

more building degrees with less theory, the result of too much influence of architects.

One electrical engineering firm felt that electrical engineering courses should have "a strong mechanical bias"; and that

radio and electronics should be divorced from engineering and become more scientific.

In gas engineering:

Leeds is the only place.

The following comments were made on chemical engineering courses:

The universities have slipped rather on chemical engineering and we are behind Germany and the U.S.A.

Chemical engineering courses are restricted to certain universities. The universities should do more about this.

A graduate entering the gas industry ought in theory to have taken chemical engineering, but I don't think it matters provided he is given some scientific basis on which he can build if he is a man of intelligence. . . . We want a man who can think.

A course combining light engineering and physics had recently been introduced at the technical college level to meet the needs of the precision instruments industry, but it was suggested that it should be raised as soon as possible to the university level.

On production engineering the following comments were made:

Certain techniques have been developed by industry and the universities have done practically nothing to educate production engineers in them. The country needs help on the production side, but the universities are terribly slow to suit the curriculum to the needs of industry. Birmingham is the only university to help here. The others by-pass the problem by saying that another subject can't be added to the courses.

Production engineering should be more prominent. The technical colleges are a long way ahead of the universities.

Courses on industrial management

Twenty-five suggestions were made bearing on the teaching of what may be broadly defined as industrial management. This was a subject of particular concern to firms in the consumer-goods industries, which were largely or mainly interested in arts graduates, but it was raised also in relation to all types of graduates recruited by industry.

At universities the teaching of industrial management may, broadly speaking, take three forms. At the undergraduate stage students may be required to give some time and attention to industrial management as part of their first degree studies in other subjects, whether for a degree in science, technology, or an arts subject. Or they may take a special course wholly devoted to management in addition to their first degree studies. As has been pointed out in an admirable survey of management education in the United Kingdom,

British universities do not offer degrees specifically labelled "Business Administration", but subjects of use in management, and in particular certain aspects of economics, law, psychology and accountancy, are to be found in many degree courses. In some universities teaching for scientific degrees includes some teaching in management subjects. In some modern universities the degrees in Commerce are deliberately designed as a preparation for a business career.*

At the post-graduate, or rather post-university stage, university courses in management may be taken at various distances in time from graduation. (Only those taken immediately after the first degree are post-graduate in the narrow sense of the word.) There are also large numbers of other bodies, including technical colleges, which provide courses in industrial management. Of these, the Administrative Staff College at Henley is the outstanding example, and it differs from the others in being wholly devoted to the study and teaching of management.

Except for isolated pioneer efforts, however, the teaching of industrial management, at whatever level, developed in this country only after the end of the war, and at the time of the survey those interested in it were feeling their way, as indeed they still are. It is, therefore, perhaps not surprising that the replies of some members of management do not always make clear what form or level of industrial management they had in mind and that their answers do not always lend themselves to precise classification.

Half of the suggestions had to do with the question of including management subjects in existing first degree courses, or with special courses or lectures on them. The distinction between the two was not always made. Five members of management thought that students heading for industry, whether arts men, scientists or technologists, should give some time in the course of their studies to "management" subjects. These were mostly not closely defined:

The difference between here and America doesn't lie in technology, it lies in management. What is needed is administrative education as taught in America, where all men have the basic tools of management.

Others suggested "Commercial training" or "Some lectures on economics and management"; "Some business training". Three were in favour of "More management studies" or "General economics and personnel management" for technology students.

* David K. Clarke. "A Survey of Management Education in the United Kingdom", *Journal of Industrial Economics*, Volume IV, No. 2, February 1956. Page 95.

No member of management had any suggestions to make regarding scientists; and, as has been seen, none mentioned them in pressing the need for securing that students should get some experience of industry before entering it. This different point of view regarding scientists and technologists indicates perhaps an acceptance of the proposition that scientists may properly be left in an "ivory tower" but that engineering students should be regarded, rather, as being in the same class as medical students: as needing to undertake, at the university stage, work bearing directly on their future vocation.

For arts men, opinion was in favour of special courses, separate from the first degree studies. Five members of management—all those making specific references to arts men—gave this as their view. One member of a giant firm said:

It is a frightful error to introduce business courses into arts curricula.

Another in a firm interested almost wholly in arts men said:

There is an abysmal ignorance of industry in graduates—for example, its vocabulary is unknown to them. Some sort of course could surely be organised which gave the history of industrial development in this country, together with knowledge of its terms and usages.

The remainder of the replies had to do with the question of a first degree in "administration" or "management" (as distinct from courses or lectures in this subject tacked on to or taken alongside studies for a degree in another subject, just considered); and of post-graduate or, more precisely, post-university, courses, that is, courses taken at some period after the first degree. At each successive stage in his career the objects of study may be progressively less concerned with improving specialist techniques and more with widening the horizon and interests of the "potential manager".

One man was in favour of making "administration" a degree subject; two were against this: "You can't have a management degree". Nine, of whom five were concerned with arts graduates, were in favour of post-university courses, though one with reservations:

The need for administration is growing and with it the need for . . . post-graduate courses in administration.

We send a lot to Henley [the Administrative Staff College].

A post-graduate year in business training would be preferable [to any undergraduate study of the subject], but a man would be less worth while after this added delay from the point of view of good basic material for the firm.

Four, of whom two were concerned with arts graduates, were in favour of post-university courses on American lines:

More courses should be available for specialist training in commerce and industrial activities [immediately] after the degree, as in the United States.

Harvard post-graduate courses in business administration might be good for British industry as well.

In short, the few members of management who mentioned the subject were almost equally divided in their views. Some were in favour of including something on administration or management in or alongside studies leading to a first degree in another subject, others preferred study of management at some stage after graduation.

Very closely allied to this subject were two others, also raised by members of management in the course of replying to the question whether universities should do more to meet the needs of industry: better liaison between senior members of universities and industry; and the acquisition by undergraduates of a more practical or direct knowledge of industry before entering it.

Knowledge and experience of industry

The need for better relations between universities and industry was brought up by fourteen members of management from thirteen firms. The ideas put forward took various forms, but all had in common an explicit or implicit assumption that it was for the universities to take the initiative:

Some universities need closer contact with industry, especially with middle management. There is no attempt, except for Social Science, to see what industry's problems are.

The universities must find some way of avoiding a too academic approach. The provincial universities are probably better at this.

Two members of management called, more specifically, for a greater effort to keep abreast of advances in industry; two for a more "practical interest" in local industry. The following suggestions were made:

F

All university professors should be made to read economic history.

University appointments boards could well spend more time finding out what industry wants; they are too theoretical.

There should be greater collaboration between universities and industry in the development of chaps not technically but socially— in the attitude graduates who enter industry should adopt towards the men they are going to control.

Practical experience of industry before graduation

Twelve members of management were concerned rather with the need for universities to provide opportunities for undergraduates to obtain some practical experience of industry before entering it. All but two, who were interested in arts graduates, had engineering students in mind. Solutions varied. Seven thought "courses" or "work" in industry during vacations might be the solution. For example:

Vacation courses of three months should be compulsory and a condition of a degree.

Men don't know sufficient about industry when they leave the university. In long vacs. boys take jobs where there is most money— haymaking or bricklaying. Universities should control more the jobs taken in the vacs. and see that engineering students go into industry.

The others were in favour of a longer period in industry than a long vacation would provide. For example:

There should be a period in industry in the middle of the course— more like the system in a *Technische Hochschule*.

The problem of forearming the graduate who is to enter industry with some theoretical and practical knowledge of its administrative and other processes, itself raises in an acute form the problem how far university education for those who will go into industry should be vocational. But the fact is that, unlike those who are going to be doctors, for example, undergraduates who eventually go into industry do not have to make up their mind to do so before going to their university, and the men who were the subject of the surveys were by no means exceptions.

Those who had studied full time were asked when they decided to go into industry. Four hundred and thirty-two of the 552 graduates in the graduate interviews (the more representative survey), that is, 78 per cent, had decided to do so before completing their university studies—63 per cent of the arts graduates, 71 per cent of the scientists and 93 per cent of the technologists.*

Those who had done so were asked what steps they had taken while studying to acquaint themselves with industry either by attending lectures, or by visiting factories or firms (other than those specified in their normal academic courses), or by working in a factory during vacations in order to prepare themselves for work in industry.

Of these 432 men, 35 per cent had attended lectures, 60 per cent had visited factories and 57 per cent had undertaken vacation work in industry. The engineering graduates among them were more active than the others. Altogether 92 per cent made some attempt before graduating to acquaint themselves with conditions in industry, as compared with 72 per cent of the science graduates and 66 per cent of the arts graduates.

The type of preparation most germane to the suggestions put forward by management is vacation work. Eighty per cent of the technologists, 40 per cent of the scientists and 27 per cent of the arts men spent some vacation time in industry in order to prepare themselves for it. Moreover, those who undertook vacation work were relatively more assiduous in attending lectures or visiting factories. Approximately three-quarters of the graduates in each faculty who did this vacation work either attended lectures on industry or paid visits to industrial establishments or both, whereas only just over half of those who did not do so took these additional steps to forearm themselves.

If these preparations were to any purpose, these figures suggest that something at any rate was already being done, particularly by engineering students, to meet the suggestions put forward by some members of management that undergraduates heading for industry should be better acquainted with its methods of organi-sation and processes before entering its employment. The question therefore arises whether something more thoroughgoing than can be achieved in vacations might not meet the case rather better. It was with this possibility in mind that members of management were asked what, from their experience (and in the light of their views on what would be the ideal first degree course for their purposes), would be the ideal order in which a man eventually

* The figures for the case study graduates were: arts 80 per cent, science 72 per cent and technology 91 per cent.

joining their firm should acquire his education and training—including national service.

In the event, many members of management, in fact, half, proved to be so much concerned with the problems raised by national service that they confined themselves to this subject.* Twenty-three addressed themselves to the phasing of experience in industry in relation to university studies. There were thirteen suggestions that there should be a period in industry before the university. They came mostly from the metal manufacturers and electrical engineers; three had earlier recommended work in industry in vacations.

> The right order is industry, national service, university, industry. I feel a boy at that age is willing to be pushed around the works more readily.

> A young man ought to have a period in industry before going to a university so that he can get practical experience of what he's learning.

Nine members of management were in favour of sandwich schemes; one considered them, only to turn them down. They were all in engineering or building firms and raised the point only in relation to technology students.

> The sandwich scheme is best: six months at a university, six in industry and so on. The second best is a year at the works first, then university and apprenticeship, with national service last.

> A boy should get national service over after leaving school, go into the works as a tradesman and get a degree through a sandwich course.

---

* Thirty-two were in favour of getting national service over before the university; their argument was most frequently either that this made the student more mature before starting at the university, or that the graduate could come to his job fresh from his studies, not rusty. Twenty-five were in favour of national service after the university, largely because this would achieve continuity of study. Four considered that there should be some period in industry after graduation and that national service should come after this. Five wanted national service abolished, either altogether or for technologists. Eight said the order should depend on the individual; two gave miscellaneous replies; five had no views; twenty-two did not answer.

The Government's recent decision (set out in the White Paper *Call-up of Men to the Forces, 1957–60*, Cmd. 175 (H.M.S.O.), 1957, 4d.) to abolish National Service in successive stages by the end of the present decade now makes these arguments appear somewhat remote but they were strongly held at the time.

The member of management who was critical pointed out that there was a difficulty inherent in any systematic sandwich scheme. "When does a boy really make up his mind what to do?" A sandwich scheme implies that the choice is made at the outset, and in favour of industry.

Summary of views on courses

Only half the suggestions put forward in considering what further steps the universities could take to meet the needs of industry or in considering what would be the ideal first degree course for the firm bore on the content of any university course; and they were put forward by a small minority of the members of management. Only some 7 per cent had suggestions to make on the general objectives of university teaching, 10 per cent on science subjects, 16 per cent on technology and 20 per cent on industrial management. The other half had to do with ways of achieving a better understanding of the administrative and technical processes of industry among undergraduates heading for industry, and among the university teaching staff concerned. The majority, when asked what their ideal first degree course would be, named some existing course or subject of study.

These results should be considered alongside the graduates' views on their undergraduate studies. They were asked whether, in the light of experience since graduating, they would choose to take their first degree course again. Seventy-six per cent of the 594 men in the graduate interview sample said "Yes".* But it was the technologists among them who were the most content and the arts men the least. Only 15 per cent of the technologists would have liked to have taken a different course; 26 per cent of the scientists and 31 per cent of the arts men.† Only a very small number, 5 per cent of the 594, would have liked a "more specialised" course and 7 per cent a "more practical" one.

These figures do not take things very far, but they suggest a

* This proportion was reflected in the replies to a similar question put to the graduates in the case studies.

† The replies to the consequential questions, according to whether the graduate answered "Yes" or "No" throw little light on the sort of alterations they would have liked, or on the subject of study they would have preferred. This was largely due, no doubt, to the form taken by these consequential questions. These disappointing results unfortunately make impracticable further examination of the views of graduates on their university education.

substantial measure of satisfaction regarding the first degree course taken, as seen in the light of subsequent experience, though it should be remembered that this was of, at most, four years' employment.* They seemed to show little call for the more practical approach to which, as has been seen, importance was attached by some members of management.

INFLUENCING UNIVERSITY COURSES

MANAGEMENTS' views on courses should also be considered in conjunction with their replies to a question whether they had done anything at any time to influence the content of any university courses. It was considered important to discover the extent of any steps taken by members of management to put before the universities any views they might have on courses.

Forty-two, a third, had done something; half said they had done nothing. (Eighteen did not answer.) Of these forty-two, fourteen, though they said they had influenced courses, made it clear that they had done so only indirectly, for example, through lecturing at their local university or being associated with the founding of a chair or the giving of a grant by their firm. (One firm made untied grants, two had founded chairs in subjects in which they were interested.) Twenty-four members of management had had informal contacts with professors and other senior members of universities and had made suggestions or had attended a conference to discuss courses. (Six had done so on the initiative of universities.) A few of these contacts appear to have been of a somewhat tenuous nature. For example: "Yes, but only light-heartedly"; "Yes, but not seriously"; "Only behind the scenes—the university is very autocratic". Four, however, could point to a specific course already in being at that time and in the formation of which they had played some part. Two of these were post-graduate courses for engineers—one of them on production engineering, another on concrete; two were non-technical courses —one on personnel management and another on industrial administration.

THE VALUE OF HIGHER DEGREES

A FURTHER subject bearing on university education for industry, and the last of those raised in the course of the questions put on

* See Appendix E.

this subject, is that of the higher degree—a degree, generally for a Doctorate, which can be gained only by undertaking research resulting in some original contribution to knowledge. It is in essence an aspect of the main problem what kinds of graduates and what numbers of each kind industry wants—and needs—to get from the universities. The larger the amount of fundamental and applied research being undertaken in industry, and the more complex processes and materials become, the greater the need must be to increase the number of employees with academic achievements going beyond the first degree. The proportion in which people with these additional qualifications are needed, in relation to those with a first degree, is one question. Another is the form or forms these additional qualifications should take.

The need for a larger proportion of graduates with additional qualifications has been widely recognised, and immediately after the war government policy included provision on a liberal scale for grants to enable graduates to take a higher degree. At the time this was considered to be an effective means of providing for industry's needs. But by the time this survey was undertaken there was some evidence that this policy was not working out altogether happily. The Department of Scientific and Industrial Research, the Federation of British Industries, besides other bodies, were already questioning it. Criticism was directed towards the type and level of research undertaken and also towards its effect on the outlook of the student and his capacity to adapt himself to industrial conditions. It was decided therefore to sound members of management and graduates during the course of the present survey on the value to them of a higher degree. The former were asked: *Have you any views of the value to you of a higher degree in science or technology?* The latter were asked: *On balance, do you think it has been worth while taking a higher degree in relationship to* (a) *your career, and* (b) *the work you have to do?*

Graduates with higher degrees*—there were thirty-five among the 594 in the graduate interviews and the same proportion among those in the case studies—were inclined to take a favourable view of the value to them of their higher degree, but they were by no

* By "higher degree" is meant a Doctorate or a Master's degree conferred by a university in Great Britain. Master's degrees which are first and non-post graduate degrees, as in Scotland, and Master's degrees which are granted without further examination, as at Oxford and Cambridge, are excluded.

means unanimous.* They had had little time to test their view in a career in industry. But twenty-six, some three-quarters, were satisfied that this degree was worth while in relation both to their career and to the work on which they were then engaged; four for their career, but not their work; one for his work only. Three thought it had not been worth while in either respect and one did not answer. The few case study graduates with a higher degree took a less rosy view. Only half felt that it was worth while, both from the point of view of their career and the work on which they were then engaged and they were inclined to qualify their views in various ways.

Members of management were rather more sceptical. Eleven firms and one gas board had no graduate with a higher degree and, on this account, perhaps, a rather high proportion either did not answer this question (twenty-two) or had no views (twenty-five). Of these, a third came from the undertakings known to have no graduate with a higher degree. All but two of these were small firms and all but one were new employers of graduates.†

Of the remainder, twenty-eight, nearly a quarter of all the members of management to which the question was put and a third of those expressing some views, thought a higher degree in science and technology of no value to them. Of these, ten were from undertakings with no men with a higher degree. Of these ten, one looked to its research association and two to the laboratories of their head firm to make the running on much or all of their research and development and explained their views on higher degrees on this ground. Only a minority of those to whom a higher degree was of no value were outspoken in their criticism of it. One said it was "unserviceable"; another, an electrical engineer, who advocated post-graduate courses for engineers on the ground that the normal first degree course was not good enough for his purposes, thought a higher degree "no use at all". The others were less emphatic. For example: "No—prestige

* The 6 per cent of the 594 graduates who had obtained a higher degree after graduating in 1950 is roughly in line with, but a little higher than, the 4 per cent with a higher degree given for graduates in fifty engineering firms examined in the Report on the *Recruitment of Scientists and Engineers by the Engineering Industry* (H.M.S.O.), 1955. 1s. 6d.

† The replies from the gas boards were to a large extent governed by the fact that research is reserved to the Gas Council. None of the eight firms classed as employing a graduate only incidentally had a graduate with a higher degree and none was asked this question.

only"; "It spoils a man for the rough and tumble [of a production department]".

Thirty-two said that a higher degree in these subjects was of value to them, but qualified their reply in one way or another. Two-thirds of these thought a degree of this sort of use only in research or, less frequently, in research and development, and another six thought it of use for "limited purposes"—"in physics only ... a higher degree engineer is too big for his boots", or "for production", or "for the little job in a sheltered life", for example. Three saw some value in this type of degree, but thought that the delay it entailed to entry into industry a mistake. Miscellaneous answers were given by a small number; of these, three, though they did not deny value to such a degree, considered experience in industry more valuable.

Only ten members of management—less than 10 per cent— gave an unqualified or a nearly unqualified "Yes". Five confined themselves to a simple affirmative or such answers as "Yes—clear thinkers", or "Yes, it impresses others". The remaining five replied more fully:

A higher degree is of very considerable value. We have a number of people with higher degrees, particularly in the research departments. In so far as people taking higher degrees are often amongst the most able graduates, we find among men with higher degrees some of the most promising recruits for higher positions. (A member of management in a chemical manufacturing firm.)

The top people in an organisation should have a higher degree. It is evidence of ability to apply themselves. But it is not essential. (Another from the same firm.)

They are essential to some jobs. We must have a leaven of people with higher degrees. Some are on production and sales. (Another chemical manufacturing firm.)

They are of very considerable value. We would hire all people with higher degrees if there were enough. But large numbers of jobs wouldn't satisfy a man with a higher degree—though he'd do them better! (A metal manufacturer.)

They are of value for a number of jobs. But a Ph.D., rather than a Master's degree, is useful. Work for a M.Sc. is to a rigid syllabus— Ph.D. gives a clue to a man. (A firm of civil engineers.)

These five members of management were alike not only in

their full acceptance of the value of a higher degree in science and technology, but also in their acceptance of the value of employing men with a higher degree in work other than research.

Broadly speaking, therefore, of the 126 members of management to whom the question was put, only a third said they saw some value in a higher degree, but of these a small band were enthusiasts. These results must be viewed, in part, in the light of the fact that the value of a higher degree to a firm must depend to a large extent on the standard and the level of scientific and technological work undertaken, not only in research departments.

SUMMING UP

IN considering the relationship between university education and the needs of industry all but two members of management appear to have assumed that no fundamental change in existing university policy was called for or, rather, that any suggestion they might make would not give rise to the need for any such change.

Seeking the views of the universities did not fall within the scope of the enquiry, and it is possible therefore only to speculate on their reaction to the variety of opinions held regarding the relative advantages of a university education to industry, particularly the strong emphasis on advantages other than the academic. University teachers, no doubt, would not quarrel with those members of management who thought the advantage lay in the ability of the universities to train the mind. But their reaction to the idea that the chief advantage lay on the social side might be rather mixed. Nevertheless, it is true that the universities are giving a great deal of attention to the whole question of the bearing of extra-curricula activities on the general development of students. Halls of residence at thirteen universities and university colleges are included in the universities' building programme over 1957-59. A sub-committee of the University Grants Committee has been considering the wider question of the function of halls of residence, and attention is also being given to other means of increasing the "student day", as it is called, by extending the hours during which libraries are open and meals are available in unions and refectories. The main points raised under this head are, therefore, already very much in mind.

The call for more university men for industry will no doubt gradually be met, at least to some extent, by the proposals put forward in the autumn of 1956 by the universities to increase their student population to 106,000 by the mid-1960s—as compared with some 82,000 at the time of the survey. It is expected that about two-thirds of this increase would study science or technology.* Even more would be done were the universities to agree to go beyond this figure in response to the Government's view that even this substantial increase might not be likely to meet the need:

> But, large though this increase is, the Government believe that the universities should be encouraged to expand even more. The University Grants Committee has advised us that a larger expansion would be desirable if resources can be made available. It would like to invite the universities to consider still further expansion to meet national needs. . . . It is certainly our intention to ensure that the universities and the technical colleges will, together, be able to produce at least the number of qualified scientists and engineers . . . recently estimated to be needed over the period ten to fifteen years hence.†

Many suggestions were put forward on existing curricula in the course of the interviews made for this survey. Perhaps the main deduction to be made from them is that there was a large measure of acceptance of the principle that the universities should not be asked to cater in first degree courses for the specialised interests of particular industries. Indeed, there was some slight indication of support for making the established first degree courses in science and technology more "fundamental", reserving specialisation for post-university courses, and of leaving to industry the responsibility for seeing that the knowledge acquired at the university is fruitfully applied to the work undertaken. Typical of this point of view is a remark from a member of management in an electrical engineering firm:

> I do not think universities should feel that training is part of their job. Fundamental science with a certain amount of broadening—the history of industry for example—should be taught. We'll do the rest.

On the other hand, the suggestions put forward regarding the

* Statement by the Financial Secretary to the Treasury, *Hansard*, 21 November 1956, Cols. 1750–51.
  † ibid.

need for experience of industry before graduating in a technology subject and the need for courses in industrial management for all students who are to enter industry present certain difficulties.

The systematic adoption of any method of providing students with some experience of industry before entering it would tend to reinforce the vocational as against the academic aspect of the university courses followed. It would involve, among other things, the student deciding in favour of industry before beginning his university studies. A development on these lines would be one on which the universities might not see eye to eye with industry. On vacation work, as such, university views have already been expressed. The greater number of vice-chancellors and principals have stated that they were not in favour of paid employment during vacations.

Be this as it may, there are, broadly speaking, three methods of acquiring industrial experience before graduation: by spending a period in industry before embarking on university studies; by a sandwich system of alternating periods of six months or so in industry and at a university; or by vacation work in industry. The academic year does not lend itself very readily to a sandwich system and there was little evidence of support for it from members of management.

In practice, therefore, the alternatives are a pre-university period in industry and vacation work. The former is already being developed to some extent, mainly by larger firms; and this system clearly presents the least difficulty to universities. Vacation work is another question. A large proportion—80 per cent—of the engineering graduates had spent some time in industry in vacations, but the comments made by members of management on the need for more experience in industry before graduating, though few in number, suggest that something further needed to be done to ensure that the undergraduate in fact derives all the advantages he should from his vacation work. Except for some small-scale enquiries on the question of vacation work in general, no systematic examination has been made of this subject. An enquiry concerned primarily with vacation work in industry as a means of preparing for future employment in it might well be worth while.

The call for courses in industrial management also raises difficulties bearing on the question of the essential purpose of a university—whether it is to advance knowledge or to provide vocational education or training. The universities now send more men into industry than into any other walk of life. Should the universities set out to provide industry with managers—just as they provide the medical profession with doctors? The answer hangs largely on their assessment of management as a subject worthy of their attention.

University teaching staff vary very much in this assessment, but there are indications that the trend is in the direction of accepting the proposition, at least in principle, that a management discipline, were it to be evolved, would not be incompatible with the true function of a university.

Admittedly, there is still a long way to go. As Professor Hunt has pointed out, the scope of the subject and the building of the discipline itself are still being evolved:

> Much of the building material must come from other disciplines, such as economics, psychology, sociology, law, political science, accounting and the applied sciences. The traditional and orthodox treatment of these subjects may, however, be unsuitable for management purposes, and a courageous tackling of this problem by university teachers and managers, together, is urgently needed. . . . the social implications of business must not be overlooked. . . . Business problems overlap so many different academic disciplines that in this matter of university education [for management] co-operation between the various social sciences is absolutely essential. . . . The answer to the problem of management lies not merely with the economist but also with the psychologist, the sociologist, the scientist, the accountant, and the theologian as well, for the problem is, at its root, a spiritual one.*

Progress is indeed being made, if slowly, towards the development of the study of management. With it a clearer understanding of the possibilities and limitations of undergraduate and post-university study of it is emerging. The general concensus of opinion appears to be that the greater part, at least, of the study should be reserved for the post-university stage when the student is more mature and freer to concentrate on it. The level of experience is now seen as the criterion by which to judge what should be taught, and at what stage. Courses for young executives

* Professor Norman C. Hunt. "The Role of the University in Education for Management", *British Management Review*, October 1954.

of not less than about twenty-seven years of age are now available at some universities and reflect the general trend of opinion and experience on this subject in recent years.

The value of higher degrees was regarded with some scepticism by many of the members of management interviewed. It is possible that when they have had time to make their impact, the new arrangements for centralising in the Department of Scientific and Industrial Research awards of research studentships in science and technology may eventually meet some of the criticism made of the usefulness of higher degrees.* Perhaps even more hopeful, the department's new advanced course studentships awards—in "a specialised subject, a training in which is expected to add substantially to the value of the degree already taken"—will meet the needs of those members of management who would have liked their graduates to receive specialised training in the branch of science or technology in which the firm were interested, after a broad first degree course. These awards may also be an indirect means of meeting criticism of higher degrees by providing an alternative which would take the form of training, not research for a doctorate. These new provisions are the result of lengthy discussion not only with the Committee of Vice-Chancellors and Principals, but also with industry, and mark an important and promising new stage in the development of policy governing post-university awards.

In conclusion, it may be said that on several of the more important heads raised by members of management, significant progress has already been made since the survey was carried out.

* These studentships were formerly known as Maintenance Allowances. Their administration was earlier shared by the department with the Ministry of Education and local education authorities in England and Wales. Announcement of the new arrangements was made by the Ministry of Education and the Department of Scientific and Industrial Research, 6 November, 1956.

CHAPTER III

SELECTION

SELECTION is both the last phase of recruitment, the final step in the process of persuading candidates to apply for work with the firm, and the first step towards ensuring their efficient use and good relationship with their employers.

A successful selection policy involves three things: a clear conception of the kind of work for which candidates are to be chosen, together with the qualities and qualifications needed to carry it out; knowledge of where to look for possible recruits; and means of recognising and assessing, in the candidates presenting themselves, the qualities and qualifications sought.

Some indication of the purposes for which graduates were sought and of the qualifications and personal qualities looked for has already been given.* It has been seen that the work for which they were recruited was also offered to suitable non-graduates in most cases. Almost all the small firms recruited for a specific vacancy, but many of the larger ones, especially those offering training courses, sought graduates for a range of possible vacancies. As a consequence, the qualifications and qualities sought were generally expressed in broad terms. Another reason, no doubt, arises from the fact that particular emphasis was placed on the importance of the right personal qualities, which do not lend themselves to exact definition.

For most firms, therefore, until they were confronted with a possible candidate or an application from one, the situation was fluid. Once this had happened, the situation had to be considered in terms of the firm's assessment of the qualifications and qualities offered. This assessment was generally made in the light of some other information about the candidate, gained from his application form, or through an introduction, or from his having worked in the firm during the vacation. But it is the stage following this, the stage of selection proper, that is crucial.

It is the object of this chapter to examine the methods adopted in the actual selection of candidates, and the views of members of management and of graduates on them.

* Chapter I, pages 4-18.

THE FIRMS' METHODS

THE practice of each firm, the ways in which interviews were conducted, and the views of managements and graduates on the various procedures which were followed, were examined in the course of the case studies.

Managements of the forty-three undertakings with a deliberate graduate employment policy were asked how they selected graduate recruits for jobs. Procedure varied according to the individual circumstances of the appointment and the graduate, and sometimes departments or units of a firm used different methods. But generally speaking, firms had one particular approach to selection; and in most the method which was stated by management to be the most usual was similar to that described by a majority of the graduates interviewed.

All the firms used interviews of some kind for the selection of graduates. Very occasionally these were combined with intelligence or psychological tests, and one firm sometimes used group tests of the kind popularly known as the "country house" method. The interview, however, stands out as the most widely adopted method.

Two forms of interviewing predominated: the panel interview, sometimes referred to as a board, where an applicant was seen by two or more people together; and the series of single interviews, that is two or more interviews, each with a different person. Twenty firms used a panel interview, eleven as part of a series of interviews, and nine used it on its own. Nineteen used a series of single interviews. In three firms, graduates had a single interview with one man; and one small firm with only two graduates had chosen a school-leaver before he had entered a university. The distribution of the firms according to the method adopted and the total number of employees is given in Table 6.

A panel interview was the most widely adopted method of selection among the largest firms. Of the twelve with more than 10,000 employees, nine used a panel or board as part of their selection procedure. About half the firms in the medium-size categories used a panel interview. Only one of the twelve firms with fewer than 2,000 employees used a panel. Fifteen of the twenty concerns which employed fifty graduates or more, including three of the six giant employers, used this method.

TABLE 6

SELECTION METHODS—CASE STUDY FIRMS

Number of firms using method, grouped according to total number of employees

Method	Under 500	500-1,999	2,000-4,999	5,000-9,999	10,000 and over	Total
A single interview						
with one interviewer .	—	1	1	1	—	3
with panel . . .	—	1	4	—	4	9
Series of interviews						
each with one interviewer .	5	4	5	2	3	19
including panel . .	—	—	3	3	5	11
Other methods . . .	1	—	—	—	—	1
TOTAL	6	6	13	6	12	43

A series of single interviews was most often used in the smaller firms. Three-quarters of those with fewer than 2,000 employees used two or more interviews, each conducted by one person. About a third of the medium-sized firms and a quarter of those with more than 10,000 employees made their selection by means of a series of single interviews.

Although the panel interview was the most frequently encountered method of selection among the larger concerns, it should be noted that a fifth of those which employed more than fifty graduates used a series of single interviews rather than a panel interview; this included the remaining three of the six giant employers of graduates.

Three firms, all in the building and contracting industry, selected graduates by means of a single interview with one man. Two of these firms employed under twenty graduates, but the third had more than a hundred.

Interviews at universities

Nine firms said that part of the selection process took place at universities. All but one of these employed more than fifty graduates. Six of the concerns belonged to the electrical engineering industry, that is, all the electrical engineering firms in the survey with the exception of the two smallest, which employed under ten graduates. The three other firms which said that selection was undertaken partly at universities were in the metal trades, textiles,

G

aircraft and vehicles industries. In all but one case the interviews at a university were followed by a visit to the firm itself, where there were generally further interviews. The practice varied from firm to firm, but it was clear that in many cases an important part of the selection process was completed at the university, and in one instance selection was entirely carried out at universities by a panel composed of the training officer and departmental heads.

Specialised selection methods

Only four concerns referred to the use of any kind of test in the selection of graduates. All these firms employed more than fifty graduates. An electrical engineering firm said that intelligence tests were generally used and occasionally selection tests; but none of the graduates interviewed in this firm had experienced them. At the headquarters of a large food concern it was said that group tests were used; but these were not applied in the unit which was visited. One of the area gas boards said that at its headquarters a group selection of the type used by War Office selection boards was sometimes employed. Only in one firm had any of the graduates who were interviewed undergone the tests described by managements. The comments of the management and graduates on these psychological tests will be considered in a later section.

INTERVIEWING PROCEDURES

In view of the preponderance of the interview among the methods used in the selection of graduates, it is important to examine its content and supervision. Senior members of management in the forty-three firms were asked whether they used a standard series of questions during their interviews. Only one motor car firm and a unit of one of the gas boards did so, and in the latter only for some candidates. The concerns in question employed only a few graduates, and in each case interviews were based on a plan formulated by the National Institute of Industrial Psychology. The management of the motor firm said that the qualifications of the applicants were known, and that in a very full interview they therefore tried to discover qualities. The firm was satisfied with the results of selection, and considered that the method was "reasonably safe and scientific".

In the majority of the firms, selection procedures were mostly unstandardised, and the element of personal judgment was high. A number of firms, however, said that although no set of questions was laid down, the same sort of question was often asked. Typical comments were:

> Some of the questions become standardised, having been asked so many times.

> They settle into something of a similar pattern. We ask the fellow to tell us something about himself, cover his hobbies, sport, and so on, and military service.

Completed application forms were mentioned by the managements of a number of firms as providing the basis for the interview, which then varied according to the entries which had been made.

Managements were asked: *Are members of the firm in charge of selection specially trained for the work?* In seven large or medium-sized firms, members of the staff who had received special training took an active part in the selection process. These included three large electrical engineering firms, in which a panel interviewed candidates at universities, followed, in two of the three, by interviews at the works; one of these firms often used intelligence tests, sometimes selection tests. Two medium-sized firms in the metal trades chose graduates by means of a series of interviews in which a member of the staff trained in selection methods generally took part. A medium-sized firm used specially trained staff in its selection process, which included a board interview and psychological tests. The unit of one of the gas boards which sometimes used specialised selection techniques had trained staff.

In two small firms, personnel officers advised on but did not actually take part in the selection of graduates. Two medium-sized firms were shortly to appoint trained officers to assist in the selection of graduates, and one medium and one large firm were appointing officers who might be concerned with graduate selection.

Interviews were generally conducted by those closely concerned with the work the graduate would do: the head of a small firm, heads of departments, training officers. Nearly half the firms volunteered the information that they had trained personnel for the selection of non-graduate staff, but not for the selection of graduates. The use of specialised interviewing and selection techniques was exceptional. Even when people with a special training were concerned with the selection of graduates the procedure was not usually complex or strictly applied. There is little evidence to explain why specialised selection techniques were so seldom used. Managements were not asked to justify their use or otherwise of specially trained staff, but a third of those which did not have specially trained officers in charge commented on the long experience of those concerned with selection in their firm. Typical remarks were:

A personnel officer with twenty years' experience is on the selection board.

The education officer is always present; he is very experienced.

Interviewers are not specifically trained, but have much experience.

I have been trained in the hard school of experience for twenty-five years.

A medium-sized firm in the metal trades had experimented with professional selection and rejected it. This management said:

We did experiment with the professional selection of people, but we have now kicked out the personnel officers. They develop a professional callousness and aren't sufficiently sensitive; they are not interested in the person or the job, too impersonal. They may have good results in enormous concerns, but not in a family affair depending on team spirit and atmosphere.

I trust personal judgments. Everything ultimately depends upon whether you like a person. The only time I went against my judgment I made a fatal error, and this confirmed my belief.

The methods of selection which were afterwards used by this firm varied according to the job. Candidates were seen by two or three people, including the technical director, and then ideas were exchanged.

The management of a large firm, a giant employer of graduates, also expressed doubt about the usefulness of professional selection methods, saying:

I am very dubious about tests and such—very misleading. They provide gladiatorial fun for the onlooker, but I am far from happy about group selection.

The importance of a personal assessment was stressed by the

management of a medium-sized firm in the consumer-goods industry:

> All systems should in the end bow to personal judgment. Everything ultimately depends on whether you like a person.

Most firms approached selection in an informal way and their methods generally reflected the sort of attitude expressed by the management of a medium-sized chemical firm:

> Interviews are intentionally very informal, because we think that in that way we can size up a person better.

VIEWS OF MANAGEMENT ON RESULTS

THE managements of the case study firms were asked: *Does your method of selection give good results?* Of the 107 members of management in the forty-three firms who answered the question, only four, belonging to three firms, said that they were not satisfied with the selection methods used by their firm. In six firms a member of management gave a qualified answer; in each of these, other members of management were satisfied with the selection methods. Ninety-seven members of management said that they were satisfied with their selection procedure as such. In each of the categories a few members of management, totalling thirteen from ten firms, mentioned the narrowness of choice open to them.

Satisfied majority

The vast majority of members of management were satisfied with the methods of selection which were used by their firms. The answers of those who elaborated their comments show the various ways in which the success of a selection method was assessed. Some members of management expressed enthusiasm for the method itself. For instance, the managing director of a firm with over a hundred graduates, which used board interviews as part of a series, said:

> Within five minutes I think every one of us has a fairly clear idea of a man that continues through his training. We are fairly satisfied with the result—the trouble is the loss of trained men to competing firms.

In another firm the interview rating system was described as reasonably safe and scientific. One firm compared its rate of turnover favourably with that of industry as a whole, while another firm said that it had had only two failures so far. A number of members of management took rather negative views—that the method was "as good as any other", that it was satisfactory "because it isn't left to one person's judgment", or that it was "on the whole satisfactory, but is constantly being revised".

Further illustrations of the approach to selection are given in the following sections, which include the comments of members of managements of those firms in which qualified or critical comments were made.

Qualified replies

In six firms a member of management gave a qualified answer to the question; other members of management in these firms, however, were satisfied with the methods used. Two of the firms were in the largest size category, that is with 10,000 or more employees. In one of them, graduates were generally selected by a board of three; if they were first seen locally they always had a further panel at the headquarters of the organisation:

> I am satisfied that it is as good as any other method. (The general manager.)

> The university intake has as many disappointments as any other. (The staff manager.)

> Though we complain of the general calibre of graduates, this is perhaps the result of the recruiting system. But chaps stay and do quite nicely. They just don't make the progress one would like. (The training officer.)

A large electrical engineering firm arranged panel interviews at the universities. Most candidates were given a simple intelligence test and some were given simple selection tests; if candidates about whom the panel was doubtful obtained very good results in these tests they might be taken on. All candidates visited the firm before they were accepted. The personnel director referred to a graduate shortage:

> It is impossible to say whether our method of selection gives good results; if there were a greater supply we could judge. We tend to take a lower standard.

The chief engineer of one of the departments, although satisfied with the method of selection, also referred to a shortage:

> I am not getting enough engineers; it may be because mine is not a clean job. The ones I am getting are of the right type, but I want more. Those we have appointed are holding down good jobs.

Members of management in two medium-sized chemical firms commented on the difficulty of assessing candidates' suitability. In one of these the head of a research department said:

> It is very difficult to select for any job on the strength of a written application and a brief interview. Academic qualifications are only half the story. Personality doesn't come out in a short interview, and only after a man has been working with you for a few months is it possible to make a correct assessment of his value. A personnel officer has been appointed; he should be a better judge, but I doubt whether it will overcome the difficulty.

Selection here was made by a board and, except in the case of junior men for the training pool, by interview with the managing director. Four other members of management were satisfied with the results.

A series of informal friendly interviews, occasionally with intelligence tests, was the method used by another chemical firm. The final decision was left to the head of the department concerned:

> I can't answer scientifically; the human element is fallible. We hope perhaps to evolve a better system, but probably won't. (A director at the headquarters.)

> People are passed down from headquarters for interview, or sometimes interviewed locally and the appointment confirmed from H.Q. We talk over general conditions, both what they know and what they are. People are taken round the labs., and some attempt is made to get them talking there. It is often worth while to take them out to a meal, because there are some people with a line to shoot or who will sooner or later not fit in well with this ship.

> We have some fatalities, but the results are mostly good. The firm takes infinite trouble with misfits. It is practically impossible to be fired. If you chase a director with a carving knife, the firm will merely send you to a psychiatrist at their expense. (Member of management outside headquarters.)

A medium-sized firm manufacturing a non-metalliferous

mining product, a new employer of graduates but with over fifty
of them, sometimes used a board interview, sometimes an interview with one man. The emphasis was on men with previous
industrial experience. The managing director said: "Your successes
can't be measured for ten years". Three other members of
management were satisfied with the results of selection:

> The turnover of the firm as a whole is under three per cent; the
> average for industry as a whole is over six per cent.
>
> The general average is satisfactory. Less than ten per cent are failures.
>
> Immediately, the results are good. Ultimately, we have not had long
> enough to tell; but some we have taken on have already fulfilled
> their promise.

In a medium-sized engineering firm, candidates were interviewed separately by a number of people who later combined to
discuss their suitability. An executive at the headquarters of the
firm was reasonably satisfied with the results, but a director at the
unit said:

> It's not scientific, but there's so little choice. We are very short of
> chemists.

Dissatisfied minority

Dissatisfaction with their selection methods was expressed by
four members of management in three firms. The managing
director of a medium-sized firm in the metal trades employing
fewer than fifty graduates and taking on about four a year from
a local university, was not satisfied that the firm's method of
selection gave good results. He said, without elaborating, "It is
too haphazard". The education officer was more expansive. He
said:

> Selection is by means of informal interviews with the works manager
> and the head of the department concerned. I have been specially
> trained for the work of selection, but am not officially in charge.
> There is no common procedure. Methods could be improved, but
> I am fairly certain that this is subject to the availability of graduates.
> I hope it would exclude some who now turn over. A committee is
> looking at the whole question.

This education officer had earlier said that graduates did not
stay with the firm, and that good graduates were not available in

sufficient numbers. He felt that perhaps the firm did not get the best. The works manager was satisfied with the selection methods in use.

There was a similar divergence of opinion in a medium-sized electrical engineering firm employing more than a hundred graduates: an executive at headquarters, who had earlier commented that enough graduates of the right kind were not being attracted to the firm, said:

> We go to the universities and select the ones who seem possible. They are invited to a preliminary interview with a small panel, which includes heads of the laboratories or production departments. The man who wants the graduate selects him. This is a better way than any other, but I am not satisfied with the results.

A factory manager in the same firm was satisfied with the results of their selection method, and said that it had been most successful during the previous four years. The works manager of another factory, however, was critical:

> The methods of interviewing and checking are haphazard. The specification from departments of their needs is not clear; I feel that a real job could be made of the interview. There are too many dabblers, and no one with enough experience.

In a medium-sized motor vehicle firm employing under fifty graduates, candidates for the headquarters were interviewed by a small panel. The final decision was taken by a senior member of management, who had himself at one time undertaken selection at a university. He said that there had been some mistakes and he had decided not to take the blame in future. A committee of three was then set up to interview at the firm, but he said that it had had no more success. The managing director said:

> At one of the establishments they have selection boards. I don't think they are good, but we must resort to them here if we have many more graduates. I don't think our method of selection gives good results, but I don't know of any that gives better.

Limited choice

When asked whether their method of selection gave good results, thirteen members of management in ten firms referred to the narrowness of choice open to them. Comments were made on this in five of the eight electrical engineering firms in the sample; four of the five employed more than a hundred graduates. Some of the comments are given below:

> We are only satisfied with the results of selection of graduates to a limited extent because there are not enough of them; there is no choice. We have lowered our standards, but still do not get enough of them. We will probably appoint a full-time university liaison officer, and an education and training officer.

> Selection doesn't come into it at the moment.

> It is impossible to say whether our method of selection gives good results; if there were a greater supply we could judge. We tend to take a lower standard.

> I am quite satisfied with the method of selection. The results are not determined by the method, but by the supply.

In the fifth electrical engineering firm, a very small and new employer of graduates, the managing director said:

> Results are very hit or miss; this is more due to the availability than methods of selection. We choose the best we can find. We have got some good chaps, but we do make mistakes.

In two of the five building and contracting firms a member of management referred to a shortage of graduates. Both of these were medium-sized firms, one a relatively large employer of graduates, the other employing only a few. Taking the larger firm first, their comments were:

> I don't think it's a matter of selection. We must take what is possible owing to the shortage.

> I would be glad to hear of any interview which would give good results. I don't feel convinced it's the method of selection that is at fault; it's the narrowness of choice.

The remaining three firms in which a member of management referred to the effect of restricted choice on selection belonged to different industries, and were relatively small employers of graduates. Two of these have already been considered: one was the firm in the metal trades in which a member of management thought that perhaps they were not getting the best graduates; the other, the engineering firm in which reference was made to a shortage of chemists. Finally, there was a small firm, employing very few graduates, which had experienced some difficulty because of the location of their factory and the working conditions entailed by the manufacturing process.

STATISTICAL ANALYSIS

Replies in the graduate interviews

The 561 men who obtained their first industrial job after graduation were asked how they were selected. Their replies will be considered in the following sections before turning to the comments of the graduates in the case study firms. The results are shown in Table 7.

TABLE 7

METHOD OF SELECTION

	No. of graduates	Per cent	Graduates given tests	
			No.	Per cent*
One interview .	332	59	12	4
Series of interviews	188	34	24	13
Other methods .	41	7	45	12
TOTAL . .	561	100	41	7

* The proportion of those who experienced a selection method who were given a test.

Interviews of various kinds were by far the most usual method of selection; tests and specialised selection techniques were used relatively infrequently. Ninety-four per cent of the graduates said that they were chosen by means of an interview or interviews of various kinds. A single interview, whether with a board, panel, or one man, was more usual than a series. Seven per cent said that they were chosen by some other method. Eight men in this class said that they were chosen by a group interview; this was understood to mean the interviewing of a number of candidates at the same time. Two men were given group tests of the "country house" type, one took a competitive entrance examination, and one was given a practical test in statistics. The other twenty-nine had already had some sort of contact with the firm; twelve had previously worked for the firm or taken a vacation course there; seven said without elaboration that they were already known personally to the firm; five had entered a family business; four said that they had not undergone the normal method of selection because they had a relative in the firm, and one because he was himself a director.

When they were being considered for the job, 7 per cent of the graduates were given some sort of test. Seven men were given group tests and four were given practical tests of their knowledge. Intelligence tests were most usual, however, forming part of the selection of thirty-four of the forty-one men who were given a test, including four who also had another kind of test.

Analysis by size of firm

The following section examines the selection methods which were experienced by graduates in firms belonging to groups of various size. The distribution of graduates according to the size of the firm which they joined, in terms of the total number of employees, is shown in Table 8.

TABLE 8

SELECTION METHOD BY SIZE OF FIRM

| | Per cent of graduates in firms employing: | | | | | Total | |
Method	Under 500	500– 1,999	2,000– 4,999	5,000– 9,999	10,000 and over	No.	%
A single interview							
only . .	56	69	52	55	56	320	57
with tests . .	2	2	1	2	2	12	2
Series of interviews							
only .	20	22	32	38	30	164	30
with tests . .	2	2	10	1	5	24	4
Other methods .	20	5	5	4	5	41	7
	100	100	100	100	100	561	100
Number of graduates							
in firms . .	54	62	79	79	256	561*	

* In the case of 31 graduates, the size of the firm is not known. These have been included in the total figures only.

In each size group except the smallest about 95 per cent of the graduates said that they were selected by means of interviews of various kinds; in the smallest size group the corresponding figure was 80 per cent. In each group a single interview was experienced more often than a series; between 53 and 58 per cent were given a single interview in each group except that of firms with between 500 and 2,000 employees, where the proportion was 71 per cent. In all groups, less than 4 per cent of the men who had one interview combined it with any form of test.

A series of interviews was more usual with the larger firms than the smaller, although in no group was it used more often than the single interview. About 40 per cent of the graduates in firms with more than 2,000 employees were given a series of interviews, compared with 22 per cent in firms with less than 2,000. One in eight of the men who had a series of interviews also had a test, usually an intelligence test. One in four of those in firms with between 2,000 and 5,000 employees, and one in seven of those in firms with 10,000 or more, were given an intelligence test in addition to a series of interviews. In the other size groups, fewer than one in ten were given a test of any kind in addition.

A fifth of the graduates who joined a firm with fewer than 500 employees did not have a formal interview. This was nearly always because they had had some previous contact with the firm. In the other size groups, fewer than 5 per cent of the men said that they were chosen without an interview.

TABLE 9

SELECTION METHOD BY PRODUCT OF FIRM

		Per cent of graduates given:				
		Single interview		Series		
Product	No. of graduates	Only	With tests	Only	With tests	Other Methods
Mining and quarrying	19	53	5	26	11	5
Oil	14	50	—	50	—	—
Non-metalliferous manufacturing .	23	61	—	30	—	9
Chemicals . .	118	40	4	40	7	9
Metal trades . .	53	59	2	28	4	7
Shipbuilding and vehicles . .	39	85	—	15	—	—
Non-electrical engineering . .	37	54	—	38	3	5
Electrical engineering .	131	60	1	28	5	6
Consumer goods .	54	48	2	31	6	13
Building and contracting . .	22	73	—	13	5	9
Public utilities . .	32	85	6	9	—	—
TOTAL . .	561*	57	2	30	4	7

* That is, the 561 who obtained their first industrial job after graduation: the 33 graduates who were employed in industry while reading for a degree part-time have been excluded. In the case of 19 graduates the product group is not known. These been included in the total figures.

Analysis by product group

In all product groups the great majority of graduates were chosen by means of an interview or interviews, generally unaccompanied by tests of any kind. The distribution of the graduates according to the product group of the firms they joined is shown in Table 9.

One interview was the most usual method in each product group except chemicals (where 44 per cent of the men were given one interview, 47 per cent a series), and in the oil industry, where half the graduates experienced each method. In the other product groups the proportion of men selected by means of one interview varied from 50 per cent in consumer goods to 85 per cent in shipbuilding and vehicles and 91 per cent in public utilities.

The numbers of graduates in the individual product groups are not large, and no great reliance can be placed on comparisons between them. But there is little doubt that in all groups most graduates were selected by interviewing, and that in most the single interview was the predominant method, generally unaccompanied by any supplementary procedure. The proportion of graduates chosen by means other than interviewing exceeded 10 per cent only in the consumer goods industry; but in three industries (non-metalliferous manufacturing, chemicals, and building and contracting) the proportion was only just below. This was generally due to some sort of prior contact between the graduate and his firm.

Interview replies summarised

To summarise this analysis of the replies obtained in the graduate interviews, the answers of these 561 graduates show that selection was generally carried out by means of interviews, seldom accompanied by any more specialised method. In all size and product groups, most graduates were chosen by means of an interview or interviews of various kinds. The proportion selected by methods other than the normal interview procedures was more than 10 per cent in only one size group (that of firms with fewer than 500 employees) and one product group (firms in the consumer goods industry). One interview was experienced more frequently than a series of interviews in each size group and all but two product groups of firms; a series was used most often in the larger firms. Tests, generally of intelligence, were given only to a small proportion of graduates. Group tests were given to seven graduates, five of whom entered firms in the chemical industry. A more detailed examination of the experience of graduates is contained in the following sections.

EXPERIENCE IN THE CASE STUDY FIRMS

THE methods of selection adopted by the managements of the case study firms have been considered in an earlier section of this chapter. It was shown that selection was generally by means of interviews without tests of any kind; in the larger firms, a panel or board interview was most usual, sometimes alone and sometimes as part of a series. The replies of the 561 graduates, considered in the preceding sections, confirmed that interviews were generally the method of selection experienced, and that one interview was more usual than a series.

The replies of graduates in the case study firms showed that a high proportion of single interviews were with a panel or board and also that in many instances a series of interviews included a panel or board. The experience of the graduates was broadly in accordance with the stated policy of managements. There were variations from the general rule, however, particularly in the number of graduates who were selected by means of a single interview with one man. In view of the doubts which are sometimes expressed about this type of interview, the circumstances in which selection was carried out in this way will be considered.

Some thirty of the 183 graduates interviewed in the case study firms said that they had been selected for their job by means of a single interview with one man.* They included two arts graduates, six scientists and twenty-two technologists. A third of the graduates belonged to the three building and contracting firms which adopted this form of selection as a general policy. A third were in two firms which had since revised their methods. Of the remaining graduates, one said that he had been interviewed only by a personnel officer, two by the head of a research department; three men said that there should have been another interviewer who could not be present at the time; two had done vacation work in the firm; and two scientists belonged to a firm which had said that interviews were sometimes conducted by one man.

* Twenty-three of the graduates in the case studies entered their firm before graduating and were therefore not questioned on selection.

It should be added that there was no evidence to suggest that either the managements or graduates concerned thought that an interview by one man was less satisfactory than other methods.

Graduates' comments

Graduates in the case study firms were given an opportunity to comment on the methods by which they had been selected. Of the 172 graduates who replied to this question, 145 or 85 per cent made no kind of adverse criticism; twenty-eight graduates, 15 per cent of those replying, made comments in which there was an element of criticism. Most of the graduates simply affirmed that they had got the impression that the people by whom they were interviewed had a clear idea of what they wanted to get out of the interview. A number elaborated their answers by descriptive or appreciative comments, for instance:

> It was a good board; they were interested both in my technical qualifications and my personality.

> The executive director conducted most of the interview. He certainly knew what he wanted to get out of me.

> I was very much impressed with the interviewing compared with what I had met before.

A few graduates, although satisfied that interviewers knew what they sought from the interview, added comments which contained an element of criticism. For instance, one man said that he was the first to go into a department and he had the impression that they didn't really know what to ask him.

A graduate who was interviewed by a staff manager and afterwards by a manager of a department said:

> The company says that you start in a particular way, and then it depends on how you do where you go. I am not sure they know what they are going to do with me. I think the manager of the department was more concerned with getting someone of use in his department than with an idea of my place and future in the company as a whole.

A research chemist thought that it was a difficult question to answer: "It is difficult for anybody to get a full impression of someone seen for only two hours". Another graduate in the same firm thought that his interviewers had a clear idea without being exact, but criticised the method of selection by means of a series of short interviews. He said:

> A long succession of short interviews is ridiculous. I would prefer one very good interview, or one and a board.

As stated earlier, the vast majority of graduates were selected by means of interviews of various kinds, but, apart from the few comments quoted above, little was said which had a direct bearing on the particular interviewing machinery that was used. Comments and criticisms were more generally concerned with the form that the interviews took, the broad approach and the type of questions asked, rather than with the number of people who carried out the interviewing or with the question whether it was a board or series of interviews.

Psychological tests

Only five graduates had psychological or intelligence tests in addition to interviews. All were satisfied with their selection as a whole, but there was some rather critical comment from three of them. One described the tests as "questionnaire sheets with time limits, including cubes, pictures, piecing problems, and a test of English". He thought that the selection procedure had been effective in selecting him for the right kind of job, but at a later stage in the interview he remarked that he did not think that the personnel department served any useful purpose, and that interviews of engineers should not be conducted by the personnel department. Another man said:

> I was given psychological tests similar to those used in the forces during the war. There were questions on English, little problems, filling in patterns, and structures of bricks to estimate. It all seemed rather ridiculous.

The third graduate who commented on the tests said that he did not think that any notice was taken of them, and that in any case what mattered was the interview with the man in whose department he was going to work. He said:

> The interview with the personnel officer was non-technical, and I don't know what he was after.

The graduates' rather flippant attitude to the tests is in marked contrast to that of one personnel manager, who regarded interviewing as being concerned only with establishing a man's acceptability as a person, as a check on the tests. He said that if someone was shown by the tests to be unstable, the interview was much of a formality. In borderline cases interviews were intensive. If the test result was good the interview served as a means of confirming it. He thought that the method of selection gave satisfactory results, and said:

> We have done considerable research lately. The genuine failure rate is negligible, but we are anxious to cope with the possibility of rejecting good men.

CRITICISMS OF SELECTION METHODS

TWENTY-EIGHT graduates, 15 per cent of those interviewed in the case study firms, commented adversely on the manner of their selection. In each of the faculties about 15 per cent of the graduates were critical of their selection; the proportions were: arts 15 per cent, science 17 per cent, and technology 14 per cent. There was no significant difference between graduates who received a training course and those who did not; 13 per cent and 17 per cent respectively were critical. A higher proportion of those who had already had some industrial experience since leaving their university were critical—21 per cent against 13 per cent of those who were seeking their first industrial job. Criticisms were not confined to those who had had any one particular type of interview; nearly half of those who were critical had had a series of interviews, five had had a board interview, and four a single interview with one man (six could not be classified). The numbers are not large enough to make a valid comparison between those experiencing the various methods of selection, but it would appear that the number of interviewers or the number of interviews did not of itself have any great significance.

The comments of the twenty-eight critical graduates can be grouped in four broad categories, which to some extent overlap. Half the men had the impression that those who interviewed them were not sure what they wanted to get out of the interview, or had not been searching enough; five men thought that certain of their qualifications or qualities were not sufficiently considered; two thought that interviewers were not properly qualified to consider them; and seven thought that the attitude of interviewers was strongly influenced by a feeling of labour shortage.

Impression of uncertainty

The impression that interviewers were not sure what they were seeking provided the largest body of criticism. Five of the six critical arts graduates fell into this category; their comments were as follows:

They had a vague rather than a clear idea of what they wanted to get out of the interviews.

It was not clear after two interviews what I was going to do.

They were a bit vague. I think they felt that a man of my supposed intelligence should be useful, but they didn't know in what way. They still don't know.

They had no idea what they were looking for. I had the impression that they didn't really want graduates, but had been told to get some. I achieved the right kind of job by accident.

I got the impression that they did not know what they were looking for—and certainly not me.

Three of the eleven critical scientists commented as follows:

They seemed to have no clear idea. It was an odd interview. I was very surprised that I was not introduced to anyone who I'd work for or with, nor taken into the department where I would train or be. I would have felt they'd like me to be questioned by the people who would be over me.

I was interviewed by the personnel manager and various group leaders, and was asked which group I'd prefer to work for and went to it. I felt that the group leaders were not sure what qualities they wanted—just knew that they wanted someone to work. This struck me compared with other firms.

They gave me the impression that they didn't know what they were after.

Six of the eleven critical technologists were doubtful whether interviewers had a clear idea of what they wanted, or were exhaustive enough in their questioning. They said:

It was haphazard. I was seen by five people in turn in one afternoon. The first knew something about me, the next a little, and the next three nothing about me. This was not as good as the two-day selection board I had for my last job.

I was not subjected to as searching a test as I would have liked. I had to sell myself—faults and merits. Perhaps the work study department is activated by snob motives only: "I too have a graduate, and from Cambridge".

They asked very few questions, and those not really about my knowledge. They could have found out much more about what I knew and where I'd been.

The personnel manager had a clear idea of what he wanted, but the head of the department did not.

It was largely a matter of chance.

I got a clear idea that they didn't know what they were after. They were striving to be broad-minded and up to date, but didn't know how. I felt that their action in employing graduates had been stimulated by someone saying, "The gas board must be up to date and employ graduates".

Qualifications not fully considered

Five graduates thought that certain of their personal qualifications or qualities were not sufficiently considered at their interviews. Two were scientists, three technologists. Four were straight from a university, one was from another industrial firm. Four of the comments were to the effect that the interviewers had not been interested in technical matters, and had been more concerned with personal character and qualities. The criticism was only implied in three of the comments, but one scientist said:

They weren't interested in my research work. Some firms I have been to did want an account of this. I resented this unconcern.

One technologist thought that too much stress was laid on academic qualifications and not enough on his personal qualities:

I was not impressed with the interview. He was only interested in my academic qualifications; he was not interested in my powers of taking control and leadership gained from war experience.

Interviewers not properly qualified

Two graduates suggested that those who interviewed them were not in a position to be able to judge their suitability. An arts graduate said that he had only a lukewarm interview because the firm needed a statistician and didn't know much about the subject. A scientist was also dissatisfied because he thought his interviewer had not sufficient knowledge. He said:

The chief engineer was off sick. I was interviewed by someone else who didn't know anything of the technical side of the job.

Effects of graduate shortage

Seven graduates, in six firms, gained the impression that their interviewers were making a selection under the pressure of a labour shortage, and for that reason were less critical than they might otherwise have been. Five scientists made remarks to this effect, and two technologists, but no arts graduates. Three were given a training course after joining the firm. There is, however, no evidence to suggest that these graduates were in fact given less thorough consideration than others. Some of their comments probably arose because the interviews were less rigorous than expected. For instance, one scientist said that he had hated his previous work, teaching, and was desperate for a job of any kind. He said that his interview was not very formal, and he was left with the impression that they wanted graduates at all costs.

One scientist in a specialised field also said that he wanted a job badly and was clutching at straws. He seemed surprised that his interview led easily to an appointment and commented:

They were pushed for people; what they really wanted was bodies.

Another scientist in an electrical engineering firm thought that his firm would have taken anyone:

It was a sham of a selection. They were desperately trying to get people, and would have taken anyone. I spent a day there and met people. I had no formal interviews; they didn't even ask for references. They more or less just wanted to get me as cheaply as possible.

This judgment, however, must be viewed in the light of the fact that the graduate was exceptionally well qualified and had had appropriate experience with another firm.

In a firm in the metal trades, two graduates referred to a shortage:

They can't get sufficient graduates, therefore they don't worry very much about you. They are short of chemists.

They just wanted graduates. They were told to get graduates by high-ups, and graduates they got.

In a firm of electrical engineers, a scientist said:

At the time I got the impression that they were not very critical due to the fact that they were having difficulty in getting people to move here from another branch of the firm.

In another electrical engineering firm, an engineer taken on for training thought that too many graduates had been recruited:

I don't think the interviewer had a clue what he or the firm wanted. I found out very quickly that this company didn't know what to do with us, and they still don't know. They took in too many. Someone must have said, "It is good to have graduates". I came because they offered more money than anywhere else; but I have become very interested in a field which has developed since I joined.

SUMMING UP

THE approach of management to the selection of graduates clearly depended very much on the circumstances—the purposes for which they were being taken on and what was already known about them. The interview was the procedure adopted in almost all firms. It was only occasionally combined with intelligence or psychological tests. Group selection of the W.O.S.B./C.C.S.B. type was very rare indeed.

One interview was experienced more frequently than a series by graduates in each size group of firms, and all but two product groups; a series of interviews was found most often in the smaller firms. Six out of every ten graduates had one interview, three in ten a series. Examination of the case study firms indicates a considerable use of the panel interview, particularly by the larger firms and those employing more than fifty graduates. It is clear that a high proportion of the single interviews took the form of a panel or board, and that a series of interviews often included a panel or board. Three of the six largest employers of graduates, however, used a series of interviews, each with one man.

There is little evidence either from managements or graduates to suggest disadvantages in any particular method. The great majority both of graduates and of members of management appeared satisfied with interviews as the means of selection, and with the form the interviews took. Such criticisms as there were among graduates did not generally concern the number of interviews or the number of interviewers but rather the course of the interview and the type of questions asked.

Most members of management were satisfied with the methods of selection used by their firms, although a number qualified their answers in various ways. The difficulties of making an objective assessment of the methods and their results were widely recognised. It was sometimes suggested that a reliable assessment could be made only in the light of long-term results. Some members of management stressed that the results of selection depended more on the quality of the candidates than on the method which was used. A few recognised the difficulties of assessing a candidate during the course of a short interview, or stressed the fallibility of personal judgment. A few firms were contemplating changes in their selection methods, but generally speaking managements appeared satisfied that selection by means of interviews, although not perfect, was the most satisfactory method available.

The selection methods used in the forces during the war are well known, and have been widely discussed, and their principles applied, not only in the Civil Service but to a greater or lesser extent in some industrial concerns also. This survey has shown that the use of specialised selection techniques was not widespread among the industrial undertakings studied nor experienced by the graduates entering industry a few years ago.

It is of interest to consider some of the conclusions of other studies on methods of selection.

In outlining the main principles underlying the large-scale procedures devised for the forces, Vernon and Parry* point out that "tests and measurements are important, but their role in classification should not be exaggerated", and that interviews are often more economical than an elaborate psychometric programme and more acceptable to the persons undergoing classification and to their employers. A few members of management in the present study expressed doubts about the efficacy of tests, but most did not comment on them favourably or otherwise. Great faith was placed in interviews, however, as the most useful method.

The reliance on the interview, however, was founded not on the basis of its being more economical than tests, nor on its being considered to be more acceptable to applicants, but on the importance which was given to personal qualities and the conviction

* P. E. Vernon and J. B. Parry. *Personnel Selection in the British Forces.* (University of London Press), 1949, 20s.

that these qualities could best be judged by a personal assessment. Added to this, it was often pointed out that people must be acceptable to those for whom they would work and this attitude is perhaps reflected in the fact that interviews were generally conducted, at least in part, by those likely to be directly concerned.

It is of interest that a study group of the British Institute of Management which considered the recruitment and training of men intended for management positions had no unanimous view on the most effective method of selection. The three companies represented on the group which used group selection were convinced that it was worth the trouble and expense. The report stated:

> No absolute rule on methods of selection can possibly be laid down, but, in the majority of cases, a small but fairly widely drawn panel is likely to prove the fairest and most effective instrument in arriving at a right judgment, especially with the marginal cases where a variety of experience may be needed to arrive at a correct assessment.*

Selection by means of a single interview with one man was the general policy of only three of the firms examined and all three belonged to the building and contracting group. Some graduates in other firms were also chosen in this way, but they were exceptions to the rule. Often there were special reasons for their having been treated exceptionally. There was nothing to suggest that those graduates who experienced this form of selection were critical of the method as such, or were more critical in other ways because of it.

There was little evidence that interviews took a predetermined course or were based on systems of rating for the qualifications and qualities sought. Vernon and Parry, in the work already quoted, as well as other more recent writers, suggest that, though mechanical rules cannot be laid down, the technique of interviewing can be formulated and greatly improved by training, and that interviewers should be carefully selected. Although in a number of firms people with training in selection methods took part, the general approach was of a personal assessment of an

---

* *The Recruitment and Training of Men intended for Management Positions.* (British Institute of Management), 1955, 5s.

individual's character and capabilities by people with wide experience of selection or with direct knowledge of the field in which the candidate might be engaged. It is impossible to say from the evidence yielded by the survey whether this approach was as successful as more specialised interviewing methods might have been. A few graduates were not sure that interviewers knew what they were looking for, but the vast majority were satisfied.

Where criticisms were made they appeared to arise not because the methods themselves were at fault but because both managements and graduates had preconceived ideas about the soundness of any method of selection. Managements sometimes felt that choice was restricted beforehand because of a shortage of suitably qualified applicants. Criticism among graduates generally appeared to arise when, for a variety of reasons, interviews were found to be less testing than expected. Whether there was substance in these views or not, managements were afterwards inclined to think that perhaps they had not got the best men, and graduates were sometimes left to wonder whether they had been chosen without due consideration, or as a second best. As Vernon and Parry suggest:

> The value of vocational and educational classification schemes lies not merely in the closer co-ordination of human capacities with job . . . requirements, but also in their effects on morale. Bad selection leads to lack of confidence between employers and employees. . . . Selection that *appears* good has the opposite effects, even if, judged by scientific standards, it is far from efficient. To appear good it must include consideration of each individual's interests and abilities by a sympathetic interviewer, and the tests or other instruments employed must be obviously relevant to the job.

This survey of methods of selection has indicated the practices current in the years following the end of the war, and up to the time of the survey in the winter of 1954-55, and has thrown some light on the views held on these practices both by members of management and by the graduates experiencing them. If it has not established how far these practices were effective, this could hardly have been achieved within the compass of a survey concerned with conditions prevailing over so short a period—and was in fact not attempted. It is, however, worth noting that the systematic following up of the assessment made at the time of selection, in the light of the recruit's subsequent performance, is receiving increasing attention. It is now normal practice in the Civil Service, for instance.

The process of selection, however, as many members of management pointed out, and as is, indeed, obvious, did not stop at the stage at which candidates were taken on the strength, but was continued subsequently in the course of settling graduates into the firm and of training them—whether through a course or more informally. These stages are the subject of the following two chapters.

CHAPTER IV

INTRODUCTION TO THE FIRM

THE transition from university to industry is an important milestone in the graduate's career. The purpose of this chapter is to examine the ways in which managements introduced graduates to their firm, the views of graduates on the procedures followed, and the attitudes of members of the firm at various levels towards the graduates.

By "introduce" is meant the steps taken, either formally or informally, but at any rate deliberately, to enable the graduate recruit to learn about the purposes, organisation and physical geography of the firm, to meet the people with whom and under whom he will be working and to understand the part in the firm played by them and to be played by him. It can be, and is often, thought of as an aspect of training and an integral part of it. Introduction is, however, clearly distinguishable from training, which is the subject of the next chapter. The former is primarily concerned with the preliminary impact of firm on graduate and graduate on firm; the latter with the equipment of the graduate for the work on which he is to be set.

The introductory period in the firm is important not only to the new recruit but also to his employer. From the point of view both of management and of graduate it is clearly desirable that the process of settling into the firm should be accomplished as quickly and smoothly as possible. It is in the interests of management that a good relationship should be established from the outset between the graduate and those with whom he will work or come into contact, and that the graduate should know what his place in the firm is and have the right conception of it: he should come as rapidly as possible to identify himself with the firm.

The employer wants the recruit to pull his weight as soon as possible. Ideally, the introductory process must ensure that the graduate knows not only all the things about the organisation and personnel of the firm that the employer thinks he ought to know, but also, within limits, all those that the graduate himself thinks he ought to know. This is not at all simple. The employer does not and cannot know, except very broadly, what the graduate knows about the firm on arrival. Again, what the graduate needs to know will depend to some extent on the work which he is to do; but it may take some time before this can be determined. What he wants to know will depend on his attitude to the work and his intellectual horizon, which may be wider or narrower than his employers realise.

The graduate wishes to start off on the right foot, to feel part of the firm, at home, wanted, with a useful function to perform. His assessment of how far this is achieved may be strongly and lastingly affected by the attitude of managers, directors and other members of the firm towards him in his first few weeks at work. Closely allied to this is a desire to be well informed, and the desire to be appreciated may express itself not as such but as a demand to be given more information and to become more knowledgeable. The intellectual desire for knowledge, in turn, points to the close relationship between certain aspects of introduction and training.

The process of introducing a graduate to his firm may therefore be regarded as something more than a mere personal introduction, but in many ways different in its nature and objectives from training. The term "induction" is sometimes used to describe any formal steps which are taken as a matter of routine to acquaint the graduate with the organisation which he is joining, its purposes, and the people with whom he will work. The process was known to many graduates and firms, but often not under this label. During the interviews the term even caused some members of management to remark that their firm did not indulge in masonic rites nor believe in red tape, and so on. It seems wiser, therefore, to use the expression "introduction" taken in its widest sense.

THE GENERAL PICTURE

THIS chapter begins with a general statistical statement of the extent to which graduates were given a formal introduction to their firm, how long it lasted, and what its broad content was. This is based on information from the main series of interviews with graduates. Next there is an analysis of the introductory methods practised by the concerns of which case studies were made. In this section some indication is also given of the extent to which various methods appeared to meet the needs of graduates experiencing them. The third section analyses the answers of graduates in these firms taken as a whole and draws together the suggestions made under various heads. The fourth section deals with the relationship between the graduate and other members of the firm during the introductory period. The final section draws attention to the main points which emerge from this part of the survey.

Formal introduction

The graduate interviews give an indication of the extent to which firms adopted formal methods of introducing their graduate recruits. One hundred and twenty-six of the 561 graduates, or 22 per cent, said that some formal steps were taken to acquaint them with the organisation, personnel and purposes of the firm when they first reported for duty. Table 10 classifies the answers according to the faculty of the graduates and the size of the firms that they joined.

TABLE 10

GRADUATES GIVEN FORMAL INTRODUCTION

Firm size (No. of employees)	No. of graduates employed	Graduates receiving formal introduction:			
		Total		Arts	Science	Tech-nology
		No.	%	%	%	%
Under 500 . .	54	10	19	25	28	5
500–1,999 . .	62	19	31	42	24	28
2,000–4,999 . .	79	15	19	26	21	10
5,000–9,999 . .	79	20	25	22	36	18
10,000 and over .	256	56	22	21	29	16
Not known . .	31	6	19	17	20	20
TOTAL . .	561*	126	22	25	28	16

* That is, the 561 who obtained their first industrial job after graduation: the 33 graduates who were employed in industry while reading for a degree part-time have been excluded.

There was a marked difference between the treatment of technologists and that of the other graduates. Whereas about one in four arts and science graduates reported formal steps to acquaint them with their firm, only one in six graduates in technology did so. The pattern varied somewhat according to the size of the firm, but in all but one size group the proportion of technologists receiving a formal introduction was lower than for graduates in arts or science. In firms with more than 5,000 employees—which included over 60 per cent of the graduates in the sample—about one in six technologists received a formal introduction to his firm, one in five arts graduates, and about one in three science graduates.

Duration and form

Formal schemes for the introduction of graduates to their firms were for the most part of relatively short duration. As shown in Table 11, only 15 per cent lasted more than one week.

TABLE 11

DURATION OF INTRODUCTION SCHEMES

	Graduates given formal introduction		All graduates in sample
	No.	%	%
1 day	51	40	9
2 days . . .	19	15	3
3 days . . .	9	7	2
1 week . . .	27	21	5
Over 1 week . .	18	15	3
No answer . . .	2	2	—
	126	100	22

Where the scheme consisted of no more than an informal chat or introduction lasting less than a day it was excluded; so also were courses lasting more than two months since these were felt to be more akin to training than introduction to the firm.

In describing the nature of these schemes, nearly 60 per cent of the graduates mentioned tours of works and departments; just under half mentioned introductions to individuals; 30 per cent referred to lectures and talks; and 15 per cent to pamphlets or books. These forms of introduction were combined in a variety of ways as shown in Table 12.

Few graduates were given both tours and lectures, which may be taken as constituting the more elaborate and organised methods of introducing new recruits to their firm. Nearly half said that they went on a tour of the works or departments, but did not mention talks or lectures. A fifth mentioned lectures, but not tours. A fifth mentioned only introductions or pamphlets, or both. These last have otherwise been regarded as supplementary methods of acquainting graduates with their firm, and though a number of graduates who had tours, lectures and so on mentioned them also, in the table they have not been shown separately in relation to the more elaborate procedures.

TABLE 12

METHOD OF INTRODUCTION

	Graduates given formal introduction		All graduates in sample
	No.	%	%
Tours and lectures .	13	10	2
Tours but no lectures .	60	48	11
Lectures but no tours .	25	20	4
Introductions and/or pamphlets only . .	24	19	4
Others . . .	4	3	1
	126	100	22

In general, the graduate interviews showed that only about one in five of the graduates entering industry said that he was given a formal introduction to his firm; the proportion was generally higher for arts and science graduates than for technologists; only a tenth of those given a formal introduction had both lectures and tours, and a fifth had introductions or pamphlets only; more than half the introductions lasted only one or two days, only 15 per cent for longer than a week.

ANALYSIS OF METHODS USED

THE graduate interviews provide a general view of the practice with regard to formal introduction. For the practice and policy of individual firms in the introduction of graduates it is necessary to turn to the case studies, which also provide an indication of the views of graduates on the methods they had encountered.*

The methods used by the case study firms for the introduction of graduates included the following:
lectures on the organisation of the firm, its aims and functions
lectures by departmental heads on the work of their departments
tours of the works, visits to outlying units
introductions to the personnel of the firm (management and staff)
conversations
pamphlets and other literature.

The attitudes of both managements and graduates towards these aspects of introduction varied according to the individual circum-

* Forty-three case studies are relevant—thirty-nine private enterprise firms and four gas boards. The eight firms not employing graduates except incidentally were not asked questions on introduction or training.

stances. The size of the firm and its administrative organisation clearly affected the need for introduction and the form which it took. From a geographical standpoint, the layout of the works and its extent again affected the need for introduction. Requirements varied also according to the field of industry. The number of employees and the number of graduates in the firm were also important. Finally, the form of introduction often depended on the nature of the work to be performed by the graduates, and their prospective training and previous experience.

A systematic and comprehensive introductory programme including lectures and tours was exceptional, and where it existed was usually part and parcel of training. Most firms clearly recognised the importance of this introductory period, although many followed a less elaborate procedure or made no special or formal provision for the introduction of graduates to the firm as a whole. Several firms stressed their desire to make the introduction as informal as possible, and were strongly opposed to the concept of a rigid and formal "induction" programme.

Comprehensive schemes

Five of the forty-three case study firms which employed graduates as a deliberate policy operated a clearly distinguishable scheme. In four of these, all large firms with more than a hundred graduates, introduction schemes were closely integrated with the training programme. In the fifth, which employed under fifty graduates, the first week was spent in its headquarters.

In three of these firms all the graduates interviewed seemed well satisfied with the procedure which was followed. One of the two exceptions was a firm in which the first week of training was devoted largely to introductory procedures. There was a delay of a week or two before the start of the course, and this period does not seem to have been well organised, so that some of the graduates interviewed thought that things were rather haphazard. Others were satisfied with the course itself, but one felt that it was not important, and two would have liked a more comprehensive tour of the works. The other firm in which there was some criticism by graduates regarded its training period as a practical introduction to the firm. There was no introduction scheme for those entering research departments, nor for arts graduates as a rule; the arts graduates interviewed said they would have liked some form of introduction scheme. One of the scientists who had followed the course thought that more time might have been given to explaining why things were done. Another commented:

> The person new to industry doesn't know what to look for. A similar course at the end of a year might be more advantageous.

Less comprehensive schemes

Seven firms followed an introductory procedure which included one or two of the various elements, but did not amount to a fully comprehensive programme. Five of these were medium- or large-sized concerns in the electrical engineering industry, four of them had more than a hundred graduates.

In one firm the management described an introduction in which the emphasis was on lectures. The first week was said to be spent entirely on lectures on the history of the company, its products and organisation, and on the careers open to graduates. During the next few months there were said to be weekly talks by the heads of departments. In addition, educational and technical sound films dealing with a variety of subjects were shown.

In another firm, members of management stressed their informal approach. Graduates went through the formalities of engagement and were then handed to the training scheme supervisor for official talks about the factory. Later they met the appointments supervisor and the foreman. This was said to take up to one week. The time between talks and lectures was apparently spent informally. A member of management said:

> This is a very free and easy firm. From that point of view there is very little red tape here. We do not set any store by formal introduction. Let them pick things up on their own. It may be old fashioned, but there seems to be too much emphasis on the word teach and not enough on learn. Failure is always put down to the teacher; I do not subscribe to this view.

The management of a firm with only a few graduates said that it was "a question of individuals". Graduates were taken round the factory and given a leaflet explaining the organisation and outside activities of the firm and a works handbook.

A number of the graduates interviewed in the firms with less comprehensive schemes were on the whole satisfied with the methods they had encountered, and felt that they had helped them

I

to settle down. A few thought that their introduction had not helped them very much, although they made no suggestions for its improvement; but in each of these seven firms, at least one graduate suggested ways in which their introduction might have been improved. These comments often pointed to gaps in the introductory programme:

> I would like to have been told more about the whole firm, and to have met the heads of departments. They could tell you about their departments. Most important, I would have liked a plan of the works.

> I would have liked a better idea of the organisation and arrangement of departments.

> The place is isolated, and it takes three weeks to find your way about. It would have helped to have had a map.

> I would have liked to have gone to some of the outlying places. I will now probably never get the chance.

Some of the comments were concerned more with the organisation of the introduction than with its content:

> I had rather a crude introduction. I hung around and was then sent to the test section where I was to start my training. It did not help me to settle. I wanted a more organised rather than a more elaborate introduction. I would have liked to have been shown round the works completely, and to have had the system explained.

> I did not have very much introduction. I had to find out for myself. I would have liked more detail on the functions of the place, which still mystify me.

> I did not have an introductory course, but I think it was exceptional. They weren't ready for me; I arrived at a different time from the others. I didn't want anything different.

Introduction by departmental heads

In five firms, large and small in various sections of industry, and one gas board, the introduction of graduates was left to the heads of the departments where the graduate was to work or start his training. Typical comments of the managements of these firms were:

> Arts graduates are given a series of lectures on the firm spread over two years. For scientists and technologists the heads of departments

are supposed to ease the new recruit in, and someone is told to look after the new boy. We are introducing a graduate apprenticeship scheme which will alter all this, but I am doubtful whether induction is a good thing to go in for.

They start up in the department where their training will start. They learn quickly enough. There is no reason why they should learn the ABC stuff the hard way. I feel an introduction scheme may be a good thing. One of the troubles would be in finding a man suitable to do it. If you had a man capable enough to run it, you probably couldn't spare him. We are not seriously contemplating any change.

Introduction courses are run for young non-graduate entrants; but for graduates, localities handle locally. It is a matter of someone introducing them all round. I believe in handbooks and source material, but for the new graduate I think it is best to leave the matter in the hands of the first chiefs, who will see them on a friendly basis. We do not regiment. This is adequate for the limited arrival of graduates, and we would need a more regular flow to run a formalised scheme.

In one of the firms and the gas board all the graduates interviewed were fully satisfied with the introduction they had received; in one of these the management said that they tried to keep graduates at first free from responsibility, to give them as long as possible to find their feet. In the other four firms in which introduction was left to the heads of departments, the arrangement did not on the whole appear to have worked very well. Some graduates accepted what had been done without comment and two welcomed the absence of any organised introduction, but most were critical. Some wanted a general introduction to the firm; some mentioned specific things such as a tour of other departments, more introductions, or a knowledge of the structure of the firm; some mentioned the poor organisation of their introduction or reception.

The varied reactions that different individuals in the same firm can have are illustrated by the comments of those interviewed in a concern with a large graduate staff:

I was given a guided tour, and would not have wanted anything different. I was given my freedom and not clamped down.

I was not shown round, and was rather at a loss. I would have liked to be introduced to colleagues and shown round. I felt neglected.

I hung about. When formalities had been complied with, I was

shepherded to the factory, reported for duty, and had an interview
with the head of the department to discuss the work. This did not
help me to settle, but I was ready for anything. It took me some time
to settle into the industrial atmosphere, the hours, and the working
rate. It was a rude shock to come at 8.30 and bang a clock. This is
very annoying at first, but I came to accept it after a week.

In another firm, employing fewer than fifty graduates, there
was more agreement about what was wanted:

I would have liked a more organised show-round and more chats
about departments. This would have been beneficial and made me
feel more at home.

I would have liked to be introduced to one or two people in charge
of different sections, been told what they were doing, and got a
picture of the whole.

I was taken round the factory, that was all. It might have helped me
on a limited scale going round to each department for a longer
while.

I went straight in and started a job. It would have been helpful to go
round and see the departments.

Sponsoring by seniors

Five firms emphasised the role of what may be termed a
"sponsoring" system in the introduction of graduates. The general
procedure here was for the graduate to be put straight into a job
and for an immediate superior to be responsible for his supervision
and instruction. Three of the firms which followed this procedure
belonged to the building and contracting industry and no doubt
adopted it because their graduates often worked at outlying sites.
In one of these firms the management said:

We plunge them straight into the firm and their jobs. Any other
form of introduction is impossible owing to the scattered contracts.
They must find their own feet. Our method of learning is to put
them under someone who has been with us for some time; we find
it works very well.

In another firm the management was not fully satisfied.
Graduates started work as assistants, were introduced to people,
and shown round the works. Some talks were given and there was
a monthly bulletin. A member of management commented that
there were so many different factories that it would be very

difficult to operate a formal scheme of introduction. Another said:

> I am not entirely happy with the procedure—nor with other induc-
> tion processes I have seen at work. Too much in too little time leaves
> a man utterly confounded. We prefer to do things gradually. I feel
> that this is a weakness of so large a company. The firm's monthly
> bulletin keeps people posted with news, but long-term training
> schemes have revealed people who do not know about the firm. We
> should think of some system of coverage.

This apparently haphazard sponsoring method seems to have
worked extremely well in three of the five firms. For instance,
five of the six engineers interviewed in one firm were well satisfied
with the procedure followed and said that they: "used their
knowledge straight away", "it was very good", "it was very good
experience", "I considered I was lucky". Only one graduate was
dissatisfied. He said that this was because he had been placed under
someone who had not had the time to instruct him.

The policy of making someone who is in close and regular
contact with the graduate responsible for his introduction to the
firm has distinct advantages. The informal, personal, and more
sustained relationship may help the graduate to settle into the
firm more smoothly than would a centralised and impersonal
formal scheme, in which there must also at times be a tendency
for immediate superiors to feel that the matter of introduction to
the firm is no longer their responsibility. The managing director
of one large concern stressed the difficulty of persuading people
on the job that they must play their part in carrying out the
introduction and training scheme laid down at the firm's headquarters. The quality and effectiveness of a personal introduction
depends upon the quality of the person made responsible and the
time and attention which he can, or will, spare to the new graduate. The comments of the graduates interviewed in one firm
show the difficulties, but also some of the advantages, of this
informal approach:

> I was stuck in the laboratory and shown what to do. It did not help
> me to settle, but I wouldn't have wanted any change. It would be
> better if people could be given a better idea of the firm after a time.

> I would have liked a more general grounding in what the firm does.
> A lot could be done to improve the relations between the works and
> the research departments, which is not close enough at the moment.

There was no fuss made, and I felt my way in merely by working with people during a settling-down period of two to three months. The changeover from my previous firm was smooth and easy.

I was hitched on to somebody. It helped me to settle domestically, but settling in to work comes more slowly. A few days' introduction would have been helpful, perhaps a two-day period of discussions and lectures, but not visits.

I was taken round the labs. This helped, but one was left to oneself. A little more talk of the general purposes behind the lab., etc., would have been helpful. I was given a project to do and allowed to go my own way; no one bothered me.

Introduction at interview

One firm and a gas board considered that graduates had received sufficient introduction at the time of their selection. In one of these undertakings, several graduates would have liked a more elaborate introduction, to have met more people, or to have been given more knowledge of the structure and organisation of the company. The other had an introduction scheme for juniors, but not for graduates, who came in small numbers. It considered that since all candidates saw the conditions before and after selection and all were given administrative details, no further introduction was necessary. Four graduates were satisfied, but two made the following comments:

I would have liked a period going round. It does show where you fit in.

Perhaps wider introductions would have been better, and I would have liked to know a bit more about the industry as a whole.

Informal introduction

Eight firms, including one of the gas boards, said that they took steps to introduce graduates, but that this was done in an informal way to suit the individual requirements of the newcomer. Five of the firms were small, and employed only a few graduates; three were in the medium or large size categories, only one employed more than fifty graduates. In most of these firms managements were satisfied that their methods were adequate. In one firm, however, a member of management thought that graduates should be shown round the whole works rather than just certain parts. In another there was a suggestion that more formal arrangements were not followed because of the shortage of graduates:

> The graduate is sent to the analytical department first. Through his work there he begins to know people and places. The urgency of the graduate shortage and the pressure of work means that the new recruit is wanted desperately for the job before he gets here.

A member of management in another firm said:

> There is nothing to prevent a formal scheme, but we think it would make the others feel worried thinking that graduates are favoured. They sort themselves out.

Most of the graduates interviewed were satisfied with the informal introduction they had received. In five of the eight firms none of the graduates were critical or made suggestions for improvement. In one firm, six of the eight men interviewed were satisfied, but one said that he would have liked to have seen more of the works, and to have had a little more explanation of how it operated; another said he was lost for the first few weeks, and would have liked a plan of the works and more introductions. In another firm, several graduates would have liked a more elaborate introduction, asking particularly for more knowledge of the structure and organisation of the firm, but one of their graduate colleagues said:

> I did not want anything more elaborate. I do not think it is possible to assimilate these rapid induction courses.

Finally, in the research department of one concern three graduates were satisfied with their informal introduction, but one urged a more elaborate and systematic arrangement.

Firms with no introduction scheme

Ten firms said that they had no scheme for the introduction of graduates. As noted earlier, the methods used are not mutually exclusive, and the approach to introduction by the case study firms was in general so individual and informal that rigid classification was not possible. These ten firms, however, are alike in that they did not claim to be following an introduction scheme in any formal sense; nor did they state that the purposes of an introduction scheme were being achieved through some alternative procedure.

Three of the ten firms which did not appear to have adopted a definite procedure for the introduction of graduates were in the smallest size category, with fewer than 2,000 employees; four were of medium size; and three were in the largest size category, employing 10,000 or more. The three smallest firms employed less than ten graduates. The general attitude of their managements was that the firms were too small for a detailed and considered approach to be made to the matter of introduction, and that this was not necessary in the circumstances.

Of the seven medium or large firms, four had fewer than fifty graduates. In one of these the management said that there was no established procedure, but that there should be. In another there was a scheme on paper, but this was not used. The management, however, said that a lot of trouble was taken in telling newcomers about the background, and trying to give their work a "romantic significance". The absence of a systematised introduction was attributed in two firms to the small numbers of graduates joining them. Their comments were:

> A formal scheme is not necessary owing to the small number of graduates. It is a matter in which the works manager uses his own initiative. It may be a factor in the large turnover; we can't tell. I am not keen on over-formality; each man must be looked at differently. The only common factor would be in the length of time given to introduction.

> The introduction is not systematised enough, but we only take on one or two graduates.

Three of the medium or large firms without introduction schemes had over fifty graduates. In one of these, the research unit of a large concern, there was no formal introduction scheme, although one existed at other units and the headquarters. The management said:

> We are thinking about it, but at the moment we have too many vacancies to spare the staff to run a formal induction scheme.

The management of another firm believed that there was some room for improvement in its practice, and suggested that the new entrant should spend some time with a graduate already in a responsible job. Even among these firms with a relatively large number of graduates, the limited number joining at one time was sometimes considered to be a difficulty in the application of a formal scheme, as shown by the comment of the management of the third firm:

> Graduates come in ones and twos. If they came ten at a time we would run a scheme. Induction courses are run for those coming into our headquarters. The departmental manager, who has met the graduates at their interview, is there to receive them. Those who go into the labs. know all about the structure of the firm after a few weeks. Engineers may not get such a comprehensive picture, but I am satisfied that no formal induction is necessary.

The comments of graduates show that the absence of formal introduction schemes did not necessarily lead to dissatisfaction. Many, in both large and small firms, had nothing adverse to say about the manner of their introduction, and here as elsewhere it was clear that some steps, at least, were taken to introduce graduates and that they were carried out quite satisfactorily in an informal way. In four of the seven firms employing fewer than fifty graduates, none of those interviewed were critical or made suggestions for improvement; in a fifth the only hint of criticism came from a man who said that he would perhaps have liked to know about "the higher set-up and policy over design and so on".

In two firms a majority of those interviewed were not entirely satisfied with the introduction they had received. In one of these the comments of graduates were:

> I was more or less just put on the job. It was enough for me because I had been here in the vacation.

> I went straight to the job. I would have liked a short time in all departments. One would know people in three months instead of a year or so.

> I was put into a specific job. I would have liked an introduction to the whole business.

> It was left to the department what would happen to me. I would have liked a length of time at the works. I think the method was to get into the routine stuff and learn by experience.

In the other, criticisms were less general and milder. The graduates said:

> I started in the shop, having a little fling. It was not immediately

helpful, but would perhaps be more helpful now. A more concrete idea of what people are and do would have been more helpful.

It was only a small lab. I read a book all morning. Work was very slow at the beginning. I was taken round and introduced to the work's foremen and so on. This helped quite a bit, and was sufficient. I went on to the job immediately with introductions. I would have liked to know more about the various parts of the factory.

The extent of satisfaction among those in firms with fewer than fifty graduates did not appear to bear any direct relationship to the total number of employees. The firms in which all the graduates interviewed were satisfied with their introduction included examples from each of the three size categories, and one of those in which there was dissatisfaction was a small firm.

In one of the three firms employing more than fifty graduates, most of those interviewed were satisfied with their informal introduction. One graduate would have liked a more comprehensive tour, and two criticised their initial reception:

I was left to cool my heels in the personnel office for over one hour and was then told to fill in forms. The acting head of the department was not clear what was to happen to me.

I was not expected.

In the other two firms with more than fifty graduates, most of those interviewed were not entirely satisfied with their introduction, although there were exceptions and there was not always agreement among graduates on what they required. In one of the firms one man was pleased that he had started straight away on a new project, but four others were less satisfied. One said that he would have liked a clearer lead, but did not want anything more elaborate. Two would have liked to have gone on a tour of the works. One who had followed an elementary introduction procedure said:

I would have liked a little more formal introduction or training introductory course about what the section does; it took me some time to find out. I could have done with more conversation.

The comments of graduates in the third firm show the problems and the varied reactions of those concerned:

I went into a research lab. This definitely helped me to settle. I would have liked something more elaborate, but this was impossible because of reorganisation and we were too busy.

I was put on to routine tests. This helped me to settle because the fundamental principles of the industry were involved. I would have liked a quick look around the works; I still have no idea what is involved. Actually this industry is a world of its own.

I was not given an official introduction; I had to find my own way round. Eventually I found one or two people to give me information of a technical nature. This helped me to settle in, and I did not want more. I had a free hand to delve into information. It is a question of specialisation. I think that all that needs to be known can be put into a booklet.

I was seen by the general manager and introduced to my department. This helped me to settle, but I would have liked a tour of the works to get my geographical bearings.

I did know something about the works, but not through the generosity of the people here. I was in the lab. doing routine testing, and I went round the works in general. It would have been better to go round each department and spend a short time there. It is very difficult when you have to get jobs done through different departments. There should be a definite instruction scheme.

I knew most of the people here, being local born. But I know that one of the grouses of the other graduates is that they do not know about the firm.

GRADUATES' ASSESSMENT

THE previous sections have shown that there was no common policy among the firms on the form that the introduction of graduates should take. Most members of management interviewed were opposed to complicated, rigid and formal introduction schemes; in twenty-six of the forty-three studies they stressed that they approached introduction in an informal or individual way, although they were not asked this specific question. Apart from this, the outstanding feature was the diversity of the firms' approach to introduction. The views of the graduates interviewed in these firms were as diversified as those of managements.

The following sections analyse the answers of graduates in greater detail and draw together the suggestions made regarding the separate aspects of introduction.

Forty-three of the 183 graduates in the case study firms inter-

viewed on this subject said that they were given a formal introduction to their firm on first reporting for duty.* This corresponds
closely with the proportion in the graduate interview sample,
who said that some formal steps were taken to introduce them to
the organisation, personnel, and purposes of the firm. The graduates who said that they had been given a formal introduction
belonged to sixteen firms, which had adopted a variety of methods
of introduction; in only four of these firms, in the smallest size
categories, did all the graduates interviewed say that they had been
given a formal introduction. All but seven of these graduates were
satisfied with the introduction they received; most said without
elaboration that it had helped them to settle into the firm. Of the
140 graduates who said that they were not given formal introduction, fifty-nine were in some way dissatisfied with such steps
as had in fact been taken to enable them to settle in. The figures
are shown in Table 13 according to the faculty of the graduates.

TABLE 13
GRADUATES' ASSESSMENT OF INTRODUCTION

	Arts No.	Science No.	Technology No.	Total No.
Graduates given formal introduction:				
Satisfied . . .	21	11	4	36
Making suggestions .	1	5	1	7
	22	16	5	43
Graduates without formal introduction:				
Satisfied . . .	11	29	41	81
Making suggestions .	8	20	31	59
	19	49	72	140

In each of the faculties slightly more than 40 per cent of those
who said that they were not given a formal introduction were
dissatisfied with some aspect of the steps in fact taken to acquaint
them with the firm. These graduates were in firms of almost every
size and product group, and there was seldom agreement among
all the graduates in any firm on the suitability or otherwise of the

---

* Twenty-three of the graduates in the case studies entered their firm before
graduating and were therefore not questioned on their introduction to it.

introduction which they had been given. Of course, all the graduates in a particular firm were not necessarily treated in the same way: their reception depended upon their faculty, past experience, the department they were entering, the work they were to do, and so on. But beyond this, even when the circumstances and treatment seemed very similar, they often reacted quite differently. It seems clear that no single method of introduction is successful in all circumstances. There are several aspects to introduction, and these can be approached in a variety of ways. The emphasis that needs to be laid on each aspect varies according to the individual circumstances of the firm and of the graduate. An analysis of suggestions under various heads gives some indication of the aspects of introduction which most frequently gave rise to criticism.

Suggestions for improvement

Sixty-six of the 183 graduates interviewed in the case study firms, or 36 per cent, were in some way critical of the introduction they had been given, or made suggestions for its improvement. Their comments have been divided into eight broad categories as shown in Table 14. A number made suggestions which fell into more than one category: where these suggestions amounted to a criticism of the absence of arrangements covering several aspects of introduction, a single entry has been made under the heading "general introduction"; otherwise comments have been included under the separate headings. This gives a total of eighty-seven suggestions by the sixty-six graduates.

TABLE 14

GRADUATES' SUGGESTIONS REGARDING INTRODUCTION

	Number of graduates making suggestion:			
Suggestion	Arts	Science	Technology	Total
General introduction	5	2	6	13
More elaborate introduction	—	3	3	6
Tour	2	9	10	21
Structure and administration	2	5	6	13
More introductions	—	1	5	6
Lectures or chats	1	2	2	5
Better organisation	—	9	8	17
Miscellaneous	—	3	3	6
	10	34	43	87

Graduates were asked whether the introduction they had received had helped them to settle into their firm; if not, why not; and whether they had any suggestions to make. Nineteen, from fifteen different firms in various size and product groups, said that they would have liked a general introduction to their firm or a more elaborate introduction than the one they had received.

It will be seen that most of the graduates who made suggestions regarding introduction, however, referred to one or two specific aspects which they felt could be improved. The most frequent comment was that there should be opportunities for a tour of the firm, or for a more extensive or detailed tour than they had received. Most of the graduates had in fact been shown round their own departments or sections, but wanted a wider knowledge of the practical operations of the firm as a whole; some had been given a quite detailed introduction to their own factories, but would have liked to have visited associated works or outlying units. It was sometimes suggested that there should be a conducted tour with explanations, possibly by the heads of the departments which were being visited, and with an opportunity to speak to the people concerned. A few graduates would have liked to have spent a short time in all departments of the firm, but this may be more allied to training than to introduction. The request for a tour of the firm or particular parts of it was not limited to a particular type of firm or graduate.

Thirteen graduates would have liked to have known more about the structure of the firm and its administration, who people were and what they did, and the general purposes of the firm. A few would have liked more introductions to colleagues or senior members of their firm. One said that he would have appreciated being introduced to people at more leisure. A few would have liked lectures, discussions, or the opportunity to chat to people on the job.

Organisation

A more striking feature was the strong feeling expressed by graduates on the way in which their introduction to the firm had been organised. Seventeen commented adversely on the organisation of their reception to the firm or of the period that followed. Eleven of these, from eight firms, referred to the poor organisation when they first reported to their firm. Some of these comments have already been included in the studies of the firms earlier in this chapter. Others were:

> No one knew I was coming. I was unsettled because there was no introduction. I spent the first few days mainly in reading about the company.
>
> I had to wait twenty minutes in a waiting room. I was then issued with a lab. coat and sat down with a batch of monthly reports to discover what was going on. This did not help but merely confused the issue.
>
> Three new graduates had just joined. No preparation had been made to receive us and there had been no previous discussion of what we were to do. It is a bad thing to leave people standing around for weeks. There is no preparation of desks or seating accommodation, and no announcement that new people have arrived.
>
> There was two or three hours' delay because of confusion over the day of my arrival. After that I started on my job, learning where everything was kept and so on. I did not want induction. One cannot always remember things by the first introduction. Getting to know people gradually by working with them in jobs is better.
>
> No one knew anything about me or my arrival. I was put in the wrong department for a week before anything was found out. I was told people's names.

The poor reception arrangements of these firms do not appear to have depended upon the existence or non-existence of a formal scheme of introduction. The graduates' first impressions were disturbing, and the impressions remained after the graduates had been with their firm for some time. These comments (as were all the others) were made without prompting, and it is possible that poor reception arrangements were more widespread than is directly shown by this survey.

Eight graduates commented adversely on the organisation of their introductory period with the firm, including two of those who commented on their poor reception. The general feeling of these graduates was either that their introduction was not sufficiently well-defined and arranged, and that they would have derived more benefit from it if it had been better organised, or that there had been a period of stagnation while they waited for a course to start. A considerable number of firms stressed their informal approach to introduction and although some used this to excuse the absence of detailed arrangements, most treated introduction informally as a matter of considered policy. Informality was clearly not inconsistent with good organisation. On the whole, graduates seemed well satisfied with an informal or individual approach, but a few felt the need for more organisation and tended to regard informality as casualness.

CONTACTS IN THE FIRM

THE successful introduction of any newcomer depends to a large extent on his starting off on good terms with his colleagues. The introduction of a graduate, however, may present difficulties peculiar to itself in that he starts work in industry at a later stage in life than most other entrants and though, in theory at any rate, intellectually better equipped than they, he has palpably not "come up the hard way". The risk of the graduate recruit not hitting it off may be greater in firms new to the employment of university men or employing them in relatively small numbers. But, whatever the circumstances, the directors and the men to whom the graduate is immediately responsible can probably do much to ensure the recruit a good start. It is they who are responsible for laying down and carrying out the firm's graduate employment policy, and it is they who can do more than anyone else to create and maintain the right atmosphere for the creation of good relations between the firm and the new entrant. Moreover they are the nearest equivalent in industry to the senior members of the graduate's university with whom the new entrant will have been in direct contact throughout his years as an undergraduate.

Graduates were therefore asked whom they met when they joined their firm, and what impressions they gained of these first contacts. In the graduate interview sample, 50 per cent of the graduates came into contact with directors on entry to the firm, 70 per cent came into contact with foremen, 72 per cent with operatives, and 87 per cent with other personnel, including office staff. Most of the graduates found a favourable attitude in all these people; an unfavourable attitude was relatively rare. The results are summarised in Table 15.

Directors

Graduates were rather more sure of the attitude of their directors than of the other people with whom they came into contact. A favourable attitude was recognised in a higher proportion of cases,

TABLE 15

CONTACTS IN THE FIRM

Contact with	Graduates having contact		Attitude to graduates			If affected by being graduate		
			Favour-able	Un-favour-able	Neither	Yes	No	Don't know
	No.	%	%	%	%	%	%	%
Directors	282	50	84	2	14	49	42	9
Foremen	390	70	70	6	24	30	62	8
Operatives	402	72	72	4	24	21	70	9
Others	489	87	71	5	24	26	64	10

and fewer graduates found themselves unable to determine what the attitude had been than was the case with other contacts. Half the graduates concerned thought that the fact of their being a graduate had influenced the attitude of the directors they had met, a higher proportion than in the case of other contacts; only 21 per cent of the graduates who came into contact with operatives thought that their degree had any effect on their attitude, 26 per cent of those meeting others thought it may have had some effect, and 30 per cent of those meeting foremen. These results are based on impressions, and the apparent differences between the attitude of directors and the rest may be due to the fact that the graduate was more likely to have met a director before coming to the firm. It may also be that since a director was often responsible for appointing him, the graduate might have assumed more readily that he was regarded with favour.

The size of firm strongly affected the proportion of graduates who came into contact with directors. In small firms with less than 500 employees, 80 per cent of the graduates met directors, compared with the average of 50 per cent. The proportion fell progressively, and in firms with 5,000 or more employees only 41 per cent of the graduates met any of the directors. There was little difference in the attitude of directors of firms in the various size groups to the graduates they met, nor in the effect which graduates thought their degree had on directors. Except for the largest firms, those with 10,000 employees or more, there was a slight tendency for contacts to be more favourable as the size of the firm decreased, but this was not statistically significant.

Arts graduates came into contact with directors more often than did the graduates of other faculties. On entry to the firm,

61 per cent of the arts graduates met directors, 48 per cent of the scientists, and 46 per cent of the technologists. The scientists were the best satisfied with the contact; 90 per cent of the scientists who met directors found a favourable attitude, 10 per cent were undecided, none gained an unfavourable impression. Of the arts graduates, 84 per cent discerned a favourable attitude on the part of the directors they met, 13 per cent were undecided, and 3 per cent thought the attitude unfavourable. Of the technologists, 19 per cent found a non-committal attitude in the directors they met, 77 per cent discerned a favourable attitude, and 4 per cent an unfavourable attitude.

The information received in the graduate interviews was amplified by answers received from graduates in the case study firms. They were asked what impression they received during their first few weeks with the firm of the attitude of directors and of managers towards them as graduates. Of the 183 questioned, only about half met directors or managers during their first few weeks in the firm. Most of these received a very favourable impression of the attitude to them as graduates, but eleven of the ninety were not entirely satisfied with the result of the contact. This was due to a variety of reasons. Four technologists felt that managers and directors regarded them as not being very practical. This was not a strongly critical attitude, and many graduates themselves seemed to feel that they lacked practical experience. An engineer in a small firm said:

> Some of the people here take part-time degrees. They have greater practical experience than the full-time graduates and realise that you have a lot to learn. Some departmental heads do not have degrees, and are on the look-out for men flaunting their degrees; hence they are apt to emphasise that you know nothing and to suggest that a full-time graduate has done it the easy way.

> During the first few weeks the impression is that until you settle down to the practical side of the work you have only a limited value. (Another graduate in the same firm.)

In a medium-sized firm, two engineers gained rather dissimilar impressions of the attitudes of their managers and directors, as shown by the following comments:

> I found that the directors and managers were a wee bit suspicious. They expected me not to be very practical.

I had a very good impression. In a small firm personal relationships are possible between the heads of departments and graduates.

Two graduates complained of insufficient interest on the part of managers and directors:

The works manager did not take sufficient interest in the department, which resulted in my not having enough authority. (An engineer in a small firm.)

One director shook hands at Christmas, otherwise I did not see any. I do not know whether the directors are aware that graduates are here. I doubt whether there is any essential policy in the firm about it. (A scientist in a medium-sized firm.)

An arts graduate in a medium-sized firm felt that managers and directors did not seem sure how to treat graduates as a body:

Their treatment varied from a respectful attitude (too much so) as if I were someone precious, and again as someone who was of no importance. Possibly this was accountable to the stage of training. I found my superiors very helpful and friendly during the course.

A technologist in a large firm thought he detected a suspicious attitude in his managers:

The managers didn't like us. They thought we were there to pinch their jobs. It was practically impossible to glean anything through management.

One graduate in another firm commented favourably on the attitude of the managers and directors at the firm's headquarters, but was less pleased with the position at the unit where he worked.

I had the impression of a better attitude [at headquarters] than here. Things were particularly successful there. They are used to graduates and to training staff. Here the atmosphere is less good.

It may be noted, however, that other graduates in this firm were well pleased with the attitude of managers and directors.

The graduates in the case study firms who met directors or managers during their first few weeks were usually well satisfied with the contact but, as has been seen, 50 per cent had no such contact. It is clear from a number of the comments volunteered that lack of contact with managers and directors during the first few weeks at a firm may be a cause of strong and lasting resentment:

The directors were so remote that I wouldn't even know them by sight. (A graduate in one large firm.)

I had no contact. It would have been like talking to the King. (An engineer in a medium-sized firm.)

I've had no contact with managers and directors. I've formed the opinion now that management is sold on employing graduates, but not quite sure how to use them. It's a higher management policy leaving everyone puzzled. I think it's the influence of the B.I.M. talk about productivity. (A graduate in another large firm.)

We don't come across those in this firm. (A graduate in a medium-sized firm.)

I have never met a manager yet. (Another in the same firm.)

The attitude of immediate superiors

The person to whom the graduate was immediately responsible in his work was sometimes a director, sometimes a manager, or frequently some other member or members of the staff. This was clearly one of the most important personal relationships, and graduates were therefore asked how they got on with their immediate bosses.

In the graduate interview sample, 84 per cent of the 561 graduates found that their immediate superiors were on the whole helpful and co-operative. Detailed figures are set out in Table 16. More than half thought that the fact of being a graduate had favourably influenced their superior's attitude; nearly half thought it had had no effect or did not know; only 3 per cent thought that being a graduate had had an unfavourable effect.

Five per cent thought that their immediate superior was on the whole unhelpful or unco-operative. Nearly half these twenty-nine graduates thought that the fact that they were graduates may have contributed to this unhelpful attitude; but a few thought that being a graduate had in fact mitigated rather than caused it. Eleven per cent found a non-committal attitude in their superiors; about a fifth of these thought that their being a graduate had unfavourably affected the superior's attitude.

Taking the graduates as a whole, 45 per cent thought that being a graduate had had a favourable effect on the attitude of the person to whom they were immediately responsible; 43 per cent thought that it had had no effect on their attitude; 7 per cent thought the effect had been unfavourable; and 5 per cent did not know. The analysis revealed no statistically significant difference between the experience of graduates in the various faculties.

TABLE 16

ATTITUDE OF IMMEDIATE SUPERIOR

Attitude of immediate superior			If affected by being a graduate:			
			Yes		No	Don't know
			Favour- ably	Unfavour- ably		
	No.	%	No.	No.	No.	No.
Helpful . .	470	84	237	14	199	20
Unhelpful . .	29	5	4	13	8	4
No special attitude .	62	11	10	12	34	6
TOTAL . .	561	100	251	39	241	30

In the case study firms also, the great majority found their immediate bosses very friendly, helpful and co-operative. Only ten of the 183 graduates concerned were not completely satisfied and criticisms of immediate superiors were in the main mild; most were in some way related to the graduate's lack of practical experience. For instance:

> Some look up to you, but some are indifferent, thinking that you have not got the practical training. (An engineer in a small firm.)

> There was a general attitude that you must learn from experienced technicians before getting started. (A scientist in a research unit.)

Several other graduates made comments which seemed to reflect a feeling that they were thought to lack experience. An engineer in a medium-sized firm found a satisfactory attitude among those who directed the training, but thought others accepted students indifferently, as though making the best of a bad job. A technologist in a large firm thought that the people immediately senior to graduate recruits had a sceptical attitude, but that this did not apply to the top level. Other comments were:

> I formed the impression that my immediate superiors did not truly appreciate graduates except for their snob value. (An engineer in a small firm.)

> They were inclined to be rather schoolmasterish and to tell us what was good for us rather than to discuss things. (An engineer in one of the giant firms.)

There was very little indication of any real hostility to graduates by their immediate superiors. An arts graduate in a medium-sized firm found that one or two people were a little hostile and there was a certain amount of suspicion, but that this could be overcome. A graduate in a large engineering concern said:

> Some thought we were spies of management and said as little as possible; others were more enlightened, but all were friendly on the whole.

Only one graduate complained of a completely unhelpful attitude on the part of his immediate superiors. He was a technologist in a medium-sized firm, and his comment was:

> I was given no help at all. They seemed to have a complete lack of knowledge and understanding of what we were doing.

It is evident that the majority found on entering the firm that their immediate superiors were on the whole helpful and co-operative. Half the graduates thought that the fact that they possessed a degree had some bearing on the attitude of their immediate superiors, and that this effect was generally favourable. A high proportion thought that the fact that they were graduates had no effect on the attitude, generally friendly, of their immediate bosses.

SUMMING UP

WHAT emerges from this part of the survey is an impression, first, of a general awareness among employers of the significance of the initial period of the graduate's life in the firm, and, second, of the diversity of approach among both employers and graduates to the form it should take. Employers were frequently found to be opposed to formal schemes, and those firms which had adopted a standard procedure often applied it in an informal way. Again, though they were aware of the importance of a good start for the graduate's life in the firm, employers who recruited only a few graduates at a time felt that their number was too small to justify an elaborate introductory scheme. Further, irrespectively of the number of recruits arriving at any one time, many firms considered that the purposes of introduction were better achieved informally according to individual circumstances. Most of the firms which organised introduction in a systematic way regarded it as an integral part of the training programme.

Most members of managements were satisfied with the procedure they followed, though their attitude was not complacent; and each of the various approaches which have been described were well liked by some of the graduates experiencing them. More than a third of the graduates in the case studies, however, criticised some aspect of the way they had been introduced to their firms. Criticisms came from arts, science and technology graduates, from those coming direct from their university and from those who had had experience in industry before graduating. The critical graduates were not restricted to firms of any one size or product group, nor to those who had experienced a particular type of introduction. It is true that the nature of their criticism was often related to the individual circumstances, but even when allowance is made for the fact that there are several aspects of introduction, and that a single yardstick is not enough, it is clear that there was room in several firms for improvement in the manner in which the introductory period was organised.

On arrival at his firm, the graduate should feel that he is expected and wanted, that there is a place for him in the organisation and something worth while for him to do. If the firm does not appreciate this, or bungles the graduate's reception, it may find that the graduate will take a long time to overcome a first impression of neglect or inefficiency. Some graduates felt that there was a lack of purpose in the period which immediately followed their arrival at the firm—whether this was regarded as part of a process of introduction or as a waiting period until the start of a course—the inference being that not enough care and thought had been given to this stage. This was very much a matter of personal opinion, however: many graduates appreciated the freedom of a few days in which to get their bearings, while others would have liked to have got straight down to work. These differences no doubt reflected the rate at which any individual graduate was able to absorb his new surroundings, though other influences would also be present. The success of any introduction must lie in part at any rate in its phasing. The problem arises again in relation to training, which is considered in the next chapter.

A number of graduates expressed a desire to know more about the firm they were joining. The most frequent request was for more extensive tours of the firm; this sometimes stemmed from a practical need for knowledge of the firm and its layout, sometimes from the fact that the graduate's intellectual horizon extended beyond the sphere in which he was immediately engaged. Similarly, a number of graduates wanted to know more about the structure and organisation of the firm. A few graduates wanted more personal introductions, or chats, or lectures. A number thought that a lot of the information they wanted to have about the firm, its structure and administration, and geographical layout, could easily have been conveyed to them in concise form through suitable literature. A wider use of maps and flow-charts might meet these needs.

A long and formal induction programme did not always, or generally, appear necessary to meet the expressed needs of graduates. Relatively few wanted a longer or more detailed introduction than they had received, and this often amounted to a request for training rather than introduction to the firm. But many graduates felt that they should have been given at least some introduction to the organisation, personnel, and purposes of the firm.

Whatever method was adopted to meet intellectual requirements, it is clear that a great deal depended also upon personal relationships. Where the personal responsibility for introduction was placed on a senior or associate who was in close and regular contact with the graduate, complaints seldom arose unless this person was unable or unwilling to act as guide and mentor. As one graduate remarked: "It is other people who condition how you settle in". It was significant that some of the strongest complaints about their introduction came from graduates who had been unable to establish satisfactory personal relationships in their firms.

Graduates on the whole, however, received a very favourable impression of the attitude of the people whom they met when they first joined their firms. They were particularly sure of the favourable attitude of those to whom they were immediately responsible, and of those directors with whom they came into contact; in each case about half the graduates thought that the fact that they were graduates had influenced the attitude, a higher proportion than in other contacts. Only about half the graduates met directors or managers during the first few weeks at the firm, and to a number this lack of contact was a strong grievance. The proportion of graduates who met directors was considerably higher than the average in small firms, falling progressively as the size of the firm increased. If managers and at least one director were to make a point of seeing any graduate newcomer at some time during his early days with the firm, if only for a few minutes, and if only once, it would clearly help to make the introductory period a success. By so doing, the newcomer would be given some positive evidence that he was expected and wanted. At the same time management would benefit by getting to know newcomers.

A few of the firms which were studied had adopted introductory arrangements which clearly suited their individual circumstances very well. Other firms appeared to have made inadequate provision, and this was a cause of dissatisfaction among many of their graduates. In most firms there was a diversity of opinion among the graduates regarding the merits of the arrangements made for them, but it was clear that there was often room for the improvement of one or other of the two main aspects of introduction, the social and the intellectual. No single method of approach to introduction solves all the problems of every firm, but whatever course is adopted it is clear that the formation of sound personal relationships at an early stage is of paramount importance.

CHAPTER V

TRAINING

EARLIER chapters have described the various policies which firms had adopted for the recruitment of graduates, their selection and their first introduction to the firm. This chapter considers the next step: fitting graduates for their particular work in the firm.

The material is again derived from the graduate interviews and the case studies of firms. The graduate interviews show on a statistical basis how many graduates were given a training course, and show this also in relation to their faculty and the size and product of the firm which they had joined; the nature of the training given, and graduates' general reactions to it. The case studies show management policies and attitudes towards training, and the opinions of graduates in these firms on the type of training they received.

THE PURPOSE OF TRAINING

THE object of training is to provide a new entrant with the knowledge and experience that are considered necessary to enable him to be of the greatest benefit to the firm. Training may also be used as a buffer period in which to acclimatise a man to industrial life and the general ways of the firm; to give managements an opportunity to assess a man's ability before he is allocated to a specific job. It may even be one method of attracting men of the required calibre to join the firm.

The need to train a graduate varies according to the purpose for which he has been engaged, the function he is expected to perform, and his store of knowledge and experience as a newcomer. Before turning to the training policy of the case study firms it is therefore advisable to consider some of the broader issues which may have a bearing on the whole question of training. These factors are discussed under three headings: the job, the graduate, and the firm.

The job

The first consideration in determining whether a graduate should be given training, and if so the form it should take, must be the purpose for which he has been recruited. A double classification emerges: graduates recruited directly for specific posts; and those recruited with a view to ultimate allocation to one of a broad range of jobs. For the first category the emphasis of training is likely to be placed on the attainment of the level of knowledge and experience required for the specific job. If the post which the graduate will fill is not decided on entry, any training given may be more generalised, at least in its early stages. This type of training may be used in the case of potential managers or technical supervisors, or whenever it is thought desirable to precede specialisation by a period of more general training or experience.

There is no clear cut distinction. Whether a graduate is taken on for a specific post or not, he is engaged with a specific purpose in view. Any training will be primarily directed to this end.

The graduate

The function which the graduate is expected to fulfil is one side of the equation; the other is the graduate himself. Does his knowledge and experience match the requirements of the job? What gaps need to be filled? How can this best be done? The answer to such questions as these must depend largely on an assessment of the individual graduate. Factors which must be taken into account include his interests, age, salary, and his present and future status in the firm. The graduate's capacity to benefit from any particular kind of training and his intentions to work for an additional qualification or membership of a professional body are further important considerations.

A good training programme may be a considerable asset. The opportunity to gain a broad view of the industry of his choice, knowledge of a specialised field, or perhaps the achievement of further qualifications and membership of professional bodies, may add to a firm's appeal to the kind of graduate it is seeking. Some graduates may regard a training scheme as an indication of the firm's desire to develop abilities to the full; and, other things apart, they may find an added attraction in the existence of a training plan, however nominal it may be. Others may prefer to get down to a specific job as soon as possible.

The firm

The graduate's ability and the function he is to fulfil are not the only considerations which must be taken into account. Conditions in the industry or department concerned, its range of activities, its organisation, and the nature of its processes, all have their influence on training. Other relevant factors are the availability of training facilities and staff, other training arrangements within the firm, the number of graduates needing training at any one time, the practice elsewhere, the recommendations of professional institutions, and the requirements for the granting of professional qualifications. These basic considerations are not easy to assess precisely, and the extent and form of training which may be considered desirable in given circumstances may be largely a matter of personal interpretation.

Training courses may be expensive and to some extent disruptive; the salary paid to the graduate during his training period is only one item in the calculation. There is a risk that people may not remain with a firm after they have completed their training. Attitude to this risk may vary widely. Some firms may even see direct and indirect advantages in providing training for numbers exceeding those to be kept on afterwards. Some firms, especially those with only limited needs, may be able to satisfy their wants by recruiting those who have already gained the requisite training and experience in other firms.

It is in the light of such considerations as these, which naturally vary widely according to the circumstances of each firm, that managements must decide who requires training; whether it should be a formal course or a broad informal training while doing a necessary job of work; how long the training period should last; and whether the necessary instruction can best be given outside the firm.

The diversity of the problems presented by training, and the varied ways in which the requirements of training were met, are illustrated by the findings of the case studies of the forty-three undertakings made for this enquiry. The following sections examine the policies of these undertakings, and illustrate the interaction of the three main factors—the job, the graduate and the firm—in determining training policy.

TRAINING POLICY

MEMBERS of management were asked to describe any arrangements made by their firm or board for the training of graduate recruits, and were invited to comment on certain aspects of their policies. The significance of their replies can be fully appreciated only in relation to the individual circumstances of the firm. The following sections therefore contain brief descriptions of the practice of each firm, together with the comments of the members of management concerned.

Twenty-six of the forty-three firms reported that they had formal training schemes for some or all of their graduate recruits. Most of the schemes had been introduced or revised in or after 1945. Fourteen firms said that they trained all graduates; but several of these employed a very small number of graduates, and from the interviews it was clear that some of the others in fact made exceptions in certain cases. The twelve firms which said that they did not include all graduates in their training scheme mentioned the exclusion of men going to specific jobs, entering research departments, or working with the firm while taking their degree; two firms trained only graduates who entered sales departments; and one firm trained only graduates taken on from a university specifically for that purpose.

Seventeen of the firms said that they had no formal schemes. Absence of a formal training scheme, however, did not necessarily mean that graduates were regarded as fully competent to fulfil at once the functions for which they were engaged. Training was often considered necessary, but managements felt either that it could be most effectively carried out in an informal way, or that in their particular circumstances a formal scheme was impossible or inadvisable.

A few firms were contemplating policy changes or revisions in existing schemes, but, by and large, firms were satisfied with what was being done, although many were far from complacent about the details. Comments typical of the attitude of many firms were:

> Our people seem to emerge from their training scheme as good products.

> We find it fits them very well for their work in the firm. We can tell by the comments of the graduates.

Large firms with training schemes

Formal training schemes for graduates were operated by ten of the twelve concerns with 10,000 or more employees. The two exceptions were area gas boards, one of which had a scheme on paper which had been applied only to the extent of taking on one arts graduate, while the other intended to set up an internal training scheme which would make the recruitment of graduates from outside unnecessary.

Electrical engineering. One of the giant electrical engineering concerns, a very large employer of graduates, trained all graduate engineers except those with previous experience or those under-taking research work. The management considered that graduates were not engineers, nor trained men, until they had gained experience: the training course was essentially two years' experience, and varied according to what was available, and the job in view. Flexibility was one of the keynotes. The type of training was similar to that which the firm gave to a student apprentice during the last two years of his five-year apprenticeship, but the schemes were quite separate. In each works the head of apprentice training supervised the course; in the bigger works this was a full-time appointment, but not in the smaller works. A typical programme was:

1 month to get used to the tools

4 months' assembly work

4 months in the testing department

3 months' working on switchgear

3-6 months in a technical office associated with the work.

The remainder of the two years was spent in an engineering department.

A member of management at one of the works considered that two years' training was not nearly long enough for electrical engineering:

> Two years gives graduates the basic principles and then you must build up on it. The five-year scheme for student apprentices has advantages. Each scheme has something the other hasn't got. After seven years it is a matter of the best man getting ahead. In the graduate scheme no time is spent in the draughtsmen's office. Actually doing the type of drawings they will later interpret is an invaluable training.

Another large electrical engineering concern treated each graduate individually in its arrangement of the training programme. The management described the training as follows:

In general those direct from a university follow a two-year course. Those who have had practical training, for instance through a sandwich course or through working in industry before going to a university, are given about six months in which to get used to our products. If they have been in a similar industry they may not need this. We have no set course, it all depends on the individual. There are four phases of about six months covering basic manufacturing techniques, assembly, what the product can do, and the graduate spends the fourth period in the departments where he will go before assignment. I get the impression that our programme is quite as popular as that of any corresponding engineering company in the country. Personally I believe that there is room for improvement, although I feel we're doing better than other firms. It might be an improvement to give more technical lectures to graduates than we do at the moment. I would prefer to enlarge the induction course to two or three months with more lectures on the main subjects, and to support the lectures with visits to departments with lectures to explain points. At the moment there is a great tendency to leave graduates to pick this up.

A third large electrical engineering concern adopted a much less flexible approach. It ran a two-year training scheme for all graduates except those entering research departments. The scheme was instituted before the war, but had since been revised. Engineers all followed the same programme during the first year, and then a specialised programme for the second year depending upon the department to which they were to go. There was a distinct standardised first-year course for arts graduates, followed by a year's "specialist" course arranged in consultation with the head of the department which they would finally join. The management was satisfied with the operation of the scheme, and knew of no obvious defects.

The research unit of a large electrical engineering concern had no training scheme, although the other units of the company had one:

There is no formal training here. We recognise that this is wrong, and our ambition is to recruit into a pool for training; but we can't afford to spare the graduates' time with so many vacancies awaiting them.

Vehicles. A firm in a branch of the vehicles industry, a very large employer of graduates, had five years earlier abandoned its

training course for technologists in favour of direct appointment.
But it felt that a training scheme was a better way of obtaining
graduates, and in 1955 was re-introducing a two-year course:

> The scheme varies according to the individual, and we allow a man
> to depart from it. At any stage now, by mutual consent, a graduate
> can get out of it. I think it is quite iniquitous of some firms who
> eventually want ten men to take forty into a training scheme and
> later discard thirty. This is a fatal practice.

A three-year training scheme for arts graduates for sales departments continued to be operated. Owing to the small numbers
involved, it was found possible to keep the programme varied
and flexible.

Metal trades. A firm in the metal trades had a two-year scheme
for graduates without industrial experience who joined the firm
direct from a university. Departmental managers were responsible
for the training of graduates recruited by them for their sections,
although the training was not necessarily restricted to the section
for which the graduate was selected.

Food. In a food firm, a unit of a very large concern, the training
programme was adjusted to the individual:

> The programmes are tailored according to the job, and a personal
> interest is taken—which works both ways. The training is based on
> what a man knows and what he needs to know. Graduates are seen
> regularly and asked for comments. They are encouraged to examine
> training programmes critically, and are given projects in the early
> stages. We are satisfied with the scheme, but not complacent.

This rather informal and individual approach to training reflected the views expressed by the headquarters of the whole
concern, where a period of roughly eighteen months to two years
was considered to be about right, but responsibility for the
formulation and application of training programmes was left to
the heads of the units of the company.

Oil. A large marketing and distributive agency had a combined
induction and training course lasting about six months. The
programme usually entailed several weeks' visual appreciation, or
practical work, before going to the residential training centre for
a fortnight's course. This was followed by the training proper, or
field work. The scheme was not restricted to graduates, and was

applied equally to non-graduates at the same level. The management said that its policy was to train people to do a job of work. Specialists had the same early programme, but had a more technical bias in their later training.

Gas boards. Two of the four area gas boards said that they had training schemes for graduates. In each case the training course was planned to last about two years, but was very flexible. The management at the headquarters of one of the boards said that it was left to the undertakings in the area of their board to give the best training they could in the two years, and that any aspect of training could be cut short as the unit managers thought fit. The management stressed that it did not wish it to be felt that graduates were favoured, and that on this account its approach to introduction was also informal. Reports on trainees were sent in to the board by group managers, but a member of management thought that the scheme could be improved if an education officer were appointed and "proper selection methods" adopted:

> One of the dangers at present is that trainees may be used for routine work; that is an easy way out for managers. An education officer could keep an eye open for that, and would throw up a lot of things. But considering the state of the industry we have made good progress.

The individual interpretation of the training scheme by the units of the board was shown in the following comment:

> The board prescribes six months everywhere, but we use our discretion. It is easier to train in a small undertaking than in a large one. We make our boys specialise in one department rather than moving them all the time.

The other area gas board had only a very slight training scheme for the very few graduates who were sought for training for senior posts, but attendance at outside courses was encouraged.

Medium-sized firms with training schemes

Of the nineteen firms with between five and ten thousand employees, twelve said that they operated formal training schemes for graduate recruits. Five did not train all the graduates who joined them; seven said that they trained all graduate recruits, but in five of these one or more of the graduates interviewed had

L

not in fact been given a training course. Schemes were generally not restricted to graduates, and varied considerably in their length and nature.

Chemicals. A chemical firm employing under fifty graduates had a formal six-month training scheme only for its sales staff, and graduates were not sought as such or employed as such in sales jobs although some of the men who had been taken on had degrees. All other graduates were immediately assigned to definite jobs, generally the posts for which they were engaged. Occasionally, however, men were taken on, not to fill an immediate vacancy but with a view to later promotion to executive positions. There was no set routine for this class of recruit, but the management tried to put them into a definite job which needed doing and which would give them suitable experience and bring them into contact with a lot of people. The firm did not clearly distinguish between introduction and training.

Another medium-sized chemical firm, employing nearly two hundred graduates, had a scheme for graduates going into the factories, but not for those entering research departments or generally for arts graduates:

> Trainees have a programme of about three months. They spend time in each production department, with longest in the department they are likely to be connected with. They work first as workmen, and the junior staff are encouraged to give them as much work to do with their hands as possible. I am sometimes doubtful how well this works out under pressure of work—sometimes trainees may get overlooked—but all I have asked have expressed satisfaction. We like trainees to get into close contact with the technical problems of the plant with which they will later have to deal. This is important so that they don't lose the respect of the men on the plant for which they are working.

Metal goods. A medium-sized firm trained all its graduate recruits under a scheme adopted in 1946. The management said that all trainees would ultimately be taken on the staff. For technologists it operated a two-year graduate apprenticeship scheme, designed to meet the requirements of the Institute of Mechanical Engineers for the granting of associate membership; these graduates spent eighteen months in an engineering department doing their machine tool apprenticeship, then six months in a production department working on basic processes. On one day a week they went to a technical college to work for their diploma. This programme was considered to be the absolute minimum. The management said that in theory they should do six months in works study, but in practice this time was usually needed for report writing.

The few arts graduates were given a six-month period of job-rotation in each department, and took a diploma in industrial administration. For each arts graduate taken on, a member of the existing staff underwent the same training. The training programmes were not standardised, but very much made to suit individuals; this was thought to be particularly necessary on the technical side. The management worked on the basis that graduates should be treated, and personally known, as individuals. Two members of the staff were available to give advice and encouragement to technical trainees, one to those on non-technical training. The firm placed the greatest faith in diploma courses.

The firm was satisfied that its scheme fitted graduates well for their work and felt it had learnt very well how to train and develop the technical graduate; but it did not think it had yet learnt what was best for the non-technical graduate, and was reviewing how it could have improved the methods adopted for them. It was in fact giving up the recruitment of arts graduates.

Electrical engineering. Both the medium-sized electrical engineering firms said that they had training schemes for all graduates. One of these had only recently introduced its two-year scheme, and none of the graduates interviewed had experienced it. The other said that a two-year training was given to all graduates who had not already received practical training. The scheme went back at least to the Twenties. The training in electrical or mechanical engineering was stated to have two aims: first to give the student a comprehensive practical knowledge of general engineering workshop practice and experience in the design and manufacture of the equipment; and secondly to enable the student to discover the relation between the theoretical and academic knowledge acquired at a university and the practical problems of design, research and manufacture. The training was divided into two main stages, the first being spent in the works training centre, in the production departments, and in erection and commissioning on site; and the second stage in the technical departments. Suitable students wishing to specialise in research entered the research unit at an appropriate stage of their training to concentrate on the branch of their choice. The management said:

> The training of graduates is all centred round the requirements of the professional institutions who require that every member shall have had at least eighteen months practical working experience. Provided he fulfils these requirements we can modify the rest of the training to suit the individual. Many overseas students come for the sake of training. In the last five years we have had more overseas students than home students. The education and training officer deals with all technical training, including that of apprentices. He works to the guidance of a student training panel which consists of representatives of the various departments.

Vehicles. One medium-sized motor vehicle firm had a training scheme, but this was intended as part of a sandwich or apprenticeship course, and not for graduates. The firm brought in very few outsiders and preferred to "live on its own fat". Few graduates were employed. Another motor firm, employing some thirty graduates, approached the training of graduates in an informal way:

> Some graduates come in for a specialised job and get bunged on to it. But we have a noble desire to take any graduate and let him have a knowledge of all the factory before he settles down to earn his keep. It all too often happens that we have a man here six months and then pinch him to meet a dire need—this is a direct result of the shortage. If the two years he wastes in the army were spent on training he would be a better asset to the nation. I would say that our method is adequate, not more than that, but it is difficult to improve so long as there is a dearth. But if you have a good man you could lock him in a coal shed and he'd come out useful.

Another member of management praised the firm's training methods, which he regarded as being better than anyone else's, particularly in their freedom:

> The very formal scheme is soul destroying. Up to the first six months I play ball, after that I grab them. They take motor cars to pieces getting their hands dirty up to two years to become development engineers. The engineering department does everything to a motor car.

Textiles. The textile firm said that it trained all graduate recruits under schemes which applied also to public school boys and people promoted from within the firm. The schemes were standardised, and carried out in the various factories of the firm wherever feasible according to instructions from headquarters. Those with a science degree destined to become production chemists spent a period or twelve months, more or less, in a research department; this served as a buffer between the university and the works. They were then transferred to the works and put into a laboratory, under the charge of the technical chemist. During their training period they were doing a practical job. Those who were to join the sales staff, often arts graduates, followed a course lasting eight or nine months which gave them a practical introduction to the production side and training for selling.

Food. A firm in the food industry said that it trained all graduates, but it was clear from the interviews with graduates that those engaged for research were in fact not always given a training course. The training course for those entering production departments consisted of a comprehensive three-year programme covering all aspects of the work of the firm; this was arranged to fit in with seasonal work.

Drink. A medium-sized firm in the soft drinks industry, employing relatively few graduates, said that it trained all its graduate recruits for a period of up to two years. Programmes were made out individually and some time was spent in each department:

> Personal care is taken of all graduates. The first six months is all-important. Firms should be willing to take immense pains over people. We train dogs and horses with great care: why not people? Firms have the responsibility of training. Time is a problem. One can be dizzy with too much training and frustrated with too slow. But people seem to emerge from our training scheme as good products. There is no segregation in our training policy. We have no fetish of learning by doing or vice versa; it all depends on the man. There is no standardisation, but there is a written examination at each stage.

Building and contracting. Finally, among the medium-sized firms with training schemes were two concerns which illustrate the individual and informal approach characteristic of the building and contracting industry, already seen in their attitude to introduction, with the emphasis on learning by doing as an understudy or assistant. One of these employed fewer than ten graduates.

Arts graduates spent three months in various departments, including practical work in the factory. Technologists went into a laboratory or worked with the technical people at the firm's headquarters, for a period depending on the time they took to absorb the information.

The other firm of building engineers had a training scheme for only a few of its graduates, largely foreign graduates or men working for a higher degree. Training was arranged according to the individual, and lasted one or two years. A member of management said:

> I do feel that the question of theoretical training is not as important as experience in the departments. For instance, it is better to see something working on a site than to have lectures on it. But I do feel that a course of lectures would give a more general idea of the work of the company than can be got in the course of duties.

Small firms with training schemes

Four of the twelve small firms said that they had formal training schemes for graduate recruits. These firms, each of which had a total staff of less than two thousand, employed only small numbers of graduates.

Non-metalliferous mining products. The training method of a small firm engaged on non-metalliferous mining products was to give graduates a series of jobs in different departments. Grammar school boys followed the same sort of programme, which was fitted to the individual:

> The scheme is to give them a series of jobs, just long enough to master them and then to move on so that they do not get stuck. For instance, a trainee may spend a year in a series of departments for five years to become a reasonable master of each. We believe that men should not only be leaders, but should, through their own merits, eventually be accepted as leaders. The scheme not only aims at making trainees efficient in all possible jobs and acquainted with all sides of the business, but also at introducing them to the operatives and others in the works.

Leather. The management of a small leather manufacturing firm took much the same view with regard to training:

> All must work as workmen at the production level for a varying period, about three years. They are then appointed to a section and

put in charge, and advanced as occasion offers, but still in competition with others at a similar level.

Building and contracting. In a small firm in the building and contracting industry in which two arts graduates were employed, only one was being trained, the other having already had eighteen months' training in another firm. A year's programme was laid down with regard for the job in view, which was in the sales department. Two months were to be spent in each department in turn.

Another small building and contracting firm operated a programme of training formulated by two professional associations. It took on three graduates each year under a scheme for the training of graduate pupils organised jointly by the Institution of Civil Engineers and the Federation of Civil Engineering Contractors. Under this scheme the firm engaged to give graduates who wished to go on to practical training after completing their university studies, one year's practical work on sites and one year in drawing offices learning design and organisation. The details of the scheme were very flexible. Pupils were moved round the various departments to widen their experience, but received no formal instruction. The management held that the experience and training offered by the firm were of the best.

Small firms without training schemes

No formal training schemes for graduates existed in eight of the twelve small firms. Each of these firms employed only a small number of graduates, eleven or less, and had a total of fewer than two thousand employees. A ninth firm which just entered into the medium size category otherwise showed the same features as the small firms and will be considered with them. The managements of these smaller firms were on the whole satisfied that in view of the smallness of the firm and the fact that graduates were generally taken on at most in ones or twos and for a specific job, a formal training course was unnecessary. As one member of management put it:

The firm is too small; everything is obvious to everyone. We have no turnover of people, anyone new is a major event. We have none of the larger firms' worries.

Graduates who joined these smaller firms were treated on an

individual basis, according to their experience and the job for which they were recruited. Needs met by formal training schemes in the larger firms were here satisfied in an informal way. For instance, a small electrical engineering firm kept its graduates free from responsibility for as long as possible. Another engineering firm put graduates into the drawing office for a time to refresh their knowledge and to put them in touch before starting to specialise. A third said that engineers were sometimes given an apprenticeship by the parent firm, and occasionally they themselves trained people for specific jobs, although there was no formal scheme; the management considered the firm to be too small and the jobs too specialised. Two electrical engineering firms, very new to the employment of graduates, envisaged the introduction of training schemes when they were able to recruit in greater numbers.

Outside courses were encouraged whenever these appeared to be advantageous. One firm in the consumer goods industry mentioned that there was a need for more technical training facilities nearer at hand. Another consumer goods firm said that few suitable courses were available, although attendance was encouraged. Several of the small firms drew attention to the fact that they gave time off with pay for graduates to attend suitable courses or meetings.

The small firms' approach to training, as with introduction to the firm, was informal and individual, and in general met with the approval of the graduates concerned.

Medium and large firms without schemes

Eight medium or large firms said that they did not operate a formal training scheme. One of these has already been considered with the smaller firms in the last section. Only two were in the largest size category, that is with 10,000 or more employees. They were both area gas boards. One had planned a training scheme, but had not yet put it into practice; with regard to introduction the management said:

> The introduction is not systematised enough, but we only take on one or two graduates.

In the other gas board, graduate recruits were sent straight to their jobs. It was the intention of the management to set up an internal training scheme, but for school leavers; this scheme would make unnecessary the recruitment of graduates from outside.

Several of the medium-sized firms considered that it would be difficult or impossible to apply a satisfactory formal training scheme. The management of one said:

> Formal training is possible only in limited fields, for instance in the refineries, where they are put into the laboratory first before being in charge of workmen; it is too sudden to put them into the workshops straight from university. Generally they go as assistant to the man they are to replace. We would like to have formal training, but try to do the same job by *ad hoc* methods.

In the research station of a chemical firm, the management considered that a standardised scheme was not possible because of the variety and complexity of its work, and held that it was virtually impossible to train research staff. Graduates were taken on for specific jobs, and set to the job they were going to do.

A large firm of building contractors had no formal training scheme, but regarded the first three years of the graduate's employment as a training period:

> A formal training would be impossible. Graduates do jobs under supervision. When they are ready to take on responsibility they do. We find that this method works very well.

The management of a medium-sized firm in the metal trades was not entirely satisfied that a formal scheme was unnecessary:

> Graduates start at the works, usually as understudies. They learn by example, and are given increasing responsibility. In view of our very high turnover, however, I cannot say that this works adequately.

A medium-sized firm engaged on the treatment of non-metalliferous mining products was completely satisfied with its method of training graduates:

> Graduates are put in a job for say three months to assess their potentialities. We consider that it is better and more economical for new recruits to learn by doing.

In a medium-sized firm in the metal trades, members of management had rather conflicting opinions with regard to training; one said:

> The procedure depends on the job. Works people start in process

development; sales vary, we occasionally put them through departments. A particular member of the staff is in each case given the job of being father confessor and nursemaid, etc., to the new recruit. I do not believe in formal training. I am satisfied that a training scheme would merely repeat the mistakes of the educational system and produce uniform types. The best sort of education leaves people's originality unimpaired; therefore, why train to type? Jobs are chosen to suit pecple, and even invented when necessary. Wide interests are encouraged, but I am not keen on sending people to fancy management courses. "High-grade spivery."

Another member of management in the same firm felt that if they had more graduates they could run a training scheme. He said:

We are desperately hard up for workers. It is an absolute necessity for universities to produce more graduates so that a better use can be made of them and they can be properly eased in.

GRADUATES' EXPERIENCE

THESE studies of individual firms show the diversity of practice in the training of graduate recruits. Most of the large firms, two-thirds of the medium-sized firms, and one-third of the small firms said that they ran formal schemes. These training schemes varied widely in their nature, and few firms gave a training course to all the graduates who joined them. Most excluded certain types of graduates from their schemes, for instance those with previous experience or those entering research departments. Some firms restricted formal training to limited classes, such as recruits for sales departments or for senior posts. A number of firms, mostly of small or medium size, had no formal training scheme of their own, but many of them thought that the purposes of training were met in an informal way or through attendance at outside courses. This diversity of practice should be borne in mind when considering the statistical evidence which follows on the extent to which the main body of graduates (those in the graduate interview sample) were given training and on the length and content of the training received.

Number given a training course

Two hundred and thirty-three of the 561 men in the graduate interviews, 42 per cent, said that they were given a training course

by the first industrial firm which they entered after graduation.*
Fewer science graduates (34 per cent) were given a training course
than either technologists (46 per cent) or arts graduates (44 per
cent). This may perhaps be attributed to the tendency for a higher
proportion of scientists to enter research departments, for which
many firms suggested that training courses were inappropriate.
The figures are shown in Table 17.

TABLE 17

GRADUATES GIVEN A TRAINING COURSE

Size of firm (No. of employees)	Graduates given a training course							
	Arts		Science		Technology		Total	
	No.	%	No.	%	No.	%	No.	%
Under 500 . .	7	44	5	28	1	5	13	24
500–1,999 . .	9	47	8	32	8	44	25	40
2,000–4,999 .	6	32	15	38	7	33	28	35
5,000–9,999 .	6	33	14	50	19	58	39	49
10,000 and over .	26	54	29	32	67	58	122	48
Not known .	2	—	—	—	4	—	6	—
TOTAL . .	56	44	71	34	106	46	233	42

Fifty-eight per cent of the technologists who entered firms in
each of the two largest size categories said that they had received
a training course; this compares with an average of 27 per cent of
those technologists who joined firms in the smaller size categories.
Fifty-four per cent of the arts graduates who entered firms in the
largest size category (10,000 employees and over) were given a
training course, a higher proportion than in the other size groups;
in the two smallest size groups the proportion of arts graduates
given a course was close to the average, and below the average
among graduates entering firms with between 2,000 and 10,000
employees. The proportion of scientists given a course rose from
28 per cent of those who entered the smallest firms to 50 per cent
of those who joined firms with between 5,000 and 10,000
employees; in the largest size category, however, which for the
other faculties showed a higher proportion receiving a course, the
proportion fell to 32 per cent.

The 233 graduates who said that they were given a training
course are classified in Table 18 according to the principal product

* The question was put only to the men who had entered this first industrial
firm after graduating. (Thirty-three joined at an earlier stage.)

of the firm they entered. Five main product groups have been used: chemicals and allied trades; heavy industry, comprising the metal trades, shipbuilding and vehicles, and non-electrical engineering; electrical engineering; consumer goods, the largest categories in which are textiles, with twenty-six graduates, and food, with fifteen graduates; and others, which includes all firms not coming into the other four categories.

TABLE 18

PRODUCT GROUP OF FIRMS

Product group	No. of graduates employed	Graduates given a training course							
		Arts		Science		Technology		Total	
		No.	%	No.	%	No.	%	No.	%
Chemicals .	118	11	50	28	33	3	30	42	36
Heavy industry .	129	11	39	11	28	28	45	50	39
Electrical engineering .	131	3	21	14	33	44	59	61	47
Consumer goods	54	20	67	9	60	4	44	33	61
Others . .	129	11	30	9	39	27	37	47	36
TOTAL .	561	56	44	71	35	106	46	233	42

The numbers in many of these groups are too small to permit generalisation, but several points may be noted. In electrical engineering firms, the proportion of technologists who received a course was significantly higher than in the other product groups, 59 per cent compared with an average of 46 per cent. In the consumer goods industries, two-thirds of the arts graduates said that they were given a course, a significantly higher proportion than in the other product groups.

Assessment of courses

The overwhelming majority of the 233 graduates who had been given a training course were satisfied with it. Eighty-five per cent said that they thought that the course had been well calculated to fit them for their work in the firm. The reasons they gave for thinking this are shown in Table 19.

The fact that 85 per cent of the graduates who had received a training course thought that it was well calculated to fit them for their work in the firm largely justifies the view generally expressed by the managements of the case study firms that they were working along the right lines. But satisfaction with a course as a

TABLE 19

ADVANTAGE OF COURSES

Reasons for thinking course well calculated to fit them for their work in the firm	Graduates No.	%*
Gave good background, "overall" picture . . .	89	45
Sound practical training	59	30
Helped in work or further experience	18	9
Provided the contacts needed	14	7
Enabled the graduate or management to see to which post he was best suited	14	7
Questions encouraged; course adapted to meet the interests of the recruit	6	3
Others	6	3
No answer	18	9

* Percentage of the 197 graduates who were satisfied with their training course. Since some graduates gave more than one reply, this column totals more than 100 per cent.

whole did not mean necessarily a total absence of criticisms and suggestions, and both managements and graduates frequently felt that there was room for the improvement of certain aspects of training. In the graduate interviews, however, only the 15 per cent who were not satisfied with their course as a whole were asked to

TABLE 20

HOW TRAINING COURSES COULD BE IMPROVED

Suggestions for improvement	Number of graduates making suggestion
Better organisation	9
More specific to job	7
A set scheme	2
More lead or direction	3
Someone responsible	2
More contact with management . . .	3
More practical	5
Less routine work	4
See more, do less	1
More responsibility	3
More extensive (more departments) . .	3
Longer	1
Shorter	1
More co-ordination with production . .	2
More co-operation from technical staff .	1

47

comment further. The points that they raised were very similar to those made by graduates in the case studies, whether or not they were satisfied with their courses as a whole. The criticisms which are listed below are therefore of greater import than the figures themselves imply.

The suggestions for improvement of the fifteen per cent of the men in the graduate interviews, thirty-six graduates, who had received a training course and who thought that it had not been well calculated to fit them for their work in the firm, are classified in Table 20. Five added that the course had since been improved.

These suggestions for the improvement of training courses which graduates considered were not well calculated to fit them for their work in the firm do not take things very far. To sharpen this picture, the various aspects of training will be considered separately in later sections. First, however, it is of interest to consider the position of those graduates who did not receive a training course.

Number not given a training course

Fifty-eight per cent of those in the graduate interviews were not given a training course by their firms. The proportion of scientists not given training (66 per cent) was rather higher than for arts graduates (56 per cent) or technologists (54 per cent). The proportion of all the graduates in the case study firms who were not given a training course was very similar to the total for the graduate interviews (62 per cent against 58 per cent), but there were wider variations between the three faculties: 75 per cent of the scientists in the case studies did not receive training compared with 66 per cent; 60 per cent of the technologists compared with 54 per cent; and 44 per cent of the arts graduates against 56 per cent in the graduate interviews. Statistically, the graduate interviews are the wider and more representative sample; but for an indication of the attitude of those graduates who were not given a training course it is necessary to turn to the case studies of firms.

Table 21 shows the general attitude of the graduates in the forty-three undertakings studied who did not receive a training course, compared with the views of those who did.

The numbers in the various categories are not large, and any conclusions based on them can only be tentative, but they seem to confirm some of the impressions of firms given in earlier sections.

TABLE 21

ATTITUDE OF GRADUATES IN THE CASE STUDIES

	Satisfied				Critical			
	Arts	Science	Tech-nology	Total	Arts	Science	Tech-nology	Total
	No.	No.	No.	No.	No.	No.	No.	No.
Given a training course .	20	10	9	39	3	6	22	31
Not given a training course								
in firms with formal								
training . . .	4	14	20	38	4	6	6	16
in firms without formal								
training . . .	5	25	17	47	5	4	3	12
TOTAL . . .	29	49	46	124	12	16	31	59

Most of the arts graduates who were given a training course by their firm appreciated the training they received and the form it took; relatively few made major criticisms. One in two of the arts graduates who were not given a training course, however, were in some way critical of its absence. For scientists and technologists the reverse was true, and there was a less critical attitude among those who did not receive a formal training than among those who did. This was particularly marked in the case of technologists. Whereas more than two-thirds of the technologists who received training were in some way critical, only one in five of those without training criticised its absence. Similarly, in the case of scientists, one in three with training was critical, one in five of those without.

In assessing the generally uncritical attitude of the graduates who were not given a training course, a number of considerations should be taken into account. Some graduates had already had specific training or experience which they or the management, or both, considered made a further training course unnecessary; other graduates were entering specialised jobs for which managements thought that they were already qualified. In some jobs or firms a formal training course was on both sides thought to be inappropriate, and it was often considered that it was impossible to devise a training course for certain graduates entering the research field. Again, as has been seen, a number approached training informally, and although there was no formal course there was an initial period during which the graduate learnt his job. Apart from such considerations, relatively few firms had a training course which met with universal approval among those taking it, and some graduates felt that they would have lost more by taking a course than they would have gained. Finally, the choice whether a graduate should be given a training course in a number of cases rested in the first instance with the graduate himself. The comments of a few of the many graduates who did not feel the need for a formal training course are given below:

> It would be difficult to give a training for this particular job. Teaching by doing is the only way in my department.
>
> In civil engineering, practical experience takes the place of training. Civil engineers are given responsibility under adequate supervision.
>
> As I hadn't been in industry, they asked me to go into the laboratory for four weeks. This was not really intended as training, but in fact was a good training. I was working with people to whom I am now giving instructions.
>
> A training scheme is unnecessary, provided they don't ask too much at first; this firm does not expect too much at first.

Although many of the graduates who were not given a training course did not regret its absence, one in two of the arts graduates, one in five science graduates, and one in five technologists were in some way critical of the procedure that had been followed. They came from firms in various industries and size categories, both with and without formal training schemes for some graduate recruits.

Arts graduates who criticised the absence of formal training commented as follows:

> I would have liked to have sat back and watched for a few weeks; but this was not possible as I was brought in to relieve another man.
>
> I was told when I started that I couldn't be taught the work but would have to pick it up. But I feel that I could have been given a better insight into the set-up.
>
> I would like to have been given the combined introduction and training course which was introduced after I had joined.
>
> It would be helpful if arts graduates spent some time on the shop floor, although a long training is unnecessary.
>
> There should be a training scheme, however short, and someone should have responsibility for it. At present the people who teach really have their own work and responsibility.

The comments of science graduates who did not receive a

training course and were in some way critical included the following:

> I would have liked a training, but industry is in such a hurry to make a profit out of a graduate that there's no time.

> I would like to spend weeks in other departments, but the pressure of work prevents it. I am doing night classes in industrial administration to fill in the gap. A week of general information and a week in each department in order of process, as done for sales, would help enormously.

> I was not given training, but I was given time during which I acquired knowledge. I did not want a more formal training, but would have liked to be under someone who was an authority on the subject I was learning. No one there was an authority, and there was no one to consult in time of difficulty.

> Definitely I would have liked a training in the machinery and assembly, the whole thing in fact. Coming straight from university I was at sea. I understand they are starting a scheme at our headquarters; it strikes me there are some good ideas.

Technologists who did not receive a training course and in some way criticised or made suggestions for the improvement of the procedure they followed commented as follows:

> I would have liked a normal graduate apprenticeship. I felt very much out of water. I was given a project on which very little was known, so I had no one to turn to. It was too soon to give a new graduate such a job, but I managed it eventually. It grew to such an extent that this factory was taken over to house it.

> I would have liked a more formal training. I disagree with the way things are done. Graduates should be a link between workmen and research. Management should give graduates more responsibility.

> I think a training course would have been a good thing. They have an apprenticeship scheme now. I don't know much about it except that it is two years, which is a bit much.

> There should be a wider use of university post-graduate courses, so that those engaged on specialist research might have a readier grasp of specialist fields, higher learning, and up-to-date techniques. The nationalised industries do not understand post-graduate courses, or what they have to offer. They should have the courage to send people.

> A graduate apprenticeship scheme is essential to engineering graduates. A degree is only the beginning of work.

M

Introduction and training

The close relationship between certain aspects of training and introduction to the firm has already been noted. A number of firms regarded introduction and training as part of the same process, and some had combined courses to cover both.

A relatively small proportion of graduates, some 12 per cent, said that they were given both a formal introduction and a training course; there was little difference between the three faculties in this. Ten per cent were given a formal introduction to their firm, but not a training course; arts and science graduates figured largely in this group. The proportion only given a training course varied from 36 per cent of technologists to 22 per cent of scientists, although aspects of introduction to the firm were probably present in many of these programmes. The figures are given in Table 22.

TABLE 22

TRAINING AND FORMAL INTRODUCTION

Graduates given:	Arts		Science		Technology		Total	
	No.	%	No.	%	No.	%	No.	%
Formal introduction and								
training course . .	17	13	26	13	24	10	67	12
Introduction only . .	15	12	31	15	13	6	59	10
Training course only .	39	31	45	22	82	36	166	30
Neither . . .	56	44	103	50	110	48	269	48
TOTAL . . .	127	100	205	100	229	100	561	100

Nearly half were given neither a formal introduction nor a training course; variations between the faculties were relatively slight. Here again it may be noted that the absence of formal arrangements did not necessarily mean that needs were nor satisfactorily met in other ways.

The comments of graduates in the case studies on their experience with regard to training often point to the difficulties which may arise when introductory arrangements are inadequate or unsuccessful. This applied both in the field of personal relationships and of knowledge of the firm as a whole, as will be shown in the following sections, which deal with the various aspects of training.

THE NATURE OF TRAINING

THE training procedure, the time given to the training period, the programme followed, and the methods used may be determined by many factors. The purposes which it is hoped to achieve by training, the circumstances of the firm, and the position of the individual graduate may all have a bearing on the content and length of training. As shown in earlier sections, this diversity of circumstances may lead to wide variations in training practice, not only between different industries, but also between firms in the same industry and between different branches of the same firm.

The training procedure

The case studies revealed a wide diversity in the training methods adopted by the various firms. Although the nature of the industry and the work eventually to be performed had a marked influence on the method by which training was given, other less tangible factors were important. The five electrical engineering concerns which ran training schemes, for instance, all had a two-year training course for technologists, a period perhaps determined by the requirements of the professional institutions; but, as has been shown, there were considerable differences in their nature and method of application. The size of the firm and its general organisation had an important bearing on the way in which training was carried out. In the case of large undertakings, the administrative division into units and their relationship to the whole strongly influenced the form and application of schemes.

The principal distinction between the various types of scheme lay in the extent to which training was devised on the one hand to show how to do a job, and on the other to show how a job was done. Where the emphasis was on learning to do a job, the graduate himself worked rather than watched others working. The extent to which it was possible or advantageous for a graduate actually to learn to do various jobs depended upon the individual circumstances of the graduate and the complexities of the tasks involved. A number of the graduates in the case study firms thought that it was better to do practical and constructive work than to spend too much time watching others, a view also expressed by some arts graduates. A typical comment was that of a scientist who said that he had been allowed to spend a time in each department of the works, but only as an observer, though he was allowed to ask questions:

> I would have liked to take my coat off and do some real work. That is the only way you can really get to know a department.

In one firm, two arts graduates emphasised the value of a training which involves doing a job. Other comments were:

> In the machine shops there was a tendency for me to have too little to do because the work was too skilled to try.

> I learnt a great deal from my training. I am a scientist, not an engineering man, but I picked up a lot about engineering. It depends on yourself; if you want to learn, you can. We could have been given things to do rather than just watching.

> This is a big firm, and there is very often too little to do, but I can't think of remedies. So many graduates are going through that the men think "here's another one". There is a lot of standing around and watching, which is very boring. The course was ideal with this exception, and I can't see a remedy.

The degree of responsibility carried by a graduate during his training period is closely allied to the question of working or watching. Here again, some men seemed to feel the need to do something useful, to have a sense of purpose and achievement. For instance:

> I had no responsibility. It is very unsatisfactory to stand by and watch. It is not good for learning.

> I would like to be given some small jobs occasionally which a chap could be left to do and a superior could check. They could then see what a man can make of it on his own—but that doesn't seem to be the practice here.

> I am a little doubtful whether the course is well calculated to fit me for my work. I am learning a great deal and getting confidence in myself doing a job. But I feel that when we get down to a proper job it'll be a bit of a jolt, that we have been treated too soft. We should be allowed to have responsibility during training and allowed to stand on our own feet. On the shop floor they won't let you touch a thing and treat you as fools—which you are to them, I suppose.

Half of those in the graduate interviews who were given a training course both watched others and did work themselves.

Thirty-six per cent worked only; 11 per cent watched others working, but did no practical work themselves. In addition to these main activities, 23 per cent of the graduates attended a course at a technical college, 11 per cent were given lectures, and 10 per cent were given some other training (usually some form of course, but in some cases a form of induction such as a tour of the works). More than half of the graduates combined none of these other activities with their training (see Table 23):

TABLE 23

THE TRAINING PROCEDURE

Main activity of graduates			Technical college	Other activities Lectures	Other	None
	No.	%	No.	No.	No.	No.
Watched and worked	117	50	28	15	14	60
Worked only . .	83	36	19	5	4	55
Watched only . .	25	11	3	4	3	15
Neither . . .	7	3	3	2	2	—
TOTAL . .	232*	100	53	26	23	130

* One graduate did not reply.

Time spent in departments

Where the emphasis in the training course lay on learning by doing, there was a tendency for a longer time to be spent in fewer departments. Sometimes this led to complaints at the end of a course that only a very limited knowledge had been gained of the firm as a whole; often this amounted more to a need for a fuller introduction to the firm rather than for an extended training period. A few graduates, however, thought that their work in a department had been allowed to fall into routine, either because too long had been spent there or because the scheme was not efficiently planned or applied. One trainee said:

I felt I was being used merely to get the work done. The fact that I was learning was subsidiary to the results which were expected right away.

More typically, the comments called for a training spread over more departments. For instance:

Eighteen months was too long to spend in one department, and I would have liked to have spent some of the time in others.

I would like to have got round to more departments during my training, only staying long enough in a department to get a grasp of it and then to move on—not to stay long enough to be put on to routine work. There was no time for us to visit many departments; the average period was three to six months, but even at an average of three months only eight places out of fifty could be visited.

I would have liked to go right through the factory for one year, visiting and getting to know the different departments and the people I'd need to deal with. Eventually, when I was doing experimental work, I didn't know who anyone was. They'd say: "Who are you?"

I would like to have found out about the factory as a whole. The impression one gets is of a lot of units.

Flexibility

Nearly all the case study firms said that their training programmes were not standardised, but varied according to the job in view and the rate of progress of the recruit. Yet there was great diversity in the extent to which this was done and in the way it was done.

Quite frequently the specific job to which a graduate would go was not decided until a fairly late stage. It was pointed out that it was often difficult, particularly in large firms, to determine precisely what specific vacancies would be available at the end of a long training period. Even if requirements were fairly definitely established, the decision regarding the specific job to which the graduate should be allocated was sometimes not made until after he had completed more generalised parts of his training. This procedure gave managements more time to assess their precise needs, and a fuller knowledge of each graduate's aptitudes before it was decided to which specific job he should be allocated. A number of graduates appreciated the delay for the same reasons, or because it gave them more time to look around and decide precisely in which direction they wanted to go. Some 7 per cent of the graduates who felt that their course was well calculated to fit them for their work in the firm gave the reason that it had enabled them or the management to see to which post they were best suited.

Some graduates, however, suggested that they would have liked to have known sooner what they were going to do when their training was completed, and felt that their courses should have been more specifically directed to the job in view. A few gave this as their reason for thinking that their course was not well calculated to fit them for their work in the firm. Typical comments were:

> Half my graduate apprenticeship was a waste of time for the work I am doing. Only during the last few months, after the decision was made that I was to go to a sales department, was the training well calculated to fit me for my work. If the company knew what they wanted and gave a survey of openings earlier it would be possible to spend more time specialising.

> Parts of the course were good, but others were not. The nature of my future work should have been decided earlier. I found the greatest value of the course was in making personal contacts, but these would not have been much use if I had gone to a research laboratory.

> I think it would be better for arts men if the firm knew what they wanted them for and trained them for the specific job in view, instead of taking them on in case they will be useful.

Criticisms such as these do not necessarily show that time was wasted or that courses were not properly planned. Graduates may not have had sufficient experience to appreciate fully the purpose of the steps that were taken. In fact, a few men who made suggestions for the alteration of training programmes admitted that when they were following the courses they would not have appreciated them. It is clear, however, that a number of graduates did not always see the point of what they were doing: closer contact between the graduates and those responsible for training might have helped in this respect.

A number of firms gave the graduates themselves a considerable freedom of choice regarding the nature of their training, and this freedom and flexibility was greatly appreciated by many graduates. For instance:

> I rather like the method here, to be given a free hand to train oneself. Any information is available freely, but there is no set course. I think you get to know colleagues more than through a formal training scheme, because you do rely on them for information. I have had no experience of bigger organisations, but it would be easier there to allow for formal training and there could be a special staff for it.

> I followed a loose timetable which covered the entire factory. The

timetable was drawn up for general guidance, and I was allowed to modify it as I felt fit. The responsibility of applying it or modifying it was my own. I thought the method was excellent.

It depends on yourself; if you want to learn, you can. I was completely satisfied. I chose my own course, or rather had a great deal of say in it.

Some men, however, felt that too much was left to their own initiative, and they called for a set training scheme or for more lead or direction. Typical comments were:

I was left a little too much on my own.

There were certain difficulties. Too much was left to me. I felt a more rigid timetable would have helped. Also there could have been a weekly get-together of trainees and apprentices for a general discussion.

Length of training courses

The length of time devoted to training, again, depended upon the purpose of training, the conditions of the firm, and the position of the graduate as well as upon other factors. There were great variations according to the requirements of the job in view, the graduate's knowledge and experience, and the ability of the firm to give the training desired. Many firms had no formal training arrangements for men who came to them with suitable training or experience gained elsewhere; some felt that, because of the nature of the work or the circumstances of the firm, formal training was impossible; others varied the length of their courses to meet individual requirements.

Factors outside the firm itself sometimes determined the length, for instance, when a minimum period was laid down for membership of a professional institution. Practice elsewhere in the same industry may also have had some influence, if only from the competitive standpoint of attracting suitable recruits.

The pace and nature of the training given are relevant to any consideration of the length of courses. The significance of the period taken by a training course depends very much on the way in which the time is spent. A course may appear to be of a nominal nature, for instance one aimed primarily to provide experience which will meet the vocational requirements of professional institutions; the graduate may then be employed as productively as is consistent with this purpose and with as little disruption as possible of the day-to-day work of the firm. The following comments illustrate graduates' reaction to schemes of this type:

> It is rather a misnomer to call it a training course. It involved doing the normal work; it was a case of learning while doing a job. Trainees are not treated any differently except that because of their contract they do get preference in going out on sites for experience. But I have no complaints about the jobs which I was given to gain the experience. I don't think anything more formal could be done for this type of work.

> I don't know what the course consists of: I seem to do the same as anyone else.

On the other hand, a graduate may be used productively only in so far as this is consistent with the primary purposes of training. Differences in the length of training course do not therefore in themselves necessarily show that in the long run one firm devotes more time and attention to training than another. As one member of management said:

> Time is a problem. One can be dizzy with too much training, and frustrated with too slow.

Great variation in the length of courses and also adjustments were therefore to be expected, and were, in fact, encountered. One of the firms had reduced its training period from as much as three years to six months for a combined introduction and training course:

> We feel that men need to make a success of a job of work, and for that reason we have cut the training to a minimum.

Training courses for technologists were generally longer than those for graduates in other faculties. In the graduate interviews, 70 per cent of the technology graduates who had been given a training course by their firm said that it had lasted more than a year; the comparable figure for arts graduates was 27 per cent, and for science graduates 20 per cent. More than half the science graduates who were given training courses said that they had lasted six months or less, 43 per cent of the arts graduates; only 16 per cent of the technologists had courses lasting six months or less. The figures are shown in Table 24.

TABLE 24

LENGTH OF TRAINING COURSES

Length of training course (months)	Arts		Science		Technology		Total	
	No.	%	No.	%	No.	%	No.	%
More than 36 .	1	2	—	—	3	3	4	2
25-36 . .	1	2	2	3	12	11	15	6
19-24 . .	7	12	9	13	44	42	60	26
13-18 . .	6	11	3	4	16	15	25	11
7-12 . . .	17	30	18	25	12	11	47	20
4-6 . . .	10	18	12	17	11	10	33	14
3 or less . .	14	25	25	35	6	6	45	19
Not stated . .	—	—	2	3	2	2	4	2
TOTAL . .	56	100	71	100	106	100	233	100

Few graduates in the case study firms commented directly on the length of the training courses they had been given, although a number of suggestions made in connection with other aspects of training, if carried out, might have resulted in a longer or shorter course. There were no comments from technologists, who generally had the longest training period. The comments of arts graduates on the length of their training were:

Training should be as short as possible, so as not to bore people with routine.

I was given three weeks' training, but would have liked more, particularly on the technical side of the business. But I would not have welcomed it at the time.

I thought the course was well calculated to fit me for my work in the firm, but I was left on my own too much and could have done the course in a much shorter time.

The course was a long, drawn-out induction which lasted six months rather than two weeks.

One science graduate thought that his course was too long because it was not well organised. The varied reactions of individuals is illustrated by the comments of two scientists in the same firm:

I had eight months' training. On the whole it was satisfactory. It is a good idea to keep it short and to pass people through quickly.

In general, I wouldn't want any changes. It depends on the individual and his energy. People react differently. Training must be protracted to cover all sections.

RESPONSIBILITY FOR TRAINING

HOWEVER well the scope and content of a course is defined to meet the needs of the graduate, the final results depend upon its effective application. It is therefore of interest to examine who was responsible for training and its supervision.

Supervision and organisation

Men in the graduate interview sample who had been given a training course were asked who supervised their training as a whole. Thirty-nine per cent said that their training was under the supervision of a departmental manager. A slightly higher proportion, 44 per cent, said that a training officer or personnel manager had supervised their training. Eight per cent named a director of the firm. The figures are shown in Table 25.

TABLE 25

SUPERVISION OF TRAINING COURSES

Training supervised by				Graduates	
				No.	%
Departmental manager .	.	.		92	39
Training officer .	.	.	.	77	33
Personnel manager	.	.	.	25	11
Director .	.	.	.	18	8
Others .	.	.	.	3	1
No answer .	.	.	.	18	8
TOTAL .	.	.	.	233	100

The responsibility for training may be viewed from three angles: who formulates training schemes; who applies them; and who supervises them. The above table relates only to the supervision of the training course as a whole, and does not distinguish any division of responsibility in these three senses; the fact that 8 per cent of the graduates were unable to answer the question suggests that there may have been some ambiguity in this respect. It is clear, however, that many graduates regarded their departmental manager as responsible for the general supervision of their training, whether or not he was in fact to some extent obliged to work in accordance with schemes formulated and supervised outside the department. More than half the graduates said that their training as a whole was supervised by someone other than a departmental manager, generally a training officer or personnel manager.

The interviews with the managements of the firms studied have illustrated a variety of ways in which the responsibility for training may be apportioned, and some of the advantages and difficulties involved. A centrally formulated and supervised programme may imply a wider approach to training than if the entire responsibility is left to the department head; but this does not necessarily follow, and the broader aspects may be provided for initially by a general introduction to the firm as a whole. When someone not directly in the line of command is taking an interest in the trainee, he may perhaps help to ensure that the lines of training are being followed. The trainee on his side will be able to appeal against decisions of the department in which he is working. Some senior members of management admitted that there was a danger that graduates might be given too much work of a routine nature when the responsibility for training was left entirely to departmental heads.

On the other hand, there is a danger that too much centralised control may cause the man on the spot to lose interest in the broader purposes of training and to regard trainees as an imposition, particularly if they may not ultimately remain in his department. The supervision of training by someone outside the department to whom the graduate may appeal, may be regarded by the departmental head as a challenge to his authority.

The settlement of such problems as these must depend very largely upon the individual circumstances. Their relevance to the effectiveness of training is illustrated by the comments of graduates interviewed in the course of the case studies:

> The training was not well calculated. Whatever the idea was originally, I think it was lost in the works, where they put me down in the first available place and used me as staff to help out. I was only once taken note of by the manager of the works.

> The scheme was very thorough if followed through properly. It was too long. It could be more centralised. Factories run the training as they think fit; it should be run more from head office.

> It could have been laid out better. Too much was left to the manager of the works, who was inclined to forget. It should be better planned, and the trainee could be told from time to time what are the intentions. I never knew how I was doing or what was going to happen.

> The course was first-class; it couldn't have been better. It was the

ideal set-up; it was remarkably flexible. I attribute much of its success to the personnel officer, who was always ready to iron out any problems.

Training is a job tacked on to other people's jobs and therefore they can't devote so much time to it.

The range of subjects was good, but a good deal of time was wasted. Nothing was organised, and those in charge did not have time to bother. I think that this has since been altered.

It must be remembered that most members of management and graduates were opposed to over-rigidity and too formal an approach. As with introduction to the firm, the view was expressed by some graduates that the lack of organisation may in some ways have helped. One graduate said:

The scheme was not effectively organised, and this enabled me to find out for myself, and in my own way, perhaps more than I would have done in an organised way.

Several graduates thought that the process of handing on information could have been better organised:

A précis of processes and so on would help you to pick up information accurately. You can be misinformed by people on the shop floor and not find out your mistake for ages.

A lot of time was wasted in looking for standard information about the firm and its machines.

I feel that all you learn is learnt from chaps you work with, not from the firm as a firm. You never find a textbook which applies to the particular job; only other people with more experience could teach. But the firm could organise this process of handing on information.

Interest in progress

Closely allied to these problems of organisation is the degree of interest which graduate recruits feel is being taken in them during their training. Graduates in the sample who had been given training courses were therefore asked whether they felt that interest was shown in their progress during training, and also whether they felt that top management had taken a personal interest.

Most graduates felt that interest was shown in their progress during the training course, and a large proportion thought that top management had taken a personal interest. As shown in Table 26, nearly all the arts graduates felt that interest was shown in their progress during the course, and three out of four felt that top management had taken a personal interest in their progress; only 4 per cent thought that no interest was shown in their progress. On the other hand, 14 per cent of scientists and 14 per cent of technologists thought that no interest was shown in their progress, and about one in three thought that top management had not taken a personal interest.

TABLE 26

INTEREST IN PROGRESS DURING TRAINING

	Arts %	Science %	Technology %	Total %
Interest shown in progress . .	96	86	86	88
Personal interest of top management	77	63	65	67
No interest shown . . .	4	14	14	12

In firms with under 5,000 employees, a rather higher proportion of graduates than in the larger firms, 74 per cent as compared with 64 per cent, felt that top management took a personal interest in their training progress. This was probably because there were generally more opportunities for contact with top management in the smaller organisations.

The comments of some of the graduates in the case study firms who felt that sufficient interest was not taken in them are given below. They show once again the importance of establishing sound personal relationships between graduates and other members of the firm.

The only thing I got to know was what was going on. No interest was taken in me at all. There was a person in charge of training and I frequently went to him to get a change, but he was no good with post-graduate students. Training could be improved firstly by more interest being taken, and secondly, by the time in departments being better thought out. That is, a more specific course should be laid down. It is very haphazard.

I think that interest was taken in my progress during the course; and that top management took a personal interest, although I was not aware of it at the time.

One thing I have against the training is that when you go to a department no one explains the department to you. I feel that the foreman should spend a little time with you; it takes so long to find out for yourself.

I had an abbreviated course of two months as I had already been in industry. It covered departments I hadn't been in before. I would have found it more helpful if the managers of departments had taken more interest and advised; I feel I wasted time being left on my own so much.

Progress reports

A common practice was to require graduates to make reports on their progress during the training course. Forty-one per cent of the graduates did so. There was little variation in this between the different faculties; 41 per cent of arts graduates, 39 per cent of scientists, and 43 per cent of technologists. A number of the case study firms said that they attached much importance to the reports which graduates made on their training, and this is borne out by the above figures.

Not surprisingly, graduates who made progress reports tended to discern interest more often than those who did not have to do so. (See Table 27 below.) In each of the faculties, the proportion of graduates who felt that no interest was shown in their progress was lower when reports were required. The most significant differences were in the graduates' views of the attitude of top management. Whereas only 53 per cent of the science graduates who did not make progress reports thought that top management took a personal interest in them, 79 per cent of those who made reports did so. The proportion of technologists recognising the personal interest of top management was 10 per cent higher when reports were required, and 5 per cent higher in the case of arts graduates. The figures themselves cannot show the reasons for this, but the association is one of some interest.

TABLE 27

PROGRESS REPORTS AND VIEWS ON INTEREST SHOWN

	Reports required				Reports not required			
	Arts	Science	Tech-nology	Total	Arts	Science	Tech-nology	Total
	%	%	%	%	%	%	%	%
Interest shown in progress	96	89	89	91	97	84	84	87
Personal interest of top management	74	79	71	74	79	53	61	63
No interest shown	4	11	11	9	3	16	16	13

Despite making reports, some 11 per cent both of scientists and of technologists felt that no interest was shown in their progress. The comments of graduates in the case studies also show that the requirement to make reports does not in itself always satisfy graduates that a real interest is being taken in them. Some graduates found in their reports a source of frustration, since they believed that no attention was paid to them. This was particularly so when they had made suggestions for the improvement of their courses or the working of the departments they had visited:

> I wrote copious reports, which weren't read.

> The education department is disorganised; reports are unread, and suggestions on the running of the departments you are in are never seen by the departmental heads.

> Reports I made did not receive proper attention; since they were never commented on I had no idea whether my suggestions were good or not.

> I wrote reports on every department, but I don't think they were read.

Several of the firms mentioned that they held examinations at the end of sections of their courses, or told graduates how they were getting on. Some had regular meetings between trainees and members of management. The managements of most of the firms without training courses also seemed to take a keen interest in the progress of their graduates. A few graduates said that they would have liked to have had some sort of report on their own progress. For instance:

> It was recently decided at a trainees' conference that the personnel manager should have regular meetings with trainees with reports; if you're not told every three or four months how you're getting on, you feel forgotten. You should be told your faults so as to be able to correct them during your formative years.

SUMMING UP

TRAINING, whatever shape it may take, from the most formal to the most informal arrangements, is an important part of the process, that starts with the assessment of his calibre on recruitment, of employing a graduate newcomer as fruitfully as possible. The whole conception of training was given a tremendous impetus by the achievements in this field during the last war, largely, but not only, in the fighting services. As a result, there was a quickening of awareness in industry of the value of training. Conditions of continuing shortage of technical staff, however, might well affect the attitude of industrial firms towards training. But, though a small minority of firms felt too pressed to train their recruits as they would have liked, most appeared not to be skimping the training they gave on this account.

The evidence of the two surveys goes to show that about four men out of every ten were given a training course of some sort. But this figure must be heavily qualified, particularly in considering the relationship of training to arts men, scientists and technologists. One in three of the scientists and just under half the arts men and technologists in the graduate interviews were given a training course by the first industrial firm they entered after graduation. The number of graduates given training and the nature and length of course also varied considerably according to the size, product, and other circumstances of the firms.

Eighty-five per cent of the graduates who received a training course thought that it was well calculated to fit them for their work in the firm. This conclusion largely justifies the view generally expressed by managements that they were working along the right lines. But satisfaction with a course as a whole did not mean an absence of criticism and suggestions, and both managements and graduates frequently felt that there was room for improvement. Four out of every ten in the case study firms who had received a training course made some suggestion or criticism. Few firms were wholly successful in giving every recruit exactly the training course he would have liked. To satisfy all the recruits all the time would be too much to ask, but even if full allowance be made for this there are certain conclusions it seems fair to draw from the comments made by graduates.

As has been seen, a number of the larger firms took on some graduates without knowing precisely how they would employ them eventually, and saw the training period as an opportunity to size up their men and to watch how the work in this or that department was developing or contracting. This, no doubt, had advantages for the firm, but the graduates' reaction to it varied considerably. Some graduates would have liked to have known where they were heading sooner than their employers were ready to tell them. They thought that their training could have been

N

improved if the precise nature of the work which they were to do could have been determined earlier than it was. Others, however, were grateful for the opportunity for getting their bearings and deciding where their interests lay, and they felt that managements were given an opportunity to assess their abilities and to place them ultimately in the most suitable job.

There is perhaps no easy solution. But it seems that a minority of firms may not always have thought as hard as they might about the work to which graduates under training were to be posted; some graduates at least were left with this impression.

Secondly, graduates preferred learning by doing rather than by watching, and this is certainly supported by evidence elsewhere. It seems, however, that if the manufacturing processes are particularly complicated, learning by doing may give rise to a conflict of interest. Unless the course is superficial, it may result in a graduate knowing a lot about a relatively few departments and not enough about others. The stronger the emphasis on doing during the training course, the stronger the case would seem to be for preceding it by a thorough introduction to the firm as a whole. More generally, indeed, it seems that a good introduction may make better sense of the training course. *A priori*, it would be logical to suppose that a university man should want and need to grasp as soon as possible after joining a firm, its purposes, structure and organisation; and that this knowledge should not only affect the form to be taken by his training, but enable him to derive greater value from it.

What emerges far more strongly than anything else, however, is what may be described as the need for a sustained and intelligent relationship between the graduate undergoing training and some member of the firm suitably placed to ensure that the fullest value is derived from training, and, also, from any introductory programme that precedes it. The points already mentioned are directly relevant to this. So also are others: for instance, the desire sometimes expressed by graduates for greater flexibility in adjusting the training as it progressed to their needs and interests within, of course, the limits set by the firms' intentions regarding them; and closely allied to this is the efficient execution of any system of reporting by graduates on their progress.

Due allowance must be made for the fact that the graduate recruit was, after all, only a recruit, and could not be the final judge of the value of a course. Nevertheless, it seems that training could in many instances have been more effective and more rewarding if there had been someone whose duty it was to watch the graduate's progress, secure the fullest co-operation of those with whom he was to come into contact and lend a sympathetic ear to his suggestions and difficulties. A tutor at a university perhaps suggests more aptly the sort of sustained and friendly relationship which seems to be needed if training, whether or not it takes the form of a course, is to be as fruitful as it should be.

> One thing I have against the training is that when you go to a department no one explains the department to you. . . . Reports made were never commented on. . . . The personnel manager should have regular meetings with trainees. . . . You should be told your faults so as to be able to correct them. . . . Whatever the idea was originally, I think it got lost in the works. I was only once taken note of by the manager. . . . I never went anywhere unless I suggested it myself.

These are typical of the sort of difficulties encountered and they might not have arisen if the training course had been more closely watched. And in the graduate interviews it was "better organisation", the solution to these difficulties, that was most frequently mentioned in answer to the question how the training course experienced could have been improved.

How this relationship between a "tutor" and the graduate newcomer should be organised is not an easy question. The solution must depend not only on the size and structure of the firm or department in which the newcomer is to work, but also, no doubt, on whether or not there are fellow graduates to help the newcomer along, and on personalities at various levels. One outstanding problem is whether the tutor should be in the line of command above the graduate or be dissociated from it, as a personnel officer may be. The balance of advantage in any particular firm may lie with one arrangement or the other. In some circumstances it might be possible to combine the two. At the senior level there might be someone not in the line of command, who would be the equivalent of a "college tutor"; at a lower level there would be "subject tutors" in the various departments in which recruits received their training. The graduate recruits would be responsible to them but would have direct access also to the "college tutor". But whatever arrangement be adopted, the objective must be to secure for the graduate an easy, continuous and open relationship with some authoritative person who can, if necessary, defend the firm's policy to him, make any adjustments in the training that seem right, and generally act as a stimulating and friendly confidant and guide.

There remain the six men out of ten who were not given a training course. Though this figure at first sight seems high, both the firms and most of the graduates concerned were on the whole satisfied that a formal training course was not needed, or not possible either because of the nature of the work or the smallness of the firm, for instance. It was only among arts graduates that the lack of a training course was felt to any extent. The great majority of scientists and technologists were content not to have been given a formal training.

The impression left, therefore, is that whether or not they were given a formal training course most graduates were reasonably happy. The criticisms made about training courses were not fundamental and might often have been avoided by better oversight of graduate newcomers.

The next chapter will examine, with some related questions, the relationship of training to the question whether graduates felt themselves to be intelligently employed and the views of management on the value of graduates to them two or three years after their joining the firm.

CHAPTER VI

IN THE FIRST JOB

THE first job in the firm is a testing time both of the graduate himself and of the firm's employment policy. Has the right man been appointed in the first place? Is the best use being made of his abilities and training? Is he sufficiently adaptable? Questions such as these are the subject of this final chapter.

Consideration is first given to the attitude of managements to the sort of work they feel a graduate should do and to the question whether he should be treated differently from his contemporaries in any way, and their assessment of his abilities. Secondly, the attitude of graduates to their employment is discussed: whether they thought they were doing suitable work and were on the whole intelligently employed. Finally, since the first job is only the start of a career, a study is made of the extent to which firms indicated prospects of pay and promotion, and of graduates' own estimates of their future within the firm they had chosen.

THE ATTITUDE OF MANAGEMENTS

MEMBERS of managements were asked a number of questions to ascertain their attitude to graduates as compared with their non-graduate contemporaries. The first question was: *On entering industry, do you consider a graduate should do the same work as his non-graduate contemporaries? Or is this likely to waste his capabilities?*

Most members of management thought that graduates, on entering industry, should, in certain circumstances, do the same work as their non-graduate contemporaries. They included all those in the gas boards who answered this question. Of the 126 who were questioned, thirty-six did not give a definite answer; they included the senior member of management in five firms. Some said that the practice depended on the job, the skill of the non-graduate, or the possibility of other methods of giving training. Others considered the question was not applicable to a small firm, or when graduates were taken on for specific jobs. In one of the gas boards, for instance, a member of management said:

I feel the question is not applicable in view of the board's policy to recruit men for jobs, and not graduates as such.

Only a fifth of those who gave a definite reply said that the graduate should not start on the same work as his non-graduate contemporary. (Those who held this view included the senior member of management in eight firms, of which three were large). Four-fifths of the definite replies were in favour of the graduate doing the same work as the non-graduate at the start. This view was expressed by the senior member of management in thirty firms, seven of them large. Several added that this would not apply in the case of research.

Reasons for doing the same work as non-graduates

All the members of management who thought that, on entering industry, a graduate should do the same work as his non-graduate contemporary, regarded the practice as a form of training. It was said to be done as a deliberate policy to provide background and practical experience, or to give the graduate a chance to prove his worth. Some of the replies reflected the view that, on entering industry, graduates were not always sufficiently experienced to be able to do jobs which were done by non-graduate contemporaries.

Twenty-five members of management in nineteen firms said that, on entering industry, a graduate should do the same work as his non-graduate contemporaries in the course of training or career development. For instance:

> When they come to me I like them to spend some time on the drawing board, as their training doesn't cover this side—it is an extension of training. A graduate has to go on learning for some time before I'd call him an engineer.

> If there is a proper apprenticeship scheme he doesn't have to do non-graduate work, but otherwise a short period of that work is necessary to get his abilities and knowledge in the right perspective.

Many members of management stressed the differences in their approach to graduates and non-graduates, even though at first they might be giving them the same sort of work:

> He should do the same at first, but we feel we should watch him and groom him through a career development process.

> They haven't all the same capabilities. Often a non-graduate can succeed and a graduate can fail. The difficulty is to place the graduate

in the correct job and use his capacity. Inevitably the non-graduate does the same work often.

The level at which a graduate should start, and the rate at which he should progress, were questions that clearly engaged the attention of a number of members of management:

> Graduates expect to be three rungs up the ladder. To start them age for age would give some training; but to start exactly at the bottom would waste their capabilities, though there is something in the idea of knowing how to do everything.

> Graduates should start on the same work as their contemporaries. They get a very good general background if they start low enough and see where they fit into the jig-saw.

> It is very necessary sometimes to waste capabilities. It teaches people how things tick. No one believes now in going as far back as they used to. Dissatisfaction arises when a man can't see where he's going.

The advantages of gaining an insight into the workings of industry and the firm were stressed by fourteen members of management in ten firms as reasons for setting graduates on the same work as their non-graduate contemporaries. Experience of this kind was often seen as part of the process of training and development. The following comments illustrate the points put forward:

> A firm should make full use of graduates' capabilities, but there is no harm in giving them other work to give them a practical insight. That happens when we take them in the long vacation; any job gives them a valuable insight into industry before they come into it.

> A graduate certainly ought to have experience of workshop practice, how to operate machines and work under the discipline of a foreman, to help him learn about labour relations and so on. But it's not always necessary for the graduate to spend as long on initial practical work as many non-graduates.

> It is a jolly good thing for a graduate to have the rough corners knocked off him, and this is best done by making him work along-side non-graduates, even manual workers and artisan types, in what may seem to him menial tasks—for a short time. A graduate as such is only half-trained. In knowledge of the world and practical training in industry he hasn't a clue.

Seven members of management in six firms thought that a

graduate should be given an opportunity to prove his worth. For instance:

> Everyone must start at the bottom, to prove themselves.

> A good Higher National Certificate boy is never overtaken after five years' apprenticeship. But the job is approached in a different way. Not all graduates are ambitious but some have an exaggerated idea of their value at first. All that nonsense is taken out of them in industry. . . . They find their own level amongst other intelligent people.

Ten members of management in six firms gave other reasons for thinking that in certain circumstances graduates should do the same work as non-graduate contemporaries at the start. A few of these comments reflected the view that, despite his lack of practical experience on entering industry, the graduate is capable of doing the same work as his non-graduate contemporary. Others suggested that, because of the nature of the work, graduates and non-graduates could start at the same level:

> It's quite possible for technical boys to do the same jobs, especially in the beginning.

> Yes, because we don't specialise in highly technical work.

Two members of management suggested in their replies that their treatment of men did not depend on whether or not they had a degree:

> Men need never waste their capabilities in this firm. There is always an opportunity for enterprise. . . . It depends entirely on the individual.

> Except in the research department, they do the same jobs as anyone else because we are not interested in graduates as such.

Reasons for not doing the same work

Seventeen members of management in eight firms (three large, one medium sized and four small) said that graduates should not start on the same work as non-graduate contemporaries. In five of these firms, non-graduates were not eligible for the jobs for which graduates were employed.

Most comments were to the effect that graduates were taken on for a different type of job, or different grade, from contemporary non-graduates, and that it would waste their abilities to give them other work:

> They do better work, more difficult.

> They are engaged as specialists.

> In research, efficiency does not depend on practical experience.

> I question the idea that for an empirical approach and a quick answer you need a man who has come up with the company.

Other comments reflected the view, common to many of the replies considered in other sections, that graduates on entry to the firm sometimes had insufficient experience to be able to do the same work as their contemporaries. For instance:

> The graduate is always put below an experienced National Certificate man, but his training and knowledge are put to advantage from the first. Routine work would waste his capabilities, though he must be eased into his job. No kid gloves, though.

One member of management gave a very different reason for not putting graduates on to the same jobs as non-graduates. He said:

> They are not given manual jobs because there might be trade union objections.

Scientists and technologists doing non-technical jobs

The senior member of management in each firm was asked: *Do you ever assign science or technical graduates to non-technical first jobs?* Only six firms replied in the affirmative. Three of these firms, all with over a hundred graduates, said that non-technical first jobs were sometimes given to graduates entering sales departments, for instance:

> Some graduates are engaged on analytical work, the results of which are used to help customers deal with their problems. These experts must be potential salesmen because they will have to deal with customers. They therefore start with field training as salesmen. We find that the graduates welcome this experience.

Three, including a gas board, said that it was sometimes done in the course of training, for instance:

> A few graduates are taken on for long-term training towards executive posts. Scientific qualifications may be a suitable back-

ground. They are assigned to a series of jobs, the first of which is decided partly by the ultimate aim and partly by what is available.

A seventh firm said:

We haven't done yet, but may do so. More and more non-technical posts will go to technical graduates.

Arts graduates helping in technical administration

The senior member of management in each firm was asked: *Do you ever assign arts graduates to relieve the scientific and technical staff of administrative matters?*

Although a number of firms took on arts graduates for administrative posts, in only one, a chemical manufacturer, was it said that they were ever used to relieve the scientific and technical staff of administrative matters:

We use economics graduates to do production planning. To that extent we do use arts graduates to relieve the shortage of suitable science graduates which we experienced some years ago. But in only two cases.

Other comments made in answer to this question were:

We may use statisticians.

We are always studying how to remove the non-technical work from the scientific and technical staff. We sometimes use arts graduates. A chemist may go on for ever with sampling problems; it's better to hand it over to the statistical department who can decide how many samples should be taken. It is often better to introduce a trained brain to bring a different approach from that of the man who is directly concerned with the problem.

Not yet. We are considering some, for instance an economist. But in a gas board such intentions are limited by the obligation to publish figures about staff and the tendency of the public to watch the figures critically.

We are considering engaging an arts graduate to run an information section with the research group.

We are not very clever with arts graduates.

Technologists and routine supervision

Senior members of management were asked: *Do you ever assign technology graduates to the routine supervision and control of plant?*

If so, what do you find is the attitude of graduates to such assignments?

Sixteen firms, in various size and product groups, said that technology graduates were sometimes assigned to the routine supervision and control of plant. (It was clear, however, that a number of these replies concerned science graduates rather than technologists in the sense used in this survey.) As might be expected, there was a great difference in the nature and status of the work referred to as routine supervision and control of plant. In some firms, this was regarded as responsible and highly skilled work which could be undertaken only by an able and experienced graduate:

> Yes, shift manager's job. They have to be highly trained in order to avoid any errors in the process. It is routine supervision in a pretty large way. It's what they are there for.

> Graduates are only given a load like that after two or three years; they welcome it.

> Yes, ultimately. They are delighted; the firm has to try to keep them off.

Three, including a gas board, stressed that routine work might occur during the training period:

> For short periods they may. Even for those in charge of a retort house the work is all routine with periods on shift. They expect a certain amount of routine work and some are glad to have a job to do. Others hate to be pinned down.

Two firms said it might at times arise out of the work done by graduates:

> Only when a research scientist sees his own project through into production. A limited number are willing to do it. Most enjoy it.

> Two graduates engaged in work study and the development of processes have worked for long periods on actual production.

Two firms said that there was much routine supervisory work done by graduates, but that this was an inevitable part of the productive process:

> We have no difficulty about it. Most of the [chemical] processes we are concerned with are of such technical complexity they can rarely be described as routine. You may find on enquiry that some of the young chaps may be restless, feel they are not getting on fast enough.

They may say: "Well, I am just stuck on production." But some love it.

Some men who have taken degrees while working for the industry are assigned very much to routine; so much of the gas industry is routine. Ninety-nine per cent of the technical jobs must be described as routine. The graduate tends to turn up his nose at the routine stuff.

Remarks by the managements of other firms show that routine supervision may be a skilled and responsible function, in their view often liked by the graduates concerned; or, if not popular, appreciated by the graduates as being a necessary part of their duties. There were a few suggestions, however, that shift work was sometimes disliked, particularly by married men.

They like it. It gives them authority. (A metal goods firm.)

They work in a supervisory capacity. They are not very keen on shift work. (Chemical manufacturer.)

Yes. If he has it in him, he likes it. (Metal manufacturer.)

We recruit specially for the supervision of plant under construction.

They are quite happy, though the snag in this type of work arises if a man marries. They move about a good deal to different areas.

MANAGEMENTS' APPRAISAL OF GRADUATES

THE reasons why firms took on graduates, and the kind of qualifications they sought, were considered in Chapter I. The answers to various questions elsewhere in the survey have also given an indication of the attitude of managements to graduates. More specifically, members of management were asked how they thought graduates compared with non-graduates doing similar work. The question asked was: *After, say, two or three years with the firm, how do university men who have graduated since the war compare with others of similar age doing comparable work: intellectually; in their attitude to other people; in their attitude to the kinds of work which they, as graduates, should be asked to undertake; and in their attitude to the job in hand?*

Many members of management found it difficult or impossible to make such comparisons; more than a third felt unable to answer any part of the question. Some firms or departments of firms had no graduates and non-graduates of the same age doing similar work. Some members of management felt that others who had closer contact with graduates could answer more adequately. A number felt that it was impossible to generalise, because the answer depended largely on the individuals concerned.

Most members of management considered graduates intellectually superior to non-graduates; hardly any thought them inferior. However, about half thought no distinction could be made regarding attitudes to other people, attitudes to the kinds of work they should do, or attitudes to the job in hand. The views of those in the gas boards did not differ from those in the firms. Graduates were unfavourably compared with non-graduates most often regarding attitudes to the kinds of work they should undertake. In nine firms, however, one or more members of management thought that in all these respects graduates were better than non-graduates; other members of management disagreed with this opinion in three of the firms.

Table 28 shows the answers of the seventy-five members of management who replied to part or the whole of the question:

TABLE 28

COMPARISON BETWEEN GRADUATES AND NON-GRADUATES

	Better		The same		Inferior	
	Arts	Science/ Technology	Arts	Science/ Technology	Arts	Science/ Technology
	No.	No.	No.	No.	No.	No.
Intellectual abilities .	10	33	3	13	—	1
Attitude to people .	6	15	5	26	1	6
Attitude to kinds of work	5	8	5	23	3	14
Attitude to job in hand	4	15	6	29	1	6

Three-quarters of the members of management replying to the part of the question dealing with intellectual abilities considered that intellectually graduates compared favourably with non-graduates. Their comments were mainly to the effect that the graduate had a lead by virtue of his qualifications and the particular kind of education he had received:

The graduate can sit round a conference table, express his views, and persuade you that he's right.

Higher National Certificate men do well, but if I look down the list it's the degree men's names I see who are likely to become heads of departments.

If a good degree man sees some roofing is wrong, he can make drawings and prove his point: a non-degree man may see it's wrong, but can't tell you why.

Comments suggesting that graduates were intellectually better were made by one or more members of management in twenty-five firms in respect of scientists or technologists, and in eight firms in respect of arts graduates.

In ten firms, one or more members of management thought that no general distinction could be made between the intellectual qualities of graduate scientists or technologists and non-graduates doing comparable work. Only one member of management thought they compared unfavourably. In three firms, a member of management said that arts graduates were not in general different from non-graduates.

A third of those replying, that is, fifteen members of management in thirteen firms, thought that graduate scientists or technologists were better than non-graduates in their attitude to people; just over half, twenty-six managers in seventeen firms, thought there was little to choose between them; in six firms, managers thought graduates were inferior to non-graduates in this respect. With regard to arts graduates, opinion was almost equally divided between those who thought they were better than non-graduates and those who thought they were the same; one member of management thought they were inferior.

A number of those who thought that graduates were better in their attitude to other people commented that most graduates were good mixers at all levels:

Even the most Cambridge graduates get on better with those on the shop floor than do the non-graduates.

This was attributed on the one hand to the view that graduates no longer suffered from snobbishness, and on the other to the view that very often those who had come up the hard way either "bore the scars of the battle" or were "soured, embittered, and parochial".

In six firms, a member of management considered that scientists or technologists were inferior to non-graduates in their attitude to people, and one manager thought that arts graduates were inferior in this. In all but one case, someone else in the firm expressed a different view.

Half the members of management considered that graduate

scientists or technologists in general compared neither favourably nor unfavourably with non-graduates in their attitude to the kind of work which they should be asked to undertake; a third thought they were worse in this respect; a few thought they were better. Among those who commented on arts graduates equal numbers thought they were the same or better than comparable non-graduates; a few thought they were inferior.

There was some feeling that technicians and sandwich-scheme men scored over full-time graduates because of their practical experience of industry: graduates sometimes suffered disillusionment when they discovered how little of the knowledge they had acquired at a university was of immediate practical use in industry and they were sometimes slow to adjust themselves. Some firms found that graduates were not keen on routine work and tended to concentrate only on what interested them.

As has been seen, some thought that graduates disliked shift work; but it may be noted that no graduate mentioned an active dislike of shift work.

Arts graduates came in for a small amount of critical comment, for instance:

I am disillusioned about arts graduates. . . . They suffer from a lack of humility.

They are not prepared to knuckle under.

About a third of the members of management thought that graduates compared well with non-graduates in their attitudes to the job in hand; more than half said that no general distinction could be made; a few thought graduates were inferior. The same division of opinion applied both with regard to science or technology and arts graduates. Comments of those who considered graduates were better included:

They won't take no for an answer as to why something doesn't work.

They are articulate in expressing themselves.

They are conscientious, and don't mind overtime when necessary, even when they don't get paid for it.

Determining salaries

Managements were asked how they determined the salaries which should be paid to graduates, and whether, because of his academic qualification, a graduate was paid more than a non-graduate contemporary. A distinction was made between those firms which had a salaries policy relating to all salaried staff, and those which had not.

Firms with a general salaries policy. Twenty-seven of the forty-three undertakings had a salaries policy relating to all salaried staff. These included all but one of the undertakings with 10,000 employees or more (including the four gas boards), two-thirds of the medium-size firms, and a quarter of the firms with under 2,000 employees.

Three-quarters of the undertakings said that on entry a graduate's academic qualifications placed him higher in the scale relative to his age. This initial advantage over the non-graduate, however, was generally not maintained for more than a few years. Three years after the graduate had taken up his first job, whether on entry or after training, only seven firms continued to pay him more than his contemporary simply on the strength of his degree. Two gas boards paid more at the start but did not make any distinction later on. A number of members of management commented, however, that on his merits a graduate might progress more rapidly than a non-graduate to higher positions. The answers are summarised in Table 29.

FIRMS WITH GENERAL SALARIES POLICY

TABLE 29

Graduates paid:	Size of firms (number of employees)					Total firms
	Under 500	500– 1,999	2,000– 4,999	5,000– 9,999	10,000 or over	
More at start, then according to ability	I	I	2	3	7	14
More at start and beyond three years	—	I	3	3	—	7
On same basis as contemporary throughout . . .	—	—	2	—	4	6
	I	2	7	6	II	27

Sixteen firms said they did not have a salaries policy relating to all salaried staff; only two of these employed more than 5,000. The distinction between the two groups is in some ways unsatisfactory because some firms in each said that they had a separate scheme for graduates, whether or not this was related to a more general policy. Moreover, in each group the graduate's actual starting salary was determined by a variety of circumstances, whether or not he was afterwards given a place in a definite salary scale.

These managements were asked: *Does the academic qualification command a higher salary than that of another man of comparable age and doing similar work?* The form of the question differed from that asked in firms with a general salaries policy, and did not specify at what stage in the graduate's career the comparison should be made. Half said that salaries were higher, but two added that this applied only at the start and that graduates were later paid according to the job they were doing or their ability. One firm said that graduates were paid less than their contemporaries when they entered the firm, but they progressed more rapidly. The other firms said that the academic qualification did not in itself give graduates a higher salary, which was decided on such factors as merit and responsibility.

Reasons for paying graduates more

Most firms paid graduates more at the start than non-graduate contemporaries, but after three years a degree did not in itself usually imply a higher salary. The graduate was then treated on the same basis as his contemporaries. (Prospects of advancement are considered later in this chapter.)

From the comments of managements it is clear that the initial advantage was often given to graduates because it was considered necessary in order to attract them to the firm:

We pay what we must to attract them.

Certain types of graduates are rare birds and we have to pay more.

Salaries are always elastic. We are prepared to buy a good man.

Most of the firms which gave the graduate an initial advantage in salary did not maintain the differentiation on this basis. For example:

We have definite remuneration for the training period, followed by a three-year agreement involving regular salary increases. After that it is a matter of bargaining between a man and his director. The graduate scale is separate from the salaries policy for the rest of the firm. It is intended to attract graduates. Others come in and progress

o

according to ability. After a certain period there is no difference in treatment.

Salary arrangements for graduates are made by a points assessment for all kinds and conditions of graduates, converted into a salary range. The initial salary is inflated because of competition for graduate recruits, so the increments don't seem so good afterwards.

In most firms after an initial period, and in some firms throughout, graduates were treated on the same basis as their contemporaries with regard to salary. The salary paid was determined according to the job or the merits of the individual:

We determine salary by a merit assessment, taking certain national agreements into account, and a points assessment for all kinds and conditions of graduates. No salary advantage is given to the graduate as such at any stage. Degrees are lost in the assessment.

We take on graduates at what is felt to be a reasonable salary for the position. It is generally a matter of negotiation.

It depends on the job they are doing. We don't pay by age, but have classified all jobs and put them into three groups with minimum and maximum salaries. If, for instance, a graduate has a supervisory job he is paid accordingly. What matters is the job done.

Several firms mentioned the salary scales recommended by professional bodies as providing the basis for determining salary levels for some graduates, although according to the circumstances the actual salary paid might be above this minimum level:

The salary offered to a graduate has to have relation to the open market value. The professional standard quoted sets a pattern, gives a clue how much to offer.

Difficulties were encountered in some firms which found that they had to pay graduates more than non-graduates in order to attract them to the firm, or to stop them being drawn away:

We do as much as we can, selecting bright boys from our works and paying for technical evening courses, but we've had to go outside and bring in a few graduates. . . . Salary is also a problem. On production, key men who have worked their way up are only getting the salary that graduates will expect on starting.

If we keep on increasing salary to prevent people being tempted away, this upsets the salary structure.

Fifteen members of management commented on the position of a man who graduated while he was employed by the firm. Of these, eleven said that he would receive an advance in salary; two said that this would not be automatic, and two that although there would not automatically be an increment because of the academic qualification the chances of promotion would be improved. These policies were broadly in accordance with the attitude of the firms towards graduates recruited externally.

THE ATTITUDE OF GRADUATES

MEN in the graduate interviews were asked whether on the whole they thought they were intelligently employed by the firm about which were interviewed, that is, by the first industrial firm which they entered as a career after leaving their university: (a) in their first job on entry, or, if given a training course, on completion of training; and (b) at the time of the interview, or, if they had left this first firm, at the time of leaving. They were also asked whether they had ever done work which they felt that they should not as graduates have been asked by their employer to undertake.

Most graduates said that they were on the whole intelligently employed, and most said that they had never done work which they felt they should not have been asked to undertake. In their first job, whether on entry or after training, 76 per cent said that they were on the whole intelligently employed; at the time of the interview, or when they left the firm, the comparable figure was 80 per cent. Three-quarters of them said that at no time while they were with their first industrial firm had they done work which they felt that they, as graduates, should not have been asked to undertake.

The interviews were held some four and a half years after the men graduated. At that time, 57 per cent were still with the first industrial firm they had entered as career employment after leaving their university. The remaining 43 per cent had had a change of job at some point or other during this period. Eight per cent had come into industry from other employment; 22 per cent had moved from one industrial firm to another; and 13 per cent had left industry altogether.

Of those who had remained with their first "career employment" firm, 88 per cent said they were intelligently employed at the time of the interview, compared with 67 per cent of those

who had changed their job. Eighty-five per cent of the graduates
in the case studies said that they had on the whole been intelligently
employed since they entered the firm which they were then with,
whether or not it was their first since graduation. Similarly, in the
graduate interviews the proportion of men who said they had
never done unsuitable work was higher among those who remained with their first firm than among those who changed their
employment. But the difference, 79 per cent against 70 per cent,
was less striking. In the case studies, 88 per cent said they had
never done work which they felt they should not have been asked
to undertake.

Training and intelligent employment

Eighty per cent of the graduates who were given a training
course said they were intelligently employed in the first job after
its completion; this compares with 74 per cent of those who were
not given a training course. A few men left their firm during the
training course or on its completion; of those who took up a first
job on completion of a training course only 13 per cent said they
were not intelligently employed. The length of training courses
made no difference to the proportions who said they were intelligently employed on its conclusion.

This difference of 6 per cent is not very great, and cannot be
taken to indicate that graduates who were given a training course
were in general better employed in the long run than those who
were not. For instance, men who did not take up their first job
until after a training course had had time to settle down in the
firm, and many of their problems may have been sorted out
during the training period. A true comparison cannot, however,
be made between these men and those who went straight into
their first job on entering the firm. Much clearly depended upon
the individual circumstances, and this is confirmed when analysis
is made according to the graduate's faculty, and the size and
product group of the firm, as shown in Table 30. Those who left
their firm before the completion of training are included.

In each faculty, a higher proportion of those who were given a
training course said they were intelligently employed in their first
job. Whether they had a training course or not, arts graduates
were the least satisfied with their first job, science graduates the
most satisfied.

TABLE 30

GRADUATES INTELLIGENTLY EMPLOYED IN FIRST JOB

	After training course		No training course		Total first job	
	Graduates in group No.	Intelligently employed %	Graduates in group No.	Intelligently employed %	Graduates in group No.	Intelligently employed %
Faculty						
Arts . .	56	73	71	63	127	68
Science . .	71	87	134	80	205	83
Technology .	106	78	123	72	229	75
Firm product*						
Chemicals .	42	79	76	82	118	81
Heavy industry	50	74	79	76	129	75
Electrical engineering .	61	84	69	77	130	80
Consumer goods . .	33	82	21	43	54	67
Others . .	47	81	83	70	130	74
Firm size†						
1–499 . .	13	69	42	79	55	76
500–1,999 .	25	84	37	73	62	77
2,000–4,999 .	28	75	51	80	79	71
5,000–9,999 .	39	79	40	75	79	77
10,000 and over	122	81	133	71	255	76
TOTAL . .	233	80	328	74	561	76

* The composition of product groups is given in Chapter V, page 150.
† The size of firm was not known in every case; the effect on the figures is insignificant.

There is no such consistent pattern, however, in terms of the product and size group of the firms which they entered. The numbers in many of the groups are too small for a significant comparison to be made between those who were given a training course and those who were not. However, in the size group of firms with more than 10,000 employees, the group which accounted for nearly as many graduates as the others put together, there was greater satisfaction among those given a training course.

Taking the total number of graduates in their first job, the proportion satisfied was almost identical in each size group; there was a slight variation between the product groups. The consumer goods category, which showed the greatest difference, contained fewer graduates than the others.

Changes in attitude during employment

At the time of the interview, or when they left their firm, 80 per cent thought that they were on the whole intelligently employed. This compared with 76 per cent who said they were intelligently employed in their first job on entry to the firm or after training. As noted earlier, a higher proportion of those who remained with the industrial firm they entered as their first career employment said they were intelligently employed at the time of the interview.

Table 31 shows the proportions satisfied with their employment at the two points of enquiry, and the proportions who said they

TABLE 31

ATTITUDE OF GRADUATES
(Graduate interviews)

| | Graduates in group* | Intelligently employed | | Never given unsuitable work | Prospects† | |
		In first job	Time of interview (or on leaving firm)		Pay	Position
	No.	%	%	%	%	%
Faculty						
Arts . . .	127	68	75	71	52	53
Science . .	205	83	83	79	65	56
Technology . .	229	75	79	74	61	54
Firm product						
Chemicals . .	118	81	87	71	73	61
Heavy industry .	129	75	71	71	47	42
Electrical engineering .	131	80	84	79	58	54
Consumer goods .	54	67	69	81	57	56
Others . .	129	74	81	79	67	63
Firm size						
1–499 . . .	54	76	78	75	57	56
500–1,999 . .	62	77	77	70	48	48
2,000–4,999 . .	79	78	79	70	62	54
5,000–9,999 . .	79	77	82	81	56	52
10,000 and over .	256	76	81	76	66	57
TOTAL . .	561	76	80	75	60	55

* There were slight variations in the numbers according to the question asked, and the firm size was not known in every case: the effect on the figures is insignificant.

† This section of the table is discussed in detail later (pages 200–206).

had never done unsuitable work; the figures are again presented under faculty, the product and size group of firms. The table also shows graduates' attitudes to their prospects within the firm at the time of the interview or when they left it, a subject which is considered later in this chapter (pages 200-206).

By the time of the interview, or by the time they left the firm, the proportion of arts and technology graduates who said they were intelligently employed had increased; there was no difference in the case of scientists. Some difference remained between the faculties, but it may be noted that the men who said they were not intelligently employed in their first job and had left the firm at that time are also included in the later figures. This may have caused the apparent continuation of the difference between the three faculties, although this was less than in the first job. In the case studies, where the question related to the whole period of employment and all the men were still with the firm about which they were interviewed, there was almost no difference between the proportions of men in the three faculties who said they had on the whole been intelligently employed since they entered the firm. This was in each case some 85 per cent.

In each product and size group of firms, with one exception, more graduates considered they were intelligently employed at the time of the interview or when they left the firm than in their first job. The exception was among firms comprising the heavy industry group (metal trades, shipbuilding and vehicles, and non-electrical engineering), in which a slightly lower proportion were satisfied with their employment at the later stage.

The differences between size groups were again slight. There was some variation according to product group: graduates in the chemicals group showed most satisfaction, in heavy industry and consumer goods the least. The somewhat lower position of the heavy industry group as a whole was due to the markedly lower proportions satisfied in the metal trades and in shipbuilding and vehicles, although the numbers in these sub-groups were too small for this to be statistically significant.

Younger graduates were more often satisfied that they were intelligently employed at the time of the interview or when they left the firm: 84 per cent of those aged about twenty-six or under were satisfied in this respect. This compares with 77 per cent of those aged about twenty-seven to thirty, and 78 per cent of those of about thirty-one or over. Analysis according to the father's occupation group did not show significant differences in attitude.

Unsuitable work

Seventy-five per cent said that they had never done work which, as graduates, they should not have been asked to do. Whether considered by the graduate's faculty or the size and product group of the firm, with the exception of consumer goods, fewer graduates said they had never done unsuitable work than said they were intelligently employed at the time of the interview or when they left the firm. In other words, although a quarter of the men said that at some time they had done unsuitable work, a lower proportion said that they were not intelligently employed at the time of the interview. This may have been because some were no longer doing unsuitable work or because unsuitable work was not in itself always a sufficient reason for a man to say that he was not, on the whole, intelligently employed.

As on other counts, arts graduates complained more often than graduates in the other faculties that they had at some time done unsuitable work; scientists were again the best satisfied. The proportions who said they had never done unsuitable work were relatively low in the chemicals and heavy engineering groups, relatively high in electrical engineering, consumer goods, and others.

Age did not appear to be a significant factor with regard to attitudes to unsuitable work. A rather high proportion of those graduates whose fathers' occupations were classified as "Routine non-manual and skilled manual" felt they had been asked to do work unsuitable for a graduate (29 per cent). The proportions were relatively low in the "Professional and higher administrative" group (19 per cent), and the "Manual other than skilled" group (18 per cent), and close to the average in the fourth group, "Owners, managers, and higher non-manual" (23 per cent).

Reasons for dissatisfaction

Failure to use abilities or qualifications to the full was the reason generally given by graduates who said they were not on the whole intelligently employed or that at some time they had done unsuitable work.

Of the 25 per cent in the graduate interviews who felt that they had at some time done work which they should not have been asked to undertake, two-thirds said that no degree was needed for it; a third, and all the critical case study graduates, referred to routine or sometimes to "menial" work.

The reasons given by graduates for considering that they were on the whole not intelligently employed are classified in Table 32.

TABLE 32

REASONS WHY NOT INTELLIGENTLY EMPLOYED
(Graduate interviews)

	In first job		Time of interview (or on leaving firm)
	On entry (no training course)	After course	
	No.	No.	No.
Work not suited to personal qualifications	2	33	47
Degree not needed	13	23	38
Insufficient training or supervision .	2	11	11
Poor organisation or direction . .	7	2	6
Not enough work	4	5	9
Not enough responsibility . . .	3	1	—

There was a marked difference in emphasis between the replies given by those who had and those who had not been given a training course. Few of those without a course said that the work was not suited to their personal qualifications. But more of them said that a degree was not needed for the work. Since the possession of a degree might be described as a personal qualification, the two answers overlap. Together, they accounted for half the classified replies of those who were not given a training course, three-quarters of those taking up their first job after a training course, and three-quarters of all graduates who felt they were not intelligently employed at the time of the interview or when they left the firm. Typical comments were:

On the job, the technical work is not very great. It is more of a practical nature.

I think I could do more useful work in some other line.

It was not their fault I chose the sales side; if I had chosen the design side I would have done better.

Insufficient training or supervision was the reason given by some men for their belief that they were not intelligently employed. For instance:

> I was put into the development and research department and left to my own devices without further training. After much argument I was put into satisfactory training in a production department.

Poor organisation or direction was mentioned by some men, who generally blamed superiors for the failure to provide intelligent employment. Comments included:

> There was insufficient planning or organisation of effort.
>
> The departmental managers lack the knowledge and imagination to direct the work.
>
> Some people were too busy to help, others too jealous.

A few complained that they were not given enough work to do, that too much time was wasted, or that, after completing training, no position was available.

> This firm has very advanced training ideas, but there is a surfeit of graduates because it has taken on too many for the positions available.
>
> There was no vacancy at the moment, so I was given what was called "necessary office experience".

Finally, a few thought that they were not intelligently employed because they were not given enough responsibility or authority.

> They don't make full use of graduates' capabilities. It may be due to lack of delegation of responsibility. The chief chemist is old-fashioned. He gathers too much under his wing and we can't tie him down about our duties.
>
> I have been by no means as intelligently employed as I ought to have been, at any stage. The type of work I've been doing has been investigating problems and suggesting solutions. There has been great reluctance to allow me to think about these problems. Too often the management start from their own formulations and guess-work solutions and direct me to write the answers accordingly. And it appears like this even when it may not be happening, because I am not given the full background to the problems.

As mentioned earlier, 13 per cent of the men in the case study firms said that, although they had, on the whole, been intelligently employed since they joined the firm, there had at times been ways in which, or occasions when, they were not intelligently used.

The reasons they gave were similar to those listed above, for instance:

> Research is not used to the fullest advantage by the works.

> Often I feel I'm not exploited as much as I might be. I am not kept sufficiently in touch with things that are going on. A lot of technical meetings I'm left out of, and information doesn't get back to me that I should get via the supervisor.

Although only 12 per cent of the graduates in the case studies said they had at some time done work which they thought they should not, as graduates, have been asked to undertake, a further 33 per cent added that at some time they had done work which could have been done by less qualified workers but did not think that this was a sufficient reason why they should not have done it. The following comments illustrate the views expressed:

> It is sometimes necessary because of shortages of less qualified workers.

> There is donkey work in every job. Graduates must realise they can't do higher maths all the time.

PROSPECTS OF ADVANCEMENT

FINALLY, some questions were put both to members of management and to graduates about prospects of promotion and pay, as seen at each level at this early point in the career of the graduate recruit.

Managements' views on promotion

The senior member of management in each of the forty-three undertakings was asked: *Is it possible for the recruit to foresee chances of promotion?* The answers showed that a number of firms felt it was undesirable or impossible to give graduate recruits more than a general idea of the possibilities of promotion. But most suggested that graduates were either told what opportunities there might be, or were themselves in a position to be able to assess their chances. The reluctance of some managements to commit themselves too definitely about the future status of a graduate recruit did not necessarily mean that prospects were not good. One firm, however, acknowledged that prospects were very limited, and another that in some sections at least there was no real field for the graduate recruit. In view of the varied response to the question, the analysis is made according to the view expressed rather than in terms of the size and product groups of the firms.

In twelve firms the management said without qualification or elaboration that it was possible for recruits to foresee the chances of promotion; in four that promotion prospects were made "clear" at the start; and in one that prospects were clearly defined, especially on salary. Twenty-six qualified their answers in various ways.

In eleven firms and the three gas boards that are here relevant, graduates were told what the possibilities were, but only in general terms; or were told that promotion would depend upon their own endeavours. Typical comments were:

> We like to get to know the chap better, get to know his leanings first.

> Undoubtedly. They are clear in that, although we do not have automatic promotion, a man has an opportunity for promotion each year irrespective of his age or when he started, qualified only by his capacity.

In six firms, the management placed the onus of discovering his prospects on the graduate himself. They said that he would discover them from his early experiences in the firm or during training, and from his observation of the progress of others. Several other firms suggested that, in part at least, the graduate must make his own assessment of the chances of promotion. A typical comment (from a large electrical engineering firm) was:

> All promotion is from within, and he only has to look around to see for himself. All senior people have been promoted from inside the organisation; no one has been brought in for twenty years . . . the directors got there through ability.

In four firms, it was said that the prospects of promotion were limited or had not yet been established. In one small building and contracting firm, for instance, the numbers of graduates recruited depended on the scale of contracts undertaken; the permanent staff was small and was supplemented when necessary by temporary additions. Promotion was limited by these circumstances, but some graduates joined to get the experience they required to complete their professional qualifications. The management commented:

> Quite a number come for two or three years and then go. They would be unwise to stop longer unless they saw opportunities for promotion.

A medium-sized electrical engineering firm, which had been unable to recruit the graduates it required for its technical departments, attributed its failure to a number of factors, including the firm's unattractive location and difficulty of access, competition from other firms in more "glamorous" branches of the industry, and the fact that the salaries which the firm could offer to graduates were limited by those earned by non-graduate staff. Although the management regarded graduates as possible material for future executive positions, they thought that the prospects did not appeal:

> Graduates see our equipment and they can't see a career. For instance, a metallurgist could only get so far here; there is no real field open to him. Our product has been made in the same way for eighty years and has no appeal for him. We can't efficiently use his technical knowledge all the time; owing to our size, the work varies with our ups and downs.

Managements' views on pay prospects

The senior member in each undertaking was asked: *Is the possible rate of advancement in salary clear to graduate recruits?* The replies showed that pay prospects were not generally discussed except in broad terms, and were often regarded as being dependent on the position which the graduate achieved in the firm.

In seven firms and the three gas boards that are here relevant the management said without qualification that the possible rate of advancement in salary was clear to graduate recruits; in twelve that graduates were given only general indications, being told the framework within which they might advance according to their ability. Two firms again said that their policy with regard to the employment of graduates was insufficiently developed for them to answer the question. Twenty-one said that the possible rate of advancement in salary was not clear to graduate recruits; four added that graduates were not told because advancement was by aptitude rather than by age or length of service.

The possible future salary of the graduate recruit was in many firms regarded as a concomitant of the position that he might achieve, and some managements suggested that therefore the possible rate of advancement in salary could often not be made "clear". For example:

We say: "If you get on well we will reward you".

It depends on the individual. He can see we are an expanding firm.

Some firms, however, as a matter of policy, did not wish to disclose the level of salaries:

The salary schedule is not public, but graduates are told that there is no bar on progress and that various possible jobs are paid well.

A member of management in one of the gas boards felt that it was necessary to disclose salary prospects in order to attract graduates:

We wouldn't get them otherwise! In research it is a difficulty that promotion is not a clear line, therefore to keep them we must increase salaries without promotion. We have recently discussed that as a very real problem. And continuing in research makes them less suitable for transfer to the production side.

Graduates' views on prospects

Men in the graduate interviews were asked: *Are/were you satisfied with your prospects of further advancement within the firm?* The question related to the first industrial firm, whether or not the men were still with that firm at the time of the interview. Though, as has been seen, there may be difficulties in the way of giving firm undertakings about prospects, young men naturally want, if they can, to see their way ahead, if only so that they can aim, for example, at the size of house and size of family that would be in keeping with their prospects of advancement.

Sixty per cent of the graduates were satisfied with their pay prospects, 56 per cent with their position prospects. Satisfaction with pay and position prospects generally went together; 52 per cent were satisfied on both counts. A third were satisfied with neither their pay nor their position prospects within the firm. Nine per cent were satisfied only with pay prospects, 4 per cent only with position prospects.

As noted earlier, more than a third of these men were at the time of the survey no longer with the firm about which they were interviewed. Seventy-one per cent of those who had remained with their first industrial firm were satisfied with their pay prospects; only 45 per cent of those who had changed their employer had been satisfied in the job they had left. In the case study firms, 65 per cent of the graduates interviewed were satisfied with their prospects of promotion and advancement; all these men were still with the firm about which they were interviewed, whether or not it was their first since graduation. These facts point to the somewhat obvious conclusion that satisfaction with prospects, as with suitable work and intelligent employment, was appreciably higher among those who stayed with their firm than among those who left it.

Table 31 (page 192) shows the proportion of graduates satisfied with their prospects in each faculty and according to the size and product group of the firm which they entered.

Satisfaction with position prospects was much the same in each faculty. There was some variation in views on pay prospects; arts graduates were the least satisfied, scientists the most satisfied. This is reflected in the proportions who were satisfied with neither pay nor position prospects: 43 per cent of arts graduates, 33 per cent of technologists, and 28 per cent of scientists.

There was an appreciable difference between the product groups in the proportion of graduates expressing satisfaction with prospects. Satisfaction with pay prospects was highest among graduates in the group of firms comprising chemicals and allied trades, and this group was nearly at the head of the list in respect of position prospects. In several of the product categories which comprised the group "Others", a high proportion expressed satisfaction on each count; this was particularly so in mining and quarrying, oil, and building and contracting; but the numbers are too small for this to be statistically significant.

Satisfaction was lowest in heavy industry; and this applied to each of the categories making up the group, that is, the metal trades, shipbuilding and vehicles, and non-electrical engineering. The number of graduates in each of these sub-divisions is again too small to permit generalisation.

There was less variation between the different size groups. With regard to both pay and position prospects there was least satisfaction in firms with between 500 and 2,000 employees, and greatest satisfaction in the largest firms, with 10,000 or more employees. The lead of the largest firms, however, was slight.

The salary which a graduate is earning may have a marked effect on his attitude to prospects of further advancement within the firm. The attitude to pay prospects of those graduates who had not changed their job since entering career employment after leaving their university was therefore considered in relation to the salaries which they were earning at the time of interview. Table 33 shows the salaries which these men were earning at the time of the interview, and whether or not they were satisfied with their prospects of further advancement with regard to pay.

TABLE 33

PAY PROSPECTS—GRADUATES STILL WITH FIRST EMPLOYER

Salary at the time of the survey (1954)	Graduates No.	Graduates' pay prospects	
		Satisfied %	Not satisfied %
£200–599 . . .	46	57	43
£600–699 . . .	94	61	39
£700–799 . . .	74	74	26
£800–999 . . .	75	79	21
£1,000 and over . .	28	93	7
Salary partly in kind .	8	100	—
TOTAL . . .	325	71	29

Among graduates who were still with their first industrial employer, the proportion satisfied with pay prospects was highly correlated with the salary being earned. The higher the salary, the higher was the degree of satisfaction with prospects of further advancement within the firm, at least so far as pay was concerned. (No such correlation was possible for those who had changed their job, since their salary at the time of the survey did not relate to their pay prospects when they left their first industrial employment.)

The age of graduates had no direct bearing on the extent of satisfaction with pay prospects. The proportions satisfied with pay prospects at the time of interview (or on leaving the first industrial employer) were respectively 59 per cent, 60 per cent, and 61 per cent in the three groups aged about thirty-one or older, aged about twenty-seven to thirty, and about twenty-six or under at the time of the interview.

At each salary level, the older the graduate the lower the proportion satisfied with pay prospects. However, since the older the graduate the more he tended to earn, and because the higher the salary the greater the degree of satisfaction, the same proportions of older and younger graduates in total were satisfied with their pay prospects.

A slightly higher proportion of married than unmarried men were satisfied with their pay prospects, 62 per cent against 58 per cent. The differences were most marked in the highest salary groups; 72 per cent of married men with a salary of £800 or more were satisfied with their pay prospects, 61 per cent of the unmarried men. This difference may in fact have resulted from a number of factors unconnected with marital status.

There was no statistically significant difference between the percentage of graduates whose father came from different occupation groups who were satisfied with future prospects either as to pay or as to position within the firm.

In the more informal interviews with graduates in the case study firms the question on prospects was: *Did you get at the outset a clear idea of the possibilities of promotion and advancement?* Just over half said that they had, 49 per cent that they had not. There was little variation between the three faculties, but slightly more arts graduates than others said they had a clear idea of the possibilities.

Thirty-five of the 106 men who said they did not at the outset get a clear idea of the possibilities of promotion and advancement elaborated their answer. Twenty-two of these comments were to the effect that they accepted the fact that the firm could not be specific about prospects at that stage; thirteen thought they could have been given more information. Typical comments were:

It obviously depends on what is decided as the result of one's progress. There are no plum jobs dangling, but fresh opportunities occur. The general impression is that one will be treated fairly and justice will be done.

They gave very broad indications, but they always emphasised that the firm cannot be specific. There is no set course of advancement; it depends how one fits into the job.

A small number of graduates, ten in nine firms, commented that although they had got a clear idea of the possibilities at the outset, they now thought they had taken too optimistic a view.

P

Managements were not directly blamed for giving a false impression, but one graduate said:

> The man who painted the rosy picture has left; I feel I was deceived, but perhaps he was deceiving himself too.

In general, the replies show that graduates often did not expect managements to give them at the outset a precise indication of their future position in the firm, but were satisfied if they could gain a broad idea of the opportunities that might be open to them. Most of those who said they gained a clear idea of the possibilities of promotion and advancement at the outset were also satisfied with their future prospects of promotion and advancement at the time of the interview; this was 41 per cent of all those in the firms studied. A quarter said that they did not get a clear idea of the possibilities at the outset, but were satisfied with their prospects at the time of the interview. A quarter had not gained a clear idea at the start, and were dissatisfied with their prospects at the time of the enquiry; 10 per cent had a clear idea of the possibilities at the outset, but were not now satisfied with their prospects. Thus, of all the men interviewed in these firms, 65 per cent were satisfied with their prospects, 35 per cent were not.

The men were not asked to give reasons for their answers, and most replied with a simple affirmative or negative. Enough elaborated, however, to give an indication of the kind of factors which influenced their replies. Similarly, although the question did not refer specifically to pay prospects, some graduates mentioned salaries in their replies.

The most frequent comment was that prospects of further promotion and advancement were limited by the circumstances of the firm or the department, for instance promotion depended upon someone vacating a more senior post. A number of graduates who made comments of this type were engaged in specialised fields, particularly research:

> It is difficult to answer. Promotion in the strict sense doesn't apply in research. Should I be successful, I would probably get an increase in salary, but not a move up. But I think I am satisfied.

> I am satisfied with my prospects, though as an analyst and the head of my department I cannot improve my position except by moving away from analytical work.

Some of the graduates who thought their prospects were limited by present circumstances saw possibilities of progress by transfer within the firm, or through the development of their department:

> If I stay in my present position the prospects are not good; if I am transferred to production, the outlook might be better. How does one know how the firm will develop? If the firm decides to expand my department my prospects would be affected for the better; otherwise, no.

> I am satisfied because I have been able to make the change from the research department to the engineering side.

Unsure prospects of promotion and advancement were for some balanced by other factors such as the value of the job as experience, its vocational interest, or its higher pay:

> I think the prospects here are not very bright. I didn't come with that intention; I came for the experience.

> I am more or less satisfied with the prospects, fifty-fifty. If you go into the works as a research chemist you have better chances; but I prefer to stay in research, and in this firm the possibilities of advancement in research are more limited.

> I can't get any further here unless something happens to my superior, or the department expands. I don't expect either, but I am satisfied. The pay will increase for eight years.

A few men, on the other hand, were better satisfied with prospects of position than of pay:

> I am satisfied, but the rate of financial progress is very slow.

> I could get a higher salary elsewhere, but less security, and the eventual prospects would probably not be as good.

A few graduates, though fairly satisfied with their prospects, expressed doubts about aspects other than those considered:

> A person like myself is inexperienced and has to serve a kind of apprenticeship before being put to a position of responsibility. My personal grievance is that one gets no idea of the length of such apprenticeship; I don't feel that my work and capability is kept under review.

> The whole problem is tied up with the kind of firm it is—a private company—and things like promotion depend entirely on the whim

of the directors, both with regard to the degree of responsibility and to salary.

I have some doubts of my own ability, but I may lose those with more experience.

A relatively small number added that because of dissatisfaction with prospects they were considering leaving their firm, or had at some time considered doing so.

SUMMING UP

THE main impression gained from this examination of managements' attitudes is that graduates were, like their non-graduate contemporaries, generally regarded primarily as individuals. Most members of management who felt able to comment thought that, after a few years in the firm, graduates were intellectually better than their non-graduate contemporaries doing similar work; but that in other ways they were generally not better than non-graduates. Half the members of management who answered the question thought no general distinction could be made between graduates and non-graduates in their attitudes to other people, to the kind of work they should do and to the job in hand. In their attitude to the kind of work they should do, graduates were unfavourably compared with non-graduates by a third of those replying. In a number of firms, however, members of management considered that graduates were in all these ways better than their non-graduate contemporaries.

Although many firms paid graduates more than their contemporaries at the start, this was often not because the graduate was considered to be of greater immediate value. Rather, it reflected the competitive price which had to be paid to attract the graduate. After a few years, most firms paid graduates on the same basis as their non-graduate contemporaries.

Most members of management considered that on entering industry it was often desirable for graduates to do the same work as non-graduate contemporaries, usually to provide training and experience, but occasionally for other reasons. A few firms said that graduates should not do the same work as non-graduates, usually because they took on graduates for a different type or more advanced grade of job. Sometimes it was said that on entering industry graduates had insufficient practical knowledge and experience to do the same work as their non-graduate contemporaries who had been some time in industry.

Science or technology graduates were seldom assigned to non-technical first jobs, and then usually only in the course of training or on entering sales departments. Arts graduates were seldom used to relieve the scientific and technical staff of administrative matters, although economists and statisticians were occasionally used in this way.

In a number of firms technology graduates were sometimes assigned to the routine supervision and control of plant. In some, this "routine" work was a skilled and responsible function which could be undertaken only by an experienced graduate. Some firms said this might form part of training. Other firms suggested that the greater part of their work might be regarded as routine, and that some routine supervision was inevitable. In the view of members of management, supervision work was often liked by the graduates concerned or, if not popular, appreciated as being a necessary part of their duties. There were a few suggestions that shift work was sometimes disliked, particularly by married men. There was nothing in the replies of management to suggest that graduates' abilities were wasted when they did this type of work. Indeed, if plant is complex and costly, as it tends to be nowadays, there is a strong case for its supervision by highly-trained people able to get the maximum return from it; and in general this type of work is coming increasingly to be regarded as the high road to management for technologists.

Most graduates thought they were on the whole intelligently employed by their first industrial firm, and most said they had never done work which they felt they should not, as graduates, have been asked to undertake. The reasons given by those who were critical were generally that their abilities or qualifications were not used to the full. In commenting on this and allied matters, graduates showed themselves to be markedly objective and understanding of the position in which their employers were placed. In general, therefore, their replies serve as a reliable check on the outcome of the policy and practices followed.

Many firms did not feel able to give graduate recruits more than a general idea of the possibilities of promotion, although most suggested that graduates were either told what opportunities there might be, or were themselves in a position to assess their chances.

Pay prospects were not generally discussed except in broad terms, and were often regarded as being dependent on the position which the graduates might achieve.

Sixty per cent of the graduates were satisfied with their pay prospects within the firm, fifty-six per cent with their position prospects. Half were satisfied with both, a third with neither. The most frequent reason for dissatisfaction expressed by those who commented was that prospects were limited by the circumstances of the firm or the department. There was only a limited number of jobs to which they could be promoted, and their prospects depended upon one of these falling vacant; this applied particularly to research. The value of the job as experience, its vocational interest, or the higher pay it commanded were factors which sometimes balanced dissatisfaction with prospects of promotion and advancement. Many other factors, though not mentioned, would, of course, also affect the assessment of prospects. Besides those of individual psychology, those arising, for example, from size of family, dependent relatives or possession of private means, would also influence the answer of a graduate in replying to these questions.

What evidence there is suggests that many graduates shared the view of managements that pay prospects were in the main dependent on position prospects. Clearly there was a very close relationship between the two.

Whatever considerations may have influenced the graduates' assessment, there was a marked difference in attitude between those graduates who had entered industry as their first post-university career employment and had remained with the same firm until the time of the interview, and those who had changed their job. Satisfaction with pay prospects and regarding suitable work and intelligent employment was appreciably higher among those who stayed with this first firm, as shown in Table 34.

TABLE 34

SATISFIED GRADUATES

	Still with first employer %	Changed employer %
Intelligent employment .	88	67
Suitable work . . .	79	70
Pay prospects . . .	71	45

Certain general relationships emerge from a consideration of graduates according to their faculty and the size and product group of their firm. The proportion who said that they were intelligently employed was in most cases higher at the time of the interview or when they left the firm than it was in the initial job on entry or after training. There was a close relationship in each group between suitable work and intelligent employment; usually, more said that they had at some time done unsuitable work than that they were not on the whole intelligently employed. Pay and position prospects were closely related. No direct association was apparent between intelligent employment, suitable work and prospects. On each count, arts graduates were the least satisfied, technologists were close to average, and scientists above it.

Men in the heavy industry product group were less satisfied than the average on each count, particularly on pay and position prospects. This group comprised the metal trades, shipbuilding and vehicles, and non-electrical engineering. Men in the chemicals and allied trades were more satisfied than the average on each count except unsuitable work; there was particularly high satisfaction with pay prospects. In the electrical engineering group, satisfaction was above average on intelligent employment and suitable work, but slightly below average on pay and position prospects. There were wide variations in the consumer goods group, which was below average on intelligent employment, above average on suitable work, and close to the average on prospects. The "Others" product category taken as a whole was well above average on pay and position prospects. This, however, is composed of a wide range of industries: mining and quarrying, oil, miscellaneous non-metalliferous manufacturing, building and contracting, and public utilities. Miscellaneous non-metalliferous manufacturing was below average for satisfaction with pay prospects, and the public utilities markedly below average for satisfaction with position prospects.

Age, marital status and father's occupation were shown not to have a significant bearing on attitudes to employment and prospects.

There was little variation between size groups in the proportion of graduates satisfied that they were intelligently employed, but there were variations regarding suitable work and prospects. In firms with 10,000 or more employees, which contained nearly half the graduates in the sample, satisfaction was above the average on pay prospects, slightly above on position prospects, and average on suitable work. Firms with 5,000–10,000 employees were above average on suitable work, and below average on pay and position prospects. Firms with 2,000–5,000 employees were below average on suitable work and average on intelligent employment and prospects. In the group of firms with between 500 and 2,000 employees, graduates were less satisfied than the average on both suitable work and prospects. In firms with under 500 employees, satisfaction was close to the average on each count.

Evidence given in this chapter suggests that both managers and graduates were on the whole satisfied with the use made of graduates' abilities. Some graduates, however, had reservations, particularly on their prospects of pay and promotion within the firm. The explanation for this generally lay in the circumstances of the individual case, and on the basis of the available evidence it is difficult if not impossible to say whether such dissatisfaction arose because of some avoidable fault either on the part of managements or graduates themselves. The indications given in this chapter, however, may suggest ways of overcoming such difficulties as arise.

With this review of the employment of graduates as seen some three or four years after joining their firm, this enquiry is brought to an end. It has traced the progress of the graduates from their student days when they were thinking of a career in industry, through recruitment, selection, introduction to the firm and training, to the first job. It has also indicated the policy and practice of some industrial undertakings in seeking men from the universities.

CHAPTER VII

SUMMARY AND CONCLUSIONS

THIS report has set out the results of an enquiry into "the policy and practice of British industrial undertakings in respect of the recruitment, training and employment of university graduates".

What follows is not a miniature of the report: it attempts only to present its main findings and to draw some general conclusions from them.

The purpose of the enquiry

The underlying reason for undertaking this enquiry was concern for the need to improve industrial efficiency in this country. This could not be achieved without the employment by industry of increasing numbers of men capable of responding to the highest levels of training. But since the war a larger proportion than ever before of the nation's most intelligent children have been going on to a university, and it is therefore to the universities that industry is having increasingly to look for the men of the calibre it needs.

The immediate reason for undertaking the enquiry was to examine how industry was adjusting itself to this closer relationship with the universities. To this end, it was decided to examine how post-war graduates who chose to go into industry were recruited, selected, trained and set to work, and to match this with an examination of the policy and practice of individual firms in taking on men from the universities. The enquiry, in short, attempted to throw light on educational policy and on questions relating to the right and intelligent use of scarce human resources.

Scope and methods

The enquiry was carried out by means of two sample surveys, one of graduates in industry and the other of industrial undertakings. Both were sub-samples of a larger one, of some 4,000 graduates, the subject of a related report already published, on the employment entered by university men.

The random sample of graduates, which is representative in the statistical sense, included some 600 men, who took their degree in 1950. They were typical of those leaving the universities at that time: many were older than the normal run and had seen war service, 22 per cent had read for a degree in an arts subject, 37 per cent were scientists and 41 per cent were technologists. They were all interviewed about their first job in industry after leaving their university. The questions put to them were mostly of a factual kind.

The sample of industrial undertakings was composed of forty-seven firms in the private sector of industry situated in various parts of Great Britain. They were selected at random from the 700 odd firms to which had gone graduates in the main sample. To these were added four area gas boards, selected deliberately, to provide examples of policy and practice in a nationalised industry. The sub-sample of firms cannot be regarded as representative in the statistical sense (engineering and building and contracting are over-represented), but the evidence from both sub-samples suggests that it is representative enough to be taken alongside the larger one, of graduates.

One hundred and thirty-four members of management were interviewed in these undertakings, together with a few (some 200 altogether) of their post-war graduate recruits. Besides factual questions about the policy and practice of these firms, some questions were asked seeking views on these and allied subjects raised by the questions put at each level. The evidence derived from these "case studies" of firms serves to illustrate, and, as it were, to bring to life the somewhat dry but statistically reliable facts derived from the larger sample.

In attempting to examine, within the compass of one survey, a wide sweep of subjects bearing on the policy and practice of industry in taking on university graduates, it has been possible to achieve only a sketch, and a sketch painted largely by graduate recruits to industry, and to a much less extent by management. The results of the enquiry must be considered in the light of these limitations. They convey, nevertheless, some impression of the state of graduate recruitment, training and employment at a given juncture for the country as a whole.

The first part of the report is devoted to those aspects of the enquiry most closely touching the new relationship between industry and the universities: an examination of the views of the undertakings on the basic question of policy whether to recruit graduates, of the steps taken by those who had decided to do so; and of their views on university education for industry.

The remainder of the report is concerned with policy and practice from the stage when the employer is confronted with a possible candidate: the methods adopted in selecting graduates, in introducing them to the firm and in training them, and, finally, with an assessment of the position as seen both by members of management and by graduates, when the graduates were in their first job.

Size, product and graduate strength of the firms

There was a very wide variation, both in size and in product, in the fifty-one undertakings studied, and in their graduate strength. At one end of the scale there were three with less than a hundred employees and, at the other, nine, besides four gas boards, with 10,000 or more. Their activities ranged from building to electrical engineering, from smelting metal to the manufacture of chemicals. At the time of the survey, in the winter of 1954-55, three had no graduates (though each had had one for a time); twenty, including two gas boards, had fifty or more, and six had several hundred.

Broadly, the graduate strength increased more than proportionately with the size of the firm, and with the complexity of its processes and products. It was also closely related to the time during which graduates had been recruited. Twenty-one firms and the gas boards had adopted a deliberate policy to recruit graduates only since the end of the war. Most of these twenty-one were smaller and had a much less substantial graduate strength than the eighteen firms which had adopted a policy of this kind at an earlier stage.

RECRUITMENT POLICY

FORTY-THREE of the undertakings proved to have a deliberate policy to recruit graduates, though they varied in their enthusiasm for it.

All but one of these had some graduate scientists or technologists, a few several hundred; and almost all of them gave as a reason for recruiting them that they needed the knowledge they had acquired. Only half gave as a reason their value as potential managers.

The employment of arts graduates was on a much smaller scale,

was generally less well established and was confined to fewer
firms. Thirty-two undertakings had some arts graduates but of
these only five had more than twenty-five, and a few were giving
them up. About a third recruited them with the possibility in
mind of their eventual promotion to management, the remainder
for somewhat limited or specialist purposes, such as accountancy,
at least in the first instance.

Eight firms, about a sixth of this sample of fifty-one undertakings, employed graduates only incidentally or unwittingly.
Five were small firms and three were family firms. They argued
that graduates were unsuited to or not needed in the firm or that
the firm could not offer suitable conditions and prospects to them.

Much emphasis was given by the employers interviewed to the
importance of personal qualities. This was often reinforced by a
distinct anti-academic bias, which usually took the form of an
aversion from "brilliance" or a First Class Honours degree.
Personal qualities rather than paper qualifications seemed to
engage their attention. The personal qualities sought first and
foremost were, broadly, those having to do with personal relationships, such as ability to get on with and eventually to lead others.
These qualities were not always found in the graduates eventually
recruited. This was sometimes attributed to the lack of residential
accommodation at many universities—a matter which is now
receiving increasing attention.

The academic standards sought varied considerably, both with
the product and size of the firm. It was in the chemical and allied
trades, electrical engineering and in vehicles and aircraft construction, which mostly had large numbers of graduates, that
higher academic achievements were most frequently sought, and
in building and contracting and the gas boards least frequently
sought. Though only fifteen firms preferred, if they could, to
recruit science and technology graduates with a First or a Second
Class Honours degree both for research and for production, these
fifteen included most of the major claimants.

Again, all the major claimants for graduates undertook regular
periodic assessments of their recruitment needs. Those with only
a few graduates did not generally do so but kept their intake to
some fixed figure, or filled vacancies as they arose.

Altogether, the undertakings displayed a wide variation in their
attitude to the employment of graduates. About a third, mostly

preferring to recruit men with a good Honours degree, and including most of the major claimants for graduates, had a decidedly positive attitude: they wanted graduates as such and did not recruit them solely because they were "bright" or as substitutes for other types of qualified men. Another third looked to the universities primarily as a market for "good brains". Another third recruited with varying degrees of reluctance: some of these regarded graduates as less well suited to their needs than other types of qualified men, others regarded them as unsuited to their needs.

Broadly, the numbers of university graduates on the strength, the academic standard aimed at in bringing in new graduates, and the regularity of the steps taken to assess need, run together with the size of the firm. (The correlation of graduate strength with the size of firm is borne out by the larger graduate sample.) Moreover, as has been seen, though there were exceptions the number of graduates increased more than proportionately with the size of firm. These figures, of course, relate only to graduates; they do not include non-graduates with professional or other qualifications. Nevertheless, they bear closely on the argument, now being pressed with increasing vigour, that the progress of an undertaking (and size is one measure of it) is clearly related to its use of qualified men. This argument, as applied to the size of an undertaking, expressed very broadly and without any necessary qualification, would suggest that an undertaking will be more successful and therefore increase in size because it has a high proportion of qualified men on its books: not that it has a high proportion of qualified men on its books because it is large.

Assessment of need

The assessment of the number and kinds of staff needed immediately or in the future is a much more complicated process for industry than for the Civil Service or teaching, for example. There are more elements to be assessed and some are not easily predictable. Nevertheless, since industry is the largest competitor for scarce human resources, it has a particularly heavy obligation not to use any more university men than it really needs.

The survey shows that the general practice, though less common in smaller firms, was not to differentiate the qualifications needed for each individual vacancy, but to express them, as it were, in terms of the factors common to a range of possible vacancies. A broad specification was due, no doubt, in part to the importance attached to personal qualities, which do not lend themselves readily to precise definition in terms of vacancies to be filled. In part it may also have been due to the fact that, when training was to follow recruitment, the actual vacancies to be filled could not always be known at the stage of assessing needs. But the main reason was probably the eligibility of non-graduates over a wide field: only five firms, mostly with a small number of graduates, would not consider other candidates for the work for which they recruited graduates.

For much of their production and administrative or non-technical work and for some of their research work, most firms did not regard the recruitment of graduates as essential. For this work, the qualifications required could be and were stated in terms wider than those that would be called for if university men alone were considered. Steps may be taken (and were sometimes said to be taken) at a later stage, for example during training, to distinguish among the graduates and others recruited those of good, indifferent or poor quality. But, taken in itself, this over-lapping of the types of men acceptable for any given work opens up possibilities that the best qualified are not used to the full extent of their capacities, at least in the initial stages of their career.

The best safeguard against any waste of this sort must be a careful grading of the work on which graduates and non-graduates are set. An accurate assessment of the responsibilities carried provides a yardstick against which to measure performance.

Recruitment campaigns

Twelve firms, most of them with only a few graduates, some specially well-placed to attract them, were entirely satisfied with both the calibre and the numbers of the graduates they were getting. The rest had reservations of one sort and another, varying according to the individual circumstances of the firm.

Many firms commented on the shortage of graduates. The recruitment campaigns of most of the firms needing more than an occasional one or two graduates appear to have been conducted under a sense of pressure. The tactics employed became more complex, and were more heavily concentrated on universities, the larger the size of the undertaking. These campaigns are evidence of the extent to which industry recognises the need to employ qualified men. But the form they take must be, nevertheless, a matter of much concern since they affect university teaching staff as well as students, and not only those eventually secured for industry. The invasion of university life by an almost endless procession of talent scouts seeking to recruit scientists and technologists, is likely to be, to say the least, disturbing. The only solution is a long-term one—more graduate scientists and technologists. The universities' new programme of expansion will help towards this. In the short run, the larger firms, which are conducting these recruitment campaigns and setting the pace, might consider whether there is anything they could do to mitigate their impact on university life.

UNIVERSITY EDUCATION FOR INDUSTRY

THIS problem of increasing graduate manpower is closely related to the central problem of the new relationship of industry to the universities—reconciling the conflict between industry's specialised interests in certain fields of knowledge, and the traditional functions of a university as a seat of learning for its own sake and in all its disciplines.

The answers to questions put to members of management on university education and preparation for industry underline the considerable differences in attitude to the employment of graduates displayed by the fifty-one undertakings studied. To the opening question whether a university education, as compared, for example, with a technical college education, had advantages for industry, seventy, half the members of management, said "Yes", fifty-one would not commit themselves either way and eight said "No". The metal manufacturers, the metal goods manufacturers, and, but to a lesser extent, the builders and civil engineers, were slightly more inclined to non-committal or negative replies than the others: they tended to have relatively few graduates. Those in firms with fifty or more graduates agreed much more often that a university education had advantages over others for industry.

The relative advantages were most frequently considered to be social (in the development of personality), or educational, in the broadest sense (in the training of the mind). Only five members of management, some 4 per cent, said that they thought the relative advantage lay in any strictly academic superiority, that is, superiority of knowledge acquired. In answering the question, most of the reservations also had to do with issues bearing on the development of personality. Members of management emphasised their concern with them. The graduates were at one with management in this respect.

What the universities could do for industry

A little over half the members of management thought that universities should do more to meet the needs of industry; a third thought that they should or could do no more.

Of over a hundred suggestions put forward by those who thought the universities should do more, the greater number had to do with general objectives of university teaching and questions bearing on curricula in science, technology, and industrial management and allied subjects (these in ascending order of the interest taken in them). Others had to do with the desirability of university teaching staff improving their contact with and knowledge of industry, and of undergraduates acquiring some direct experience of industry before entering it. In fact, half the suggestions put forward were concerned with the need for closer ties with industry.

The views expressed, on whatever count, however, could not be said to amount to any serious challenge to the policy of the universities. No fundamental changes were called for, except by two members of management. The great majority appeared to see no need for any major reassessment. These results must be interpreted, however, in the light of the fact that some members of management stated explicitly, and more implied, that it was for the universities, not for industry, to set the pace.

Undergraduate work

On existing first degree courses, members of management had few comments to make. Only 10 per cent had any suggestion to make bearing on the teaching of science and only 16 per cent on technology. They had practically no suggestions on the teaching of arts men, as such. There seems, in fact, to have been a substantial measure of satisfaction with existing first degree courses, and this was echoed by the graduates themselves. There was also a large measure of acceptance of the principle that the universities should not be asked to cater in first degree courses for the specialised interests of particular industries; and some indication of a trend of opinion in favour of making the established first degree courses in science and technology more "fundamental", reserving any specialisation for post-university courses, and of leaving to industry the responsibility for seeing that the knowledge acquired at the university is fruitfully applied to the work undertaken.

These views were subject, however, to the reservations made about the need for closer contacts with industry by university teaching staff, and for the acquisition of greater knowledge of industry by undergraduates heading for it.

Members of management who wished to ensure that undergraduates, particularly technologists, heading for industry had an opportunity of acquiring some knowledge of its processes and conditions before entering it mostly favoured vacation work as the best means of achieving this. But there is a substantial body of university opinion against vacation work as such. An enquiry concerned primarily with vacation work as a means of preparing undergraduates for a career in industry might well be worth while.

Those members of management who pressed for the development of industrial management as a subject of study at the university level will have been met to some extent by the further provision which has been made for it at certain universities since the time of the survey. Half of those who were concerned to see this development, however, thought that the subject should be studied at the undergraduate stage. But the trend of thought since then has been in favour of reserving the subject until the graduate has had enough industrial experience to profit by study of it—until he is at least about twenty-seven years old.

Higher degrees

An important aspect of the problem of speeding technological advance is the proportion needed of men with academic qualifications beyond the first degree. The higher degree is one form that these additional qualifications can take and one much favoured in the years following the end of the war. Views on higher degrees, however, were in marked contrast to those on first degrees. Six per cent of the graduates interviewed had a higher degree, and, though three-quarters of them felt satisfied that it had been worth while, members of management were more sceptical. Only one in ten employers showed enthusiasm; one in four saw no value at all in a higher degree.

This dissatisfaction has already been recognised. The new arrangements for centralising in the Department of Scientific and Industrial Research awards given for research studentships in science and technology may eventually meet some of the criticisms made. The allied D.S.I.R. arrangements for entirely new advanced course studentships for post-university training in a specialised subject may also help in this direction, besides meeting the suggestions made by members of management that some specialising after a more general degree in science or technology would meet their case.

In sum, apart from questions of shortage of supply, the picture presented shows a fairly substantial degree of satisfaction with the new partnership with the universities. This was somewhat greater, however, in questions having to do with first degree curricula (though problems clearly remained here also) and somewhat less in post-university questions, including the problem of providing most fruitfully for post-university specialisation. In the nature of things this is not surprising. Just as industry first looked to the schools for sixth-form recruits, and then to the universities for first degree people, so it is now having to formulate its needs beyond the first degree stage. These needs relate both to the form and phasing of post-university study and to the proportions in which men of any given standard are required. This opens up the whole question of the proportions of each grade needed in any particular circumstance from the lowest qualified technician to the most highly qualified technologists, a question to which increasing attention must inevitably be given as the pace of technological advance quickens.

SELECTION METHODS

SELECTION, like every other step in the recruitment and employment of graduates, has direct relevance to the efficient use of scarce human resources in its widest context and the efficient harnessing of these resources to industrial progress.

In selecting graduates, the interview was the method adopted by most firms. Intelligence or psychological tests were only very occasionally used in addition. One interview was the most usual: six out of every ten graduates had one interview, three in ten a series. The one interview very often took the form of a panel or board, particularly in larger firms and those employing more than fifty graduates; and a series of interviews often included a panel or board.

Selection was generally in the hands of people with wide experience of selection or with direct knowledge of the field in which the candidate might be going to work. Only a minority of firms used specialised selection techniques although some consulted people with training in them or saw that they were present at interviews.

Both the adoption of the interview as such and the way it was conducted were justified by employers on the ground that they were best suited to the assessment of personal qualities. Both managements and graduates appeared satisfied with the interview, in whatever form it took, though reservations were made by some at both levels.

Selection techniques are still only in their infancy and there is no general body of opinion in favour of one particular method (though there is substantial support for the panel). As some members of management recognised, this does not mean that the effectiveness of any particular choice cannot be tested at some later stage in the light of progress made by the chosen candidate. Systematic periodic checks of this sort could well be adopted by all firms which have not already done so.

Introduction and training

Graduates enter industry older than their non-graduate contemporaries. Many of them are ignorant of how to attune themselves to their new life and of what to expect. Most of the employers were aware of the need to enable the graduate newcomer to grasp as soon as possible the organisation and structure of the firm and, generally, were alive to the importance of first impressions. But there was a diversity of approach among both employers and graduates to the way in which these needs should be met. Most employers were not in favour of formal introduction schemes; and, in fact, only 22 per cent of the graduates had a formal introduction to their firm. Most of the firms with systematic introduction schemes thought of them as part of their training programme.

Each of the various approaches to introduction encountered in the survey was well liked by some of the graduates who experienced it and most members of management were satisfied with their own approach.

About twice as many graduates were given a training course as were given a formal introduction. Here again, the approach varied. The number given a course was influenced by the product and the size of the firm and by other circumstances, particularly the graduate's faculty. Taking the graduate sample as a whole, about four in every ten were given a training course: one in three of the scientists and just under half the arts men and technologists. Scientists seem, in fact, to have been regarded by managements as relatively well equipped for their work from the outset. Not only did they give a training course less frequently to scientists, but they did not press, in relation to scientists, for vacation work or other opportunities to gain experience of industry before entering it or for the study of industrial management. The knowledge gained by scientists at the university would no doubt lend itself more readily to immediate use in industry and the conditions of work before and after entering industry would be likely to be much more similar for scientists than for others.

The great majority of the graduates who received a training course thought that it was well calculated to fit them for their work, and the employers who gave a course thought they were working on the right lines.

Most of the graduates who did not receive a training course recognised that a formal course was not needed or was not possible in the circumstances of the firm. Only arts graduates felt the lack of a course to any extent, no doubt because many of them would have started without immediately usable knowledge.

It may well be that this large measure of satisfaction among the graduates was closely related to the view they took of the attitude towards them held by the people whom they met when they first joined their firm. Contrary to what might have been expected, they gained on the whole a very favourable impression of this attitude, particularly that of their immediate superiors. The only source of grievance, which was often strongly felt, was lack of opportunity to meet directors and managers. This seems a fair point. It might be remedied by even a brief greeting at some juncture during a newcomer's first few weeks.

Despite this large measure of satisfaction, both the members of management and graduates thought that there was room for improvement in arrangements for introduction and for training. But, by and large, the criticisms and suggestions made, both as regards introduction and as regards training, were not fundamental. They could have been met by a closer and more sustained relationship at both stages between the graduate newcomer and his superiors, so that his needs and difficulties could be more fully appreciated and, if possible, met and the whole process of preparation for work in the firm be made more rewarding both to the graduate and to his employers.

In the first job

This survey is brought to its conclusion with the assessment by the members of management and by the graduates of the situation as it appeared to them two or three years after the graduates' joining the firm.

What emerges first and foremost is that the graduates were not considered or employed as a separate "mandarin" class. They, like their non-graduate contemporaries, were regarded primarily as individuals and treated on their merits. This is the logical outcome of the practice, common to most of the firms, of accepting non-graduates for much of the work for which university men were also recruited. The policy of most of the employers in the salaries and the prospects they offered and the work on which they set graduates all bear this out. (The difficulty of some firms in providing a statement of the number of graduates on their books does so also.)

To attract graduates, many firms paid them more than their contemporaries at the start, but, after a few years, most paid them on the same basis. Most considered that, on entering industry, it was often desirable for graduates to do the same work as their non-graduate contemporaries. Pay prospects were frequently regarded as being dependent on the progress made.

This policy was supported to some extent by the view of those members of management who held that, after a few years in the firm, though graduates were intellectually better than their non-graduate contemporaries doing similar work, there was little to choose between them in other respects. Though this evidence is slight because many members of management felt unable to comment, it is of interest also in relation to the selection policy of universities and their general handling of students.

The graduates, on their side, did not quarrel with this dispensation. Most considered that they had on the whole been intelligently employed and had never done work which they felt they should not, as graduates, have been asked to undertake. These views varied with the graduate's faculty—arts graduates were least satisfied—and his type of firm. They varied also markedly between those who were still with their first industrial employer at the time of the survey and those who had left him. The proportion of the latter who were satisfied under the heads considered (and who formed nearly half the total number of graduates) was considerably less.

Satisfaction with pay prospects varied even more markedly. More than half the graduates who had left their first firm by the time of the survey were not satisfied with their prospects of pay within their first firm, and these were generally recognised as being closely related to prospects of promotion.

As in the other aspects of firms' practice, there was room for improvement in the effectiveness with which graduates were employed in the period studied, that is, during the first three or four years with the firm: and, since industry is the largest single user of graduates, quite small margins there are of proportionately greater significance in relation to the employment of qualified manpower as a whole. It is true, for example, that only 20 per cent of the graduates thought that they had not, on the whole, been intelligently employed. Nevertheless, this represents in real figures some 800 men recruited by industry from one graduation year.

But taken as a whole, the conclusion must be reached that this assessment, as seen through the eyes of members of management— directors, departmental heads, personnel and education officers —as well as of graduate recruits, suggests a remarkable degree of satisfaction at both levels.

THE NEED FOR GRADUATES

THE most important issues arising out of this enquiry fall into two broad groups: those relating to the formulation of the need for graduates and those relating to the use made of the human resources secured.

In considering the formulation of the need for graduates, the first conclusion must be that industrial undertakings varied enormously in the extent to which they had accepted the need to recruit university men. The firms studied provide evidence of this, and the distribution by the product and size of the firm entered by the men in the larger graduate sample drives it home.* This shows that only 10 per cent of the graduates went into firms with under 500 employees, 3 per cent went into firms with under 100 employees; nearly half went into the far fewer firms with 10,000 or more. One in every four went into electrical engineering; one in every five into chemicals and oil; and, at the other end of the scale, one in a hundred into shipbuilding, for example, and much less than this proportion into railway engineering.

It is true, of course, that the need for graduates, or for more highly qualified men generally, varies with the kind of work to be done. But if the high proportion of new employers of graduates among the firms studied and the small graduate strength of these new employers compared to that of old employers be taken as a guide, some impression is gained of the immense increase likely to take place in the number of firms recruiting graduates and in the number of graduates recruited by firms already in the field.

It seems unlikely that, with the possible exception of teaching in universities, the demand from other quarters for graduates will increase proportionately as much as that of industry, which already claimed three out of every ten from those graduating in 1950.† Industry has therefore to look ahead to a relationship with the universities even closer than that which already exists and it will become increasingly important for it continually to re-examine and reassess what kinds of graduates it really wants and in what numbers, especially in view of the changes hoped for in the proportion of students reading for an arts degree or for a science degree and of the major developments now in train in the provision for technological education, both in universities and in colleges of advanced technology. The qualitative and quantitative

* Appendix F, Table F2.
† Office of the Lord President of the Council and Ministry of Labour and National Service. *Scientific and Engineering Manpower in Great Britain.* (H.M.S.O.), 1956. 1s. 6d. Page 8.

aspects of this demand by industry both have their implications for university policy. For university education, the main issues are the scope and content of first degree courses and the form and extent of provision for study after the first degree.

To take, as an example of the need for continual reassessment, the first of these. Broadly speaking, with the exception of reservations made about the study of industrial management, the scope of each faculty—arts, science, technology—was to a large extent accepted by the employers. Since the survey, however, the body of public opinion in favour of a radical reform at least of school, and possibly also of university, curricula, which would break down the barriers that have grown up between the humanities and science, has grown substantially. The argument is a general one: that the scientist and the non-scientist, in whatever walk of life, must be enabled to appreciate each other's methods and approaches. It is applied with particular force to industry.

During the span covered by the survey, the first four years' work only, this issue does not arise in its acute form; and, indeed, the practice, as exemplified in the firms studied, of using arts men only rarely to relieve scientific staff of administrative work and scientists and engineers only rarely on non-technical work seems entirely reasonable at this stage in their career. Later on, however, when more senior positions are in prospect, ability to understand the approach and methods of men of other disciplines and to work with them becomes of increasing importance. How far does industry accept this argument for itself, and what proposals would it have on measures that might be taken by universities to this end?

There is, secondly, the quantitative aspect: the question how many of any particular kind of graduates industry needs to recruit.

Whatever complications may be present, such as shortage of supply, or the smallness of the firm, the essential requirements in reaching an assessment must be measurement of work to be done, and of performance in it. With every advance in industrial science, the range of responsibility to be carried widens and the more important it becomes first, to measure the weight of responsibility carried or to be carried at any point in the range, in short, to undertake accurate job-evaluation; and, secondly, to reach an accurate and objective assessment of the calibre of each member of the staff when measured against the responsibilities he is carrying. Unless this is done, a clear conception of the proportions in which men of any particular calibre are needed is unlikely to be reached, and scarce human resources may be wasted. The principle applies equally to the first few years in the firm, though the possible range of responsibility is proportionately smaller.

These objectives must be viewed in the light of the results of the survey. One in five of the graduates did not think that they had been intelligently employed, and industry as a whole lost to other walks of life an eighth of the men it recruited from the 1950 graduation year.

This suggests that there was room for improvement in the methods of selection, the matching of men to work, in the grading of work and in the assessment of performance in it. The better this is done the more clearly defined will become the demands by industry on the universities.

THE HUSBANDING OF RESOURCES

IT HAS already been suggested that such problems as were encountered in introducing graduate recruits to the firm and in training them might be overcome by securing the establishment and maintenance by some well-chosen senior on the staff of a close and friendly relationship with each new entrant.

This proposal might also go a long way towards reducing the loss to industry. A certain amount of mobility between jobs is probably desirable as providing the best means of widening their experience for some men, accountants, for example, and mechanical and electrical engineers. The loss by industry to other walks of life suggests, however, that the turnover was higher than was really necessary. Such a proposal might enable employers to judge more accurately than might otherwise be possible the real calibre of the newcomer, by following his progress more closely and becoming more quickly aware of any frustrations and misunderstandings. By this means, also, they might be able to reduce the rather high rate of dissatisfaction with prospects of pay and promotion, which was closely related to the turnover, in itself a source of waste of manpower. This might be achieved first, by more careful placing and, secondly, by helping the graduate to appreciate more fully than he might otherwise do the difficulties often inherent in giving him firm undertakings about future progress.

Again, employers had had on the whole less experience in the employment of arts graduates than of other university men and some were clearly still feeling their way. The arts graduates themselves were generally not as satisfied as their fellows with the way things had gone, and fewer of them felt that they had been intelligently employed. The appointment of a senior to establish and maintain a close relationship with arts graduate recruits might do much also towards further developments in the ways in which they might be employed and generally in making the initial period in the firm more rewarding or at least more explicable.

FINAL IMPRESSIONS

IN looking at the results of the survey as a whole, the overriding impression is of the empirical nature of the approach made both by employers and by graduates to the whole question of university men in industry. At each stage, whether of recruitment or later on, the practice of firms was to adopt such measures as seemed most fitted to their case and to adjust them in the light of experience. The results, if they tended more to the informal than the formal, appeared to be none the less deliberate.

The graduates, on their side, were, almost to a man, openminded in their approach to their new environment and detached and objective in their views. They did not, on the whole, think of themselves as a class apart, nor did their employers so consider them. Once a graduate had joined the firm, he was considered primarily as an individual and treated on his merits, and had to make his way alongside others who had not gone to a university.

The final impression is of level-headedness. Firms appear to have resisted what may at times have been a considerable temptation to form and to carry out their policies less carefully than they might have done. Only at the stage of recruitment, of the "gold rush" for university men, did it appear that shortage of supply of qualified manpower was leading to the adoption of measures out of proportion to the results to be achieved.* At other stages, in the selecting and training of graduates, for example, firms seem to have been unflurried by shortages in carrying out the course of action they had chosen to adopt. And most of them had had at

* Since the survey was made, the system under which firms send to universities at their expense acceptable candidates from their own staff, has developed greatly. Consideration of its possible effects on recruitment drives has not, however, been attempted.

the most nine years' experience of recruitment from universities.

The period reviewed, roughly that between 1950 and 1955, was strongly affected in its earlier years by the expansions and readjustments that followed the end of the war, and throughout by the new relationship of industry to the universities and by the shortages of supply of qualified men at all levels. A response to this environment based on preconceived notions or panic measures might well have been disastrous. The response made, though by no means uniform in speed, showed a remarkable degree of adaptability. In the event, the majority of the members of management interviewed were satisfied with the outcome of their policy and practice, and the majority of the graduates were satisfied also: a remarkable achievement.

This adaptability, the essential prerequisite of evolution and of progress, is a good augury for further advance in industry's partnership with the universities, a partnership of an importance second to none for the future of the country.

APPENDIX A

THE SUB-SAMPLE OF
GRADUATES IN INDUSTRY
(The graduate interviews)

THE graduates who were interviewed about their experience of employment in industry were a random sample of those men who completed Question 20 of the questionnaire sent to the main sample, relating to graduate employment generally.*

This main sample was a random sample of one in two of the men graduating in an arts subject or in science or technology in the universities of Great Britain or through a university college or other university body (in fact, the Royal Technical College, Glasgow, and the Manchester College of Technology) in the academic year 1949-50. These university bodies are those listed in the University Grants Committee's Returns for 1949-50. Six thousand eight hundred and forty-one questionnaires were issued; 4,535 completed forms were received, a response of 66 per cent. Because of the relatively short time in which the enquiry had to be completed, the work of coding and analysis had to be put in train when only 3,961 completed questionnaires had been received. Examination of the replies to the questionnaires received too late showed no significant difference from those that were used. It is unlikely that any major source of bias is present anywhere in this sample.

The relevant section of Question 20 reads: *If you entered industry at any time after completing your university studies, would you give the following details about the undertaking you first went to....*

Industry was defined as comprising the following, whether in this country or abroad:

Mining and quarrying, including the National Coal Board
Oil extracting, refining and distribution, etc.
Manufacturing
Building and contracting and civil engineering
Public utilities: gas, electricity, water, transport by road, rail and
air.

---

* This questionnaire is set out in full in Appendix A of *Graduate Employment.*

One thousand three hundred and six graduates answered Question 20, that is, 31 per cent of the 3,961 graduates in the main sample.*

Out of these 1,306 graduates, some of whom were abroad, 750, all of whom were in Great Britain, were selected at random for interview. Out of these 750 men, 594 were successfully contacted. This represents 80 per cent of this sub-sample and 45 per cent of the 1,306. There is no reason to suppose any significant bias in this sub-sample.

They were interviewed about their first job in industry, whether they were still in it or not, and whether or not they had regarded it as a "career" or a "filling-in" job. There were only some fifty who regarded their work as a filling-in job.

The interviewing was carried out by the Social Survey, acting as the agent of P E P, between November 1954 and February 1955. The tabulation of the replies was also carried out by the Social Survey, in accordance with P E P's instructions.

---

* This figure of 1,306 is larger than the figure of 1,168 given in the Introduction, page xvi, as going into industry after graduation. The 1,306 is made up of these 1,168 who went into industry as a career job after graduating or via national service, together with some ninety men who went into industry after working elsewhere on graduating, and some fifty men who went into industry for a time to "fill-in" between or before career employment of another kind.

APPENDIX B

THE SUB-SAMPLE OF
INDUSTRIAL UNDERTAKINGS

The case studies of private enterprises

THE industrial firms to be interviewed about their policy and practice in employing graduates were a random sample of one in nine of the firms in the private sector of industry, other than those with addresses overseas, given in reply to Question 20 of the questionnaire sent to the main sample, relating to graduate employment generally.

There were some 700 of these firms. By "firm" is meant, in effect, a trading name, so that a firm which was a subsidiary of another was treated as a separate firm for the purpose of the sample. The few very large firms with large divisions in various parts of the country were, however, treated differently: each division was treated as a separate firm. This was to exclude any element of choice in picking the section of these firms in which graduates were to be interviewed. A further refinement should be noted. The firm, as defined, had in many cases a number of establishments, or sections. The procedure was if possible to interview graduates in the establishment or section thrown up in the sample from the original entry made in reply to Question 20— the so-called "unit". But this was not always possible.

No deviation was made from the unit thrown up in thirty-four out of the forty-seven firms, and in these thirty-four firms the whole firm constituted the unit in fourteen instances, and the headquarters of the firm in another fourteen. In the remaining six, the unit was a part of the firm not its headquarters.

Of the remaining thirteen firms, in which some deviation was made from the unit thrown up in the sample, a second section of the firm was added in ten cases because the section thrown up was so clearly unrepresentative of the firm. This was either on account of the original section being, for example, a purely sales section or on account of the number of graduates in it being too low in relation to the total number of graduates employed in the firm. For example, in the case of a large oil undertaking known to employ large numbers of graduates the unit thrown up in the sample contained only one graduate. So graduates at the head-quarters of the undertaking were also interviewed. In the remaining three cases in which a deviation was made from the sample, another part of the firm was substituted for that which came up in the sample. In one case the original "unit" had been sold; in another the firm would have refused to co-operate if the unit (admittedly totally unrepresentative) had been visited; and in the third, the unit thrown up then had no graduates.

Of the seventy-seven firms, as defined, drawn for the sample, fifty-seven agreed to co-operate. Because of shortness of time, only forty-seven were interviewed, roughly in order of acceptance.

The case studies of the public sector of industry

Four area gas boards, in various parts of the country, were selected from the total of twelve, after consultation with the Ministry of Fuel and Power, as it then was, to represent the public sector of industry. All kindly agreed to co-operate.

Selection of people to be interviewed

At the management level, the aim was to interview at least two senior people, of whom one was, if possible, to be a director (or a member of an area gas board), generally at the headquarters of the firm. One or two senior people were also interviewed at the section or division of the firm in which the graduates were to be interviewed, if this section or division was distinct in any way (e.g. geographically) from the headquarters. This was done in order to discover any variations in policy and practice affecting the unit in which were the graduates to be interviewed. The firms nominated the members of management to be interviewed.

One hundred and thirty-four members of management were interviewed, including fifty-four directors of firms and members of gas boards.

The graduates to be interviewed were selected by P E P according to a necessarily rather flexible formula. The aim was to interview up to six graduates in each firm who had graduated at a university in Great Britain since the war and, if possible, in or since the academic year 1948-49. They were, at any rate, to be post-war products of the universities of this country. (For details of actual year of graduation of those interviewed, see Appendix E.) Many of these had come into the firm direct from their university or via national service; others had graduated while working with the firm; others had come into the firm after working elsewhere on leaving their university. The interviews of graduates in each firm reflected, as far as possible, the proportions in which the firm's post-war graduates had been recruited from one or other of these three sources.

Two hundred and six graduates were interviewed, of whom twenty-eight were with gas boards. The remainder were in the thirty-nine firms which were found to have a graduate employment policy of a positive kind (see Chapter I, page 5-9).

R

APPENDIX C

QUESTIONS PUT IN THE GRADUATE INTERVIEWS

THESE questions were put to the 594 graduates interviewed by the Social Survey on behalf of P E P. The questions asked of the graduates who were interviewed in the firms and gas boards were almost identical, but a freer method of interviewing was adopted and answers were not precoded.

First employment in industry. . . . .   University . . . .
. . . .
Now in industry?   Yes   Degrees. . . . .
                                             No

---

1. (a) *To those with full-time first degree*
   (i) If you could start all over again would you still choose to go to a university?
                                                   Yes
                                                   No

If YES: Why?
   Better employment prospects
   Broadens outlook, social advantages
   Educational advantages
   Others (*describe*)
If NO: Why not?

(b) *To those with part-time first degree*
   (i) Why did you take a part-time degree?
   (ii) If you could start again would you prefer to go to a university?
                                                   Yes
                                                   No

If YES: Why?
If NO: Why not?

(c) *To all informants*
   (i) What course of studies did you pursue for your first degree?
   (ii) In the light of experience since then would you choose to take that course now?
                                                   Yes
                                                   No

If YES: Without any alteration?
                                                   Yes
                                                   No

If NO: What alterations would you suggest?

If NO: What do you think you should have done? (PROMPT)
   (i) Additional allied subjects
   (ii) Different subject altogether
   (iii) More practical training
Why?

2. *To those with a higher degree or post-graduate diploma*
   On balance do you think it has been worth while taking this higher degree/diploma in relationship to:
   (a) Your career?   Yes
                                                   No
       Why?
   (b) The work you have to do?   Yes
                                                   No
       Why?

3. *To those with a full-time first degree*
   Did you decide to enter industry before completing your university studies?
                                                   Yes
                                                   No

If YES:
   (a) While still studying did you attend any lectures bearing on your future industrial employment other than any specified in your course?
                                                   Yes
                                                   No
   If YES: By whom were they organised?
       University authorities
       Student groups or university clubs
       Industrial firms or bodies
       Others (*describe*)
   (b) While still studying did you visit any factories or firms, other than any arranged for in your course?
                                                   Yes
                                                   No
   If YES: Who organised your visits?
       University authorities
       Student groups or university clubs
       Industrial firms or bodies
       Others (*describe*)

(c) While still studying did you undertake any work in a factory, plant or industrial firm during vacations in order to prepare yourself for work in industry?

Yes
No

If YES: Total number of weeks?
Type of work:
Technical or practical
Clerical or administrative
Others (*describe*)

4. *To those who studied part-time for first degree*
(i) In what industry/profession were you employed while you were working for your first degree?
(ii) Did your firm allow you any time off for your studies?

Yes
No

If YES: Were you satisfied with the amount of time allowed by your firm?

Yes
No

(iii) Did your firm help in any other way?

Yes
No

If YES: In what way?

THE FOLLOWING QUESTIONS (5–14) REFER TO THE FIRST INDUSTRIAL FIRM INFORMANTS JOINED AFTER COMPLETING THEIR UNIVERSITY STUDIES.

5. What were your reasons for applying for a job in this firm?

6. How did you hear of the opening?
(i) University appointments board
(ii) Ministry of Labour Appointments Office
(iii) Technical and Scientific Register
(iv) Advertisement
(v) Visit from representative of firm
(vi) Personal application
(vii) By knowing someone in the firm
If so: Were they relatives?

Yes
No

If YES: What position did they hold?
(viii) By personal introduction
If by professor or tutor, which?
(ix) Any other method (*describe*)

7. When you were being considered for this appointment, what method/s of selection was/were used?

Yes No

(i) Intelligence test
(ii) One interview
(iii) Series of interviews
(iv) Group test ("Country House")
(v) Group interview
(vi) Other method (*describe*)

8. On first reporting for duty were any formal steps taken to acquaint you with the organisation, personnel, and purposes of the firm?

Yes
No

If YES: What form did they take?
If YES: How long did the programme last (days)?

9. (a) On the whole was the attitude of the person to whom you were immediately responsible
Helpful/co-operative
Unhelpful/uncooperative
No special attitude?
(b) Do you think the fact that you are a graduate affected his/their attitude at all?
Yes—favourably
Yes—unfavourably
No
Don't know

10. Did you come in contact with:

Yes
No

Directors
Foremen
Operatives
Others (including office personnel)?
If YES: Was their attitude
Favourable
Unfavourable
Neither?
Was it affected by your being a graduate?

Yes
No
Don't know

11. Were you given a training course by the firm?

Yes
No

If NO: What did you do on entering the firm?

If YES:

   (i) By whom were you supervised for the course as a whole? (Give position, e.g. personnel manager)

   (ii) How long did the course last (months)?

   (iii) What work did you do?

                            Yes No

       Watching others
       Working yourself
       Attending course at
         technical college
       Others

   (iv) For how long (months)?

   (v) Was any interest shown in your progress during the course?

                            Yes
                            No

   (vi) Did you feel that top management took a personal interest in your progress?

                            Yes
                            No

   (vii) Were you required to make reports on your progress?

                            Yes
                            No

   (viii) Was the training you received from the firm well calculated to fit you for your work in the firm?

                            Yes
                            No

   If YES: What makes you think that?
   If NO: How could it be improved?

   (ix) On the whole would you say that you were intelligently employed at the conclusion of your training period?

                            Yes
                            No

   If NO: Why not?

12. (a) *To those who had no training course*

On the whole would you say that you were intelligently employed on entry to the firm?

                            Yes
                            No

If NO: Why not?

(b) *To all informants*

On the whole would you say that you are intelligently employed now/ or were when you left the firm?

                            Yes
                            No

If NO: Why not?

13. Are/were you satisfied with your prospects of further advancement within the firm?

Pay   Yes
                            No
Position   Yes
                            No

14. Have you ever done work which you felt that you should not as a graduate have been asked by your employer to undertake?

                            Yes
                            No

If YES: What kinds?

15. Are there any further comments you would like to make that you think would be relevant to this enquiry?

16. Finally, what is the present/ or what was the last main occupation of your father/guardian?

APPENDIX D

QUESTIONS PUT TO MEMBERS OF MANAGEMENT

QUESTIONS seeking opinions were put to all members of management. Factual questions were put to the first member of management interviewed in each firm and also to the first member of management in the unit of the firm visited, if it carried responsibility for any aspect of the graduate employment policy or practice of the firm. Only questions under heads I and VIII were put to the eight firms classed as employing graduates incidentally.

At the end of each of the eight groups of questions, an enquiry was made whether there had been any changes of policy in the past and whether any were in mind for the future; and a question was asked, "Have we covered everything from your point of view. Is there anything you would like to add?"

A reminder was made from time to time that answers should be given in relation to arts men, scientists and technologists separately.

I. POLICY TO EMPLOY GRADUATES

1. Is the graduate recruitment/training policy
   (a) decided
   (b) carried out—at headquarters? Please describe.

2. Why do you take on graduates? (arts/science/technology/first degree/higher degree).

3. What qualifications do you seek in graduate recruits? (arts/science/technology/first degree/higher degree):
   (a) academic
   (b) personality
   (c) any other?

4. After, say, two or three years with the firm, how do university men who have graduated since the war compare with others of similar age doing comparable work?
   (a) intellectually
   (b) in their attitude to other people
   (c) (i) in their attitude to the kinds of work which they, as graduates, should be asked to undertake
       (ii) in their attitude to the job in hand?

II. METHODS OF RECRUITMENT

1. Do you recruit graduates
   (a) for a defined range of jobs in various departments,
   or (b) for specific jobs in a specific department,
   or (c) both?

2. Are these jobs confined to graduates? If not, what other types of candidates are eligible?

3. How is it decided how many graduates to take on?

4. Are the qualifications required for specific jobs or a defined range of jobs clearly defined in advance?

5. (a) What methods of attracting graduate recruits have been adopted by your firm?
   (b) In particular, have you any direct contacts with any universities?

6. Are enough graduates of the right kind being attracted to the firm?

III. SELECTION

1. How do you select graduate recruits for jobs?

2. If by interview:
   (a) By whom are candidates interviewed?
   (b) Is a standard series of questions asked each time?

3. Are members of the firm in charge of selection specially trained for the work?

4. Does your method of selection give you good results?

IV. INDUCTION

1. Has the firm a scheme for the induction of a graduate recruit when he first reports for duty?

2. What does the induction consist of?

3. Does this induction serve your purpose?
   If there is NO induction policy
N-2. What actually happens when the graduate reports for duty?
N-3. Are you satisfied that no formal induction is necessary?

V. TRAINING ORGANISED BY THE FIRM

1. Has the firm a formal training scheme for graduate recruits?

2. (a) Are all graduate recruits trained?
   (b) Are any other recruits also brought into this scheme?

3. When was the scheme introduced?

4. What does the training consist of?

5. Is the programme standardised? Or does it vary
   (a) according to the job in view?
   (b) according to the rate of progress of the recruit?

6. Is/Are any member/s of the staff responsible for training graduate recruits? If so:
   (a) Is this a whole-time job?
   (b) Does it include being available to give advice and encouragement to trainees?

7. Does the firm encourage graduates to take outside courses?

8. Are you satisfied that the scheme fits graduates well for work in the firm, both
   (a) technically and
   (b) socially?

   If there is NO training scheme
N-2. What in fact happens to graduate recruits in their early days with the firm?

N-3. Does any member of the staff keep an eye on new entrants?

N-4. Is the progress of recruits followed in any way?

N-5. Are you satisfied that no formal training scheme is necessary? That is, that the recruit is fitted both technically and socially for work in the firm as well by your methods as by a formal training scheme?

N-6. Does the firm encourage graduates to take outside courses?

VI. ASSIGNMENT

1. How does the firm assign graduate recruits to their first jobs?

2. What are the main considerations which determine such assignments?

3. Do you ever assign
   (a) science/technical graduates to non-technical first jobs?
   (b) arts graduates to relieve the scientific and technical staff of administrative matters?

4. (a) Do you ever assign technology graduates to the routine supervision and control of plant?
   (b) If so, what do you find is the attitude of graduates to such assignments?

5. Are there any types of graduate recruit that you find it difficult to assign or place?

6. On entering industry, do you consider a graduate should do the same work as his non-graduate contemporaries? Or is this likely to waste his capabilities?

7. Is it possible for the recruit to foresee chances of promotion?

8. Are you satisfied with the present procedure.
   If there is NO assignment policy
N-2. Do you feel that a standard policy is unnecessary?
N-3. In what way are graduates actually allocated to jobs?
N-4. Do you ever assign
   (a) science/technical graduates to non-technical first jobs?
   (b) arts graduates to relieve the scientific and technical staff of administrative matters?

N-5. (a) Do you ever assign technology graduates to the routine supervision and control of plant?

(b) If so, what do you find is the attitude of graduates to such assignments?

N-6. Are there any types of graduate recruit that you find it difficult to assign or place?

N-7. On entering industry, do you consider a graduate should do the same work as his non-graduate contemporaries? Or is this likely to waste his capabilities?

N-8. Is it possible for the recruit to foresee chances of promotion?

N-9. Are you satisfied with the present procedure?

VII. SALARIES

1. Has the firm a salaries policy or scheme relating to all salaried staff?

2. How are the salaries of graduates related to the scheme?

3. Does the academic qualification place them higher on the scale relative to their age

  (a) (i) on entry

      (ii) after training

      (iii) after a further three years?

  (b) (i) after obtaining their degree while working with the firm?

      (ii) after training, if any?

      (iii) after a further three years?

4. Is the possible rate of advancement clear to graduate recruits?

If there is NO salaries policy

N-2. How did the present graduate salary arrangements come about?

N-3. Do you consider a standardised salary scheme unnecessary?

N-4. Does the academic qualification command a higher salary than that of another man of comparable age and doing similar work?

N-5. Is the possible rate of advancement in salary clear to graduate recruits?

VIII. VIEWS ON EDUCATION AND TRAINING

1. Do you consider a university education, as compared with, for example, a technical college education, an advantage to industry?

2. Do you consider that the universities should do more to meet the needs of industry? If so, what?

3. What, from your experience, would be the ideal university first degree course for your purposes? What would be its content and its length?

4. (a) Bearing this in mind, what, from your experience, would be the ideal order in which a man eventually joining your firm should acquire his education and training (including national service)?

  (b) Why?

5. Have you any views on the value to you of a higher degree in science or technology?

6. Have you done anything at any time to influence the content of any university courses?

APPENDIX E
THE GRADUATE'S BACKGROUND

THIS appendix gives some details of the age, schooling, and social and academic background of the 594 graduates in the graduate interview sub-sample and the 206 graduates in the case studies sub-sample. This information is taken from replies to the *Graduate Employment* questionnaire (reproduced as Appendix B to that report) with one exception. A question on the main occupation of the graduate's father or guardian was put in the course of the present study. It was asked at the end of the series of questions to graduates, lest, if it were to cause any embarrassment, it might prejudice the results of the interview. (It was on this account that it was not included in the questionnaire sent by post to the graduates in the main sample.)

Age

All the men graduated after World War II, but because of the interruptions of the war, many were much older than the normal run. The graduates in the case studies were rather younger than the others: the distribution of the ages of the 594 in the larger sub-sample reflects that in the main sample from which they were drawn. Nearly half of the case study graduates, 45 per cent, were twenty-two years old or less in 1950, twenty-six or less when the survey was made—compared with some 30 per cent of the 594 in the graduate interview sample. Of the case study graduates, 38 per cent were aged between twenty-three and twenty-six in 1950, as compared with 49 per cent of the others; and only 17 per cent were then aged twenty-seven or more compared with 21 per cent of the others. This difference in ages is accounted for by the fact that whereas all the 594 men in the graduate interview sub-sample graduated in 1950, rather more than half the case study men graduated after that date.

Father's or guardian's occupation

The main occupation of the graduate's father or guardian was classified as far as possible according to the "Hall-Jones Grading of Occupations of Males" used by Professor Glass in his study of social mobility.* Some replies, however, failed to be precise

* D. V. Glass, Ed. *Social Mobility in Britain*. (Routledge and Kegan Paul) 1954. 36s.

enough for classification. Some graduates, for instance, said their father had been a farmer, but did not specify the size of his holding. Others said he was a manual worker without specifying whether he was skilled or unskilled. Altogether 17 per cent of the graduate interview replies and 4 per cent of those in the case studies failed to be specific enough. They were classified separately in special categories. Secondly, the numbers were too small to permit of analysis under so many categories and some grouping was necessary.

The results are given in Table E1. This is a very broad picture, but it serves to indicate the social class, as measured by the occupation of the father, of the graduates who are a subject of this report.

TABLE E1

MAIN OCCUPATION OF THE GRADUATE'S FATHER OR GUARDIAN

Hall-Jones grading	Father's or guardian's occupation	Graduate interviews		Case studies	
		No.	%	No.	%
1	Professional and high adminis-trative	149	25	38	19
2, 3 and owners, managers, unspecified	Owners, managers, farmers, executives and other higher non-manual	184	30	88	42
4, 5 and inspectors, supervisors and clerks, unspecified	Inspectors, clerks, routine non-manual and skilled manual	233	40	65	32
6, 7 and manual, unspecified	Manual, other than skilled .	22	4	8	4
	No answer	6	1	7	3
	TOTAL	594	100	206	100

Schooling

A broad picture of the last school attended by the graduates is given in Table E2. The categories of school are those current before the reorganisation following the Education Act, 1944, and the Education (Scotland) Act, 1945. The graduate interview sub-sample follows closely the distribution in the main sample of 3,961 men in this respect, as in others.

An "independent" or "public" school is one whose headmaster is a member of the Headmasters' Conference. To qualify, the school must have a certain degree of independence. Direct grant schools are included and a small number of aided schools. The schools represented are listed in *Whitaker's Almanack*. Scottish senior secondary schools correspond to grammar schools south of the Border.

TABLE E2

SCHOOLING

Type of school	Graduate interviews %	Case studies %
Grammar, and Scottish senior secondary .	61	68
Independent (public)	27	19
Others	12	13

The percentage of graduates from each type of school who read for an arts, science or technology degree is given in Table E3.

TABLE E3

SCHOOLING BY FACULTY

Type of school	Numbers G.I.* No.	C.S.* No.	Arts G.I. %	C.S. %	Science G.I. %	C.S. %	Technology G.I. %	C.S. %
Grammar . . .	331	120	22	23	40	40	38	37
Independent (Public) .	163	39	29	36	31	28	40	36
Scottish senior secondary . .	31	20	13	—	29	45	58	55
Others . . .	69	22	13	4	36	23	51	73
No reply . . .	—	5	—	—	—	—	—	—
TOTAL . .	594	206	22	21	37	36	41	43

* In this and the following tables, G.I. means graduate interviews and C.S. case studies.

University and faculty of degree

The universities to which these men went, most of them after some interruption from the war, are set out, in broad categories, in Table E4, together with the faculty of the degree for which they read.

TABLE E4

UNIVERSITY BY FACULTY

University	All faculties		Arts		Science		Technology	
	G.I.	C.S.	G.I.	C.S.	G.I.	C.S.	G.I.	C.S.
	No.	No.	No.	No.	No.	No.	No.	No.
Oxford or Cambridge	107	42	48	25	40	9	19	8
London—Internal .	103	20	16	3	35	7	52	10
London—External excluding university colleges . .	93	28	16	1	35	14	42	13
Other English including university colleges . .	211	70	41	12	79	24	91	34
Welsh . . .	25	10	3	—	14	5	8	5
Scottish . . .	55	31	8	2	15	13	32	16
Other or not known* .	—	5	—	—	—	2	—	3
TOTAL . .	594	206	132	43	218	74	244	89

* Two Irish and three not known. Irish universities, whether in Northern Ireland or in Eire, were not included in the main sample. This was confined to universities in Great Britain.

Class of degree

The class of degree obtained by these men, according to the kind of schooling they had had, is shown in Table E5. The "Other" degrees include Third and Fourth Class Honours degrees, Pass and Ordinary degrees.

TABLE E5

SCHOOLING IN RELATION TO CLASS OF DEGREE

Type of school			Percentage distribution by class of degree					
	Numbers		First		Second		Other	
	G.I.	C.S.	G.I.	C.S.	G.I.	C.S.	G.I.	C.S.
	No.	No.	%	%	%	%	%	%
Grammar . . .	331	120	12	12	45	48	43	40
Independent (Public) .	163	39	11	10	36	44	53	46
Scottish senior secondary . .	31	20	13	5	42	30	45	65
Others . . .	69	22	6	—	39	34	55	66
No reply . . .	—	5	—	—	—	—	—	—
TOTAL . .	594	206	11	10	42	43	47	47

Table E6 gives these same class results in relation to faculty.

TABLE E6

FACULTY IN RELATION TO CLASS OF DEGREE

Faculty of first degree	Total		Number First		Second		Other		Percentage obtaining First		Second		Other	
	G.I. No.	C.S. No.	G.I. No.	C.S. No.	G.I. No.	C.S. No.	G.I. No.	C.S. No.	G.I. %	C.S. %	G.I. %	C.S. %	G.I. %	C.S. %
Arts	132	43	5	1	69	27	58	15	4	—	52	63	44	35
Science	218	74	26	8	93	28	99	37	12	11	43	38	45	50
Technology	244	89	33	11	86	32	125	44	14	12	35	36	51	50
TOTAL	594	206	64	20	248	87	282	96	11	10	42	42	47	48

Part-time students

Of the 594 men in the graduate interviews, forty-two studied part-time. Of these, twenty-eight were London external and twelve London internal graduates. Of the 206 case study graduates, eight had studied part-time.

Higher degrees

Thirty-five out of the 594 graduate interview men and ten out of the 206 case study men had obtained a higher degree, some 6 per cent in both cases.

Year of graduation

All the graduate interview men took their first degree in the academic year 1949-50.

The academic year of graduation of the case study men was:

1947-48	1949	1950	1951	1952	1953	1954	Not known
8	20	57	41	33	24	14	9

Marriage

Of the 594 graduate interview men, 22 per cent had married by the end of 1950, the year in which they graduated, and 61 per cent had married by the time of the survey. Of the 206 case study graduates, 54 per cent had married by the time of the survey.

Industrial career after graduation

Of the 594 graduate interview men, some 90 per cent had entered industry as their first career job after graduating in 1950. Eighty-seven per cent were still in industry when they were interviewed during the winter of 1954-55. They were all interviewed about the first industrial firm in which they had worked, whether or not they had left it. A little over 60 per cent were still with this first firm.*

Of the 206 case study men, 86 per cent had entered industry as their first job after graduating.

They were, of course, all in industry at the time they were interviewed and were all questioned about their experience with the firm in which they were interviewed. This firm was the first industrial employer of all but thirty-eight of the 206 men.

Attitude to industry

When they were studying for their degree, most of the graduates were keen to go into industry. The figures are given in Table E7.

TABLE E7

ATTITUDE TO INDUSTRY

	Graduate interviews %	Case studies %
Keen to go into industry	60	61
Considering industry as an alternative career .	23	16
Indifferent to industry	11	11
Definitely against it	1	1
No answer	2	6
Already in industry while studying . .	3	5
TOTAL	100	100

Response to interviews in the case studies

The graduates answered the questions put to them fully and frankly and took some, but not much, advantage of the opportunities given to them to say anything more on the subjects than had been elicited by the questions.

Almost all appeared to approach the subjects raised in an objective manner. Only 1 per cent of the 206 men expressed some sort of dissatisfaction on almost every occasion when asked for their views, but they did not give the impression that they were deliberately running down the employment policy of their firm merely for the sake of putting it in a bad light.

* This includes the relevant proportion of the small number of men who went into industry as their second career employment from some other career employment, and those who had entered industry, but not as career employment.

APPENDIX F

THE PRODUCT AND SIZE OF THE FIRMS ABOUT WHICH GRADUATES WERE INTERVIEWED

THE product and size, as measured by the number of employees, of the firms about which all the 800 men were interviewed is given in Table F1. ("Firm" is not the same as "establishment", as used for Census of Production statistics. Comparison of the two is not possible.)

The size and product of, and the number of graduates, in the case study firms were obtained from each firm as a preliminary to the interviews. The size and product of the firms of the graduates in the graduate interviews was obtained from reference sources, mainly the *Register of British Manufacturers* of the Federation of British Industries, or by direct approach to the firm. For thirty-three of the graduate interview men, however, it proved impossible to discover the size of the firm, and for twenty-one the product.

The firms have been classified in accordance with their product or main product, and as far as possible in accordance with the categories used in the Standard Industrial Classification. Some firms had two or more products of apparently equal importance, none falling within the same code. To meet this problem in relation to vehicles, an "Other" category has been introduced to include firms producing more than one type of vehicle, e.g. motor and aero-engines, or aero-engines and electrical products. There may be some overweighting of the non-electrical section of engineering.

Graduate interviews

As the graduate interviews sub-sample can be regarded as representative, the distribution of the men in it is an indication of the extent to which the various branches of industry recruited graduates in 1950, or a little later. (A proportion, round about a quarter, will have done their national service between graduating and going into industry.) The largest recruiter was the electrical engineering industry, with 23 per cent of these graduates. After it came the chemical and allied trades with 21 per cent. No other

TABLE FI

NUMBER OF GRADUATES INTERVIEWED BY FIRM PRODUCT AND FIRM SIZE

Product	Number of employees							Total numbers		Percentages	
	Small 1–1,999		Medium 2,000–9,999		Large 10,000 and over		Not known					
	G.I.* No.	C.S.* No.	G.I. No.	C.S. No.	G.I. No.	C.S. No.	G.I. No.		G.I. No.	C.S. No.	G.I. %	C.S. %
Mining and quarrying, excluding National Coal Board	2	—	—	—	17	—	—		19	—	3	—
Oil	1	—	10	—	3	6	—		14	6	2	3
Miscellaneous non-metalliferous manufacture	10	3	5	5	10	—	—		25	8	4	4
Chemicals and allied trades	25	—	38	10	57	4	3		123	14	21	7
Metal trades	21	2	18	17	14	6	2		55	25	9	12
Aircraft and vehicles	4	—	21	8	17	7	2		44	15	8	7
Non-electrical engineering	16	5	16	8	7	—	1		40	13	7	6
Electrical engineering	11	2	31	17	91	22	4		137	41	23	20
Consumer goods	22	10	21	19	13	6	2		58	35	9	17
Building and contracting	9	8	4	13	6	—	3		22	21	4	11
Public utilities	—	—	—	—	36	28	—		36	28	6	13
Not known	3	—	2	—	—	—	16		21	—	4	—
TOTAL	124	30	166	97	271	79	33		594	206	100	100

* G.I. means graduate interviews, C.S. means case studies.

Size: Size relates to total number of employees, except for one firm in the electrical engineering group and one in the aircraft and vehicles group, where the size given is for the section of the firm in which the graduates were interviewed in carrying out a case study of the firm in question. These two are classed here as in the medium-size group.

group achieved more than 9 per cent. Twenty-one per cent of these graduates went into "small" firms—those employing under 2,000 people; 27 per cent into "medium-sized" firms—those employing between 2,000 and 10,000; and 46 per cent into "large" firms.*

The next table (F2) gives the size and product of the firms of

TABLE F2

MORE DETAILED ANALYSIS OF THE

FIRMS AND NATIONALISED INDUSTRIES ENTERED BY GRADUATES

IN THE GRADUATE INTERVIEW SUB-SAMPLE

Number of employees

Product	Small 1-499	Small 500-1,999	Medium 2,000-4,999	Medium 5,000-9,999	Large 10,000 and over	Not known	Total	Per cent
	No.	No.	No.	No.	No.	No.	No.	%
Coal	—	—	—	—	19	—	19	3
Oil	—	1	5	5	3	—	14	2
Other manufacturing	2	—	—	—	—	—	2	—
Non-metalliferous processing	4	3	3	1	1	—	12	2
Chemicals	10	15	24	14	57	3	123	21
Metal manufacturing	5	16	7	11	14	2	55	9
Shipbuilding	—	—	2	—	—	2	4	1
Non-electrical engineering	6	5	9	4	7	—	31	5
Electrical engineering	4	7	9	22	91	4	137	23
Motor vehicles	1	1	3	4	11	—	20	3
Aircraft	—	1	3	5	6	—	15	3
Railway engineering	—	1	—	—	—	—	1	—
Other vehicles†	—	—	—	4	—	—	4	1
Precision tools	2	3	3	—	—	1	9	2
Textiles	3	3	5	4	10	1	26	4
Clothing	2	1	1	—	—	—	4	1
Food	2	2	2	8	2	—	16	3
Drink	1	2	—	—	—	—	3	—
Tobacco	—	—	1	—	1	—	2	—
Paper and printing	4	2	—	—	—	1	7	1
Wood, cork, etc.	1	2	1	—	7	—	11	2
Building and contracting	7	2	2	2	6	3	22	4
Gas	—	—	—	—	7	—	7	1
Electricity	—	—	—	—	11	—	11	2
Water‡	—	—	—	—	9	—	9	2
Transport	—	—	—	—	9	—	9	2
Not known	3	—	—	2	—	16	21	4
TOTAL—Numbers	57	67	80	86	271	33	594	—
Per cent	10	11	13	14	46	6	—	100

* In the report, "small", "medium" and "large" are used in this sense.
† See page 248 for an explanation of this category.
‡ The graduates in water undertakings were all grouped arbitrarily in the large category.

the 594 men in greater detail. The very small number, four, in shipbuilding, an industry of growing importance, is noteworthy.

Case studies

Some details are given in Table F3 of the distribution by product and size of the case study firms and boards. It indicates also which firms had adopted a deliberate policy to recruit graduates only since 1945. These are shown in bold type.

This table gives also the total number of graduates in these firms or boards, with the following exceptions:

three firms, all large, for which it was possible to obtain a figure only for the unit of the firm in which graduates were interviewed;

one for which no figures were available. It can, however, be classed as having a hundred or more graduates;

eight firms which proved not to employ graduates, as such, as a deliberate policy or which did not employ them, as such, for various reasons, mainly the smallness of the firm, or on both accounts.

Five of the firms in the last category employed less than 500 people. At the time of the survey three had no graduates, four had one each and the remaining one, the largest, had two. All had taken on one of the men who graduated in 1950 (though quite incidentally) and had thus appeared in the sample of firms.

Disregarding these eight exceptional firms, it is seen that none of the twelve small firms with a deliberate policy to recruit graduates employed more than seventeen graduates altogether. In the medium-sized group of nineteen firms, the numbers ranged from 8 to 190; in the eight large firms and four gas boards they ranged from 28 to 500 and more. Twenty-six (including the four gas boards) had 25 graduates or more; twenty (including two gas boards) had 50 graduates or more; fourteen had 100 or more, all in the 100-200 range, except three giants with several hundred. But three of the firms for which figures are lacking or incomplete, and which are included above, certainly had well over a hundred graduates, making six giant employers in all.

These forty-three undertakings varied also in the number of men graduates they employed in relation to the total number of

s

TABLE F3

CASE STUDY FIRMS BY PRODUCT AND SIZE

Number of employees†

Product*	Small 1–499 P.	Small 1–499 G.‡	Small 500–1,999 P.	Small 500–1,999 G.	Medium 2,000–4,999 P.	Medium 2,000–4,999 G.	Medium 5,000–9,999 P.	Medium 5,000–9,999 G.	Large 10,000 and over P.	Large 10,000 and over G.	Total
Mining and quarrying, excluding N.C.B.	Q	ng§									Q 1
Oil									O	136‖	O 1
Non-metalliferous manufacture			N	4	N	80					N 2
Chemicals	C	ng			C C	28 190	C	na¶§			C 4
Metal manufacture and metal goods	MG MG	ng ng	M	6	M MG	65 21	M	35	M	115	M 4 } MG 3 } 7
Aircraft and vehicles					V V	14 29			V A	ng 488	V 3 } A 1 } 4
Non-electrical engineering, etc.	E E I	ng 2 8			R	47					E 2 } I 1 } R 1 } 4
Electrical engineering	L	7			L L L	9 134 ng	L	1068§	L L L	565 132+** 138	L 9
Consumer goods	H F	2 2	W F P	9 4 11	D	20	F T	60 166	F	595+** 22+**	P 1 } F 4 } H 1 } W 1 } D 1 } T 1 } 9
Building and contracting	B	2	B B	17 ng	B B	8 76	B	105			B 6
Public utilities									G G G C	28 45 69 62	G 4
TOTAL	11		7		14		6		13		51

* The main product of the case study firms has been classified under the twelve broad product groups used also in analysing the graduate interviews. The single code letter used for each firm is intended to denote the actual product or main product of the firm.

A Aircraft
B Building, contracting, civil engineering
C Chemical and allied trades
D Drink
E Engineering (non-electrical)
F Food
G Gas
H Leather goods
I Precision instruments
L Electrical engineering
M Metal manufacture
MG Metal goods
N Treatment of non-metalliferous mining products
O Oil
P Printing and paper
Q Quarrying
R Refining of metals
T Textiles
V Vehicles
W Wearing apparel (clothing)

The figure given after the code letter is the number of graduates in the firm.

In two studies in which the firm as a whole had a wide range of products, which fell under more than one Order of the Standard Industrial Classification, the product of the section or "unit" of the firm in which graduates were interviewed has been adopted for the purpose of this classification. One of these units is classified under chemicals and the other under vehicles.

† Size relates to total number of employees except for one firm in electrical engineering and one in aircraft and vehicles, where the size given is for the unit of the firm in which graduates were interviewed.

These two firms are classified under size group 2,000-4,999.

‡ P. means product or main product; G. means number of graduates in the firm.

§ ng—firm did not employ graduates as a deliberate policy. None had more than two.

‖ Firms in bold are those classified as new employers of graduates.

¶ na—no answer (number of graduates not available).

** Graduates in unit only. Certainly many more in firm as a whole.

people they employed. The firm with the highest ratio were electrical engineers, with 134 graduates and 2,000-3,000 employees (6·4 per cent). Next came a firm making precision instruments, with eight graduates and between 100 and 500 employees (5·4 per cent); and third came a firm manufacturing chemicals, with 190 graduates and between 3,000 and 4,000 employees (4·7 per cent). In six others, the percentage was 2-3 per cent; in eight others it was 1-2 per cent and in the remainder less than 1 per cent.

INDEX

For Product Safety Concerns and Information please contact our EU representative GPSR@taylorandfrancis.com Taylor & Francis Verlag GmbH, Kaufingerstraße 24, 80331 München, Germany

Printed and bound by CPI Group (UK) Ltd, Croydon, CR0 4YY
01/05/2025
01858391-0002